The Poet's Mistake

The Poet's Mistake

Erica McAlpine

Princeton University Press
Princeton and Oxford

Published by Princeton University Press
41 William Street, Princeton, New Jersey 08540
6 Oxford Street, Woodstock, Oxfordshire OX20 1TR

press.princeton.edu

Library of Congress Cataloging-in-Publication Data

Names: McAlpine, Erica, author.
Title: The poet's mistake / Erica McAlpine.
Description: Princeton : Princeton University Press, [2020] | Includes bibliographical references and index.
Identifiers: LCCN 2019041744 (print) | LCCN 2019041745 (ebook) | ISBN 9780691203478 (hardback) | ISBN 9780691203492 (paperback) | ISBN 9780691203768 (ebook)
Subjects: LCSH: Errors and blunders, Literary—History. | Poetry—Authorship.
Classification: LCC PN1059.E67 M33 2020 (print) | LCC PN1059.E67 (ebook) | DDC 808.1–dc23
LC record available at https://lccn.loc.gov/2019041744
LC ebook record available at https://lccn.loc.gov/2019041745

British Library Cataloging-in-Publication Data is available

This book has been composed in Adobe Garamond Pro and Fairfield LT Std

Printed on acid-free paper. ∞

Printed in the United States of America

10 9 8 7 6 5 4 3 2 1

FOR BRUCE

Contents

Preface

This book catalogs unintentional mistakes in poems in order to demonstrate that poets, even great ones, *do* make mistakes and that literary scholarship can incorporate them into its analysis of poetry without excusing, denying, or resorting to mysticism. The readerly impulse it works against—that poets *don't* make mistakes, or, at any rate, that poems cannot contain them—is pervasive among twentieth- and twenty-first-century treatments of poetry from both inside and outside of the academy. As both a writer and a reader of poems, I find this impulse misguided, though I have occasionally been guilty of it myself.

My approach here is idiosyncratic and personal. It reflects the tastes of a poet informed by historical scholarship who nevertheless resists a historically inflected method. This is not because I do not recognize that poems are created in time or that they are necessarily influenced by their historical and cultural contexts, but rather because I generally prefer to read poems in relation to a long tradition of shapes and forms that often pushes against such constraints. The scope of the material I include in my chapters—mistakes in poems from the Romantics onward—reveals my own interests as a scholar. But I should also note that it is a simpler task to write about grammatical and orthographic mistakes in poems composed after the eighteenth-century standardization of English than it would be to write about such mistakes before a clearer sense of linguistic propriety began to crystallize.

Mistakes in poems, as I see them, involve the sorts of errors that most poets, from any period, would wish *not* to make. These might include misspellings, ungrammaticalities, misconceptions of meaning, misreadings of prior poems, and historical or factual inaccuracies. They do not include purposeful errors of syntax, grammar, or logic that operate in service of creating multiple or indeterminate meanings, nor do they include deliberate breaches of code, as might be exemplified by poets writing in dialect or those whose language arranges itself in opposition to certain institutional, political, or cultural norms. Occasionally the poems about which I write seem to encompass these considerations while also erring more conventionally: the mistakes I describe in chapters on John Clare, Emily Dickinson, and Hart Crane coexist with those authors' distinct modes of antiauthoritarianism—which can seem like mistake too. Part of the work in these and other chapters is to clarify where mistake departs from license as a poetic effect.

This book contributes to a discourse about intentionality that concerns many scholars in the humanities, though it does not do so in the manner of the major theorists on the subject. Black-and-white debates about intentionality in poetry often miss the mark with regard to mistake. It is true that to call something a mistake, *definitively*, requires a knowledge of the author's intention that is impossible to have with any certainty. But it is also true that to deny mistake is to risk misunderstanding the intention it betrays. Somewhere between a poet's choice to make a poem and a reader's decision to give it meaning lies the fertile ground of error. Although the chapters in this book approach intentionality through examples (they are practical rather than theoretical), the argument they make about the poet's craft is one that addresses general theories about how and why we read. Within these pages, I am variously interested in the circumstances of a poem's coming into being (if and when they are knowable) as well as what poets' drafts can suggest about their intended meanings, but I am also aware that unconscious motives minister quietly over all compositional processes, and that poems frequently admit ideas that their poets do not consciously mean. The existence of latent or unconscious meanings in poems is an aspect of intentionality that this book tries to disambiguate from the appearance of pesky mistakes in craft.

There is no other book-length study dedicated to unintended mistakes in poetry, and my introduction suggests why this may be the case. Mistakes in novels, stories, and plays have generally been easier to digest; perhaps the length of novels, in particular, suggests the implausibility of perfection. Whatever the reason—and as books like John Sutherland's *Is Heathcliff a Murderer?*, Matthew Creasy's *Errears and Erroriboose: Joyce and Error*, and Michael Anesko's *Generous Mistakes: Incidents of Error in Henry James* have shown—readers have historically had less trouble pointing to and accepting mistakes and inconsistencies in prose than in poems. But surely poets are just as fallible as novelists and other kinds of writers. Among all readers of poetry, it has been poets themselves who are most willing to descry mistake, and indeed many of the instances I explore in these pages were first identified by literary scholars who counted themselves as poets first: Ben Jonson, Matthew Arnold, and Alfred Tennyson, among others. Apart from Christopher Ricks's important essay "Literature and the Matter of Fact," most other broad accounts of literary error from critics—Frank Kermode's *The Uses of Error*, Seth Lerer's *Error and the Academic Self*, Nerys Williams's *Reading Error*—register mistake in its more positive sense, as a tool for meaning production. The poet's uneasiness I feel at the temptation to call mistakes *good* is where this book begins.

Acknowledgments

The idea for this book came about more than a decade ago, and I have subsequently accrued many debts. David Bromwich and Langdon Hammer have modeled for me, over many years, what good scholarship can bring to poetry and the readers who live by it. Without their guidance, I could not have written this or any book. Before them came several teachers who showed me how to read, write, and think about poems when I was still an undergraduate: Jorie Graham, Lisa New, Peter Sacks, and Helen Vendler. If that isn't good fortune, I don't know what is.

Others have made lasting interventions: Leslie Brisman not only heard my opening thoughts about this project but also found the mistake in Wordsworth that inspired them. Conrad Harper demonstrated what it means to love books. Mary Jacobus reminded me to follow my nose. Paul Fry nurtured my inner Romanticist. Geoffrey Hartman's generous and joyful mind provided an example on the page and off.

Several selfless friends and colleagues read whole chapters or discussed the ideas in these pages with me at great length. Jessica Berenbeim, Matthew Bevis, Jamie Castell, Emily Coit, Stephen Gill, Tom MacFaul, Jerome Luc Martin, Bernard O'Donoghue, and Ben Westwood made this book much better than it would have been. Thanks alone cannot recuperate the hours they spent.

So many others listened to portions, offered suggestions, or endeavored to help in various ways: Laura Ashe, Katie Charles, Oliver Clarkson, Lindiwe Dovey, Merve Emre, Catherine Flynn, Alex Freer, Nicola Gardini,

Nick Gaskill, Dehn Gilmore, Andrew Goldstone, Elsa Hammond, Oliver Herford, Susannah Hollister, Doreen Hughes, Jasmine Jagger, Felicity James, Freya Johnston, Aileen Kavanagh, Henrike Lähnemann, Sebastian Lecourt, Anna Lewis, Sarah Mahurin, Stacey McDowell, Jamie McKendrick, Jim McKusick, Maureen McLane, Timothy Michael, Kate McLoughlin, Katie Murphy, Jenni Nuttall, Emily Ogden, Tom Owens, Siobhan Phillips, Lloyd Pratt, Diane Purkiss, Sophie Ratcliffe, Nicholas Roe, David Russell, Reena Sastri, Emily Setina, Sadie Slater, Helen Small, Tara Stubbs, Hannah Sullivan, Steve Tedeschi, Sarah Vanderlaan, Kate Wakeling, Dan Wakelin, Stephanie Weiner, Mark Williams, Wes Williams, and Amelia Worsley. Many hands go into the making of a book.

Much of the material here was first tested out on captive audiences at the Wordsworth Summer Conference over a number of seasons. I credit that collegial institution, now in its fiftieth year, with helping me land on my feet. Fiona Stafford has been a friend to me since I met her there in the summer of 2010; she and two other Wordsworthians, Stephen Gill and Seamus Perry, have supported me in ways I will never forget.

My colleagues in the Faculty of English at Oxford make working feel like a privilege. So do my students, who inspire me to read poems always as if for the first time. Keble College, where I began this book, welcomed me when I feared no one would. My companions in the Salutation and Cat Reading Group keep poetry alive every other week. And my new family at St Edmund Hall sustains me every day—sharing my table and steering me right.

I have wonderful friends from corners of life that do not directly involve this book, and their gifts have inevitably contributed to its completion. My three college roommates witnessed the earliest signs of my fanaticism for poems; my comrades in IGP taught me to find humor in everything, even literary criticism; and my friends from Atlanta are the dearest old friends in the world. Likewise, my family has ministered over these pages in silent ways. David and Isobel McAlpine watched much of this book materialize in their living room and cheered me on. Rachel, Jessica, and Rhona are sisters who always have my back. I cannot acknowledge adequately my debt to my parents, Carol and Steven Levy, who have encouraged my love for poems since the very beginning.

One spring afternoon a few years ago, Michèle Mendelssohn listened to a section of what would become this book's introduction and suggested I send a proposal to Hannah Paul at Princeton University Press. Her generous instinct, and Hannah's, set this project on its long path to completion. The truly extraordinary Stephanie Kelley stepped in near the end and fixed everything; there is no gratitude commensurate with her editorial gifts. Cathy Slovensky's miraculous eye scanned every page, and Ben Tate saw the project through to publication with wisdom and magnanimity. I could not have asked for a better or more receptive team of advocates at the Press. The three anonymous readers who reviewed this manuscript responded in ways that made it significantly better; I am forever grateful to them for not calling this book a mistake while simultaneously helping me improve it. There certainly are mistakes left in these pages, but thankfully many of them are not mine.

I hope young Grant and May will read this book with pleasure someday, knowing they grew up around it. Marrying Bruce was the farthest thing from a mistake I ever made.

The Poet's Mistake

The Poet's Mistake

"—Bosh!" Stephen said rudely. "A man of genius makes no mistakes. His errors are volitional and are the portals of discovery."
—JAMES JOYCE, *Ulysses*

Stephen Dedalus is defending Shakespeare when he makes this claim, and given Joyce's own predilection for error, he is probably defending Joyce too. It is an appealing idea and one partially corroborated by Freud in *The Psychopathology of Everyday Life*, where he likewise brings up volition: most of our mistakes, he says, "grant a reluctantly suppressed wish."[1] But, genius notwithstanding, it cannot always be true. Shakespeare has been known to blunder on a number of occasions: turkeys in *Henry IV, Part One*, long before such birds were known in England;[2] a striking clock in *Julius Caesar*, a thousand years before its time;[3] and, in *The Winter's Tale*, the presence of Bohemian shores, despite Bohemia's being landlocked, just to name a few.[4] Of this last error, first pointed out by Ben Jonson, scholars have been attempting to absolve Shakespeare for more than two hundred years. Some declare "Bohemia" to be a printer's mistake for "Bithynia" (which did have a coast);[5] others suggest that the play's particular "Bohemia" refers to a region in southern Italy,[6] and still others persuasively point out that comedies and romances like *The Winter's Tale* often set out to invoke and celebrate the counterfactual. A few have even suggested Shakespeare deliberately errs in order to provoke Jonson into correcting him.[7] Given the prevalence of mistaking in our everyday lives, where does this urge to deny mistakes in our literature come from, and what does it say about our conceptions of writers and writing?

Joyce's Stephen is not referring specifically to mistakes in Shakespeare's plays or poems in the lines I quote—he is thinking of Shakespeare's marriage—but the implication is that even the literary errors of great writers are shaped by intention, however unconscious. His generosity toward mistake reflects a modern view of literary making in which error and unknowingness seem to coexist with more purposed elements of form, especially in poetry, where qualities of accident and surprise play a crucial role in the process of composition. "The imperfect is our paradise," writes Wallace Stevens in "The Poems of Our Climate";[8] Robert Frost, "the initial delight is in the surprise of remembering something I didn't know I knew."[9] These artistic celebrations of error and chance coincide with twentieth-century theories of the unconscious and its creative powers to suggest for literature, and for poetry in particular, an inherent defense against mistake. Most flaws in poems appear felicitous—they "are the portals of discovery." How could a reader, upon encountering a mistake in a poem (a misused word, an incorrect fact, a grammatical inconsistency), *not* assume that whatever is wrong is also right and that whatever should not have been written, but was, is therefore meant to be? Answering how is precisely the aim of this book, but let me begin by suggesting the importance of doing so.

Our readerly temptation to justify errors in poetry has grown stronger during the last hundred years, perhaps owing to Freud's groundbreaking and systematic account of mistakes at the beginning of the century and perhaps also because of the academy's adoption of modernist-inspired ways of thinking about and encountering texts. "To divert interest from the poet to the poetry is a laudable aim," writes T. S. Eliot—an aim that becomes especially popular midcentury.[10] And how can a poet err if there is no poet, only poem? Today we nearly always begin reading poetry by assuming that what is questionable or irreconcilable in its language, history, or grammar must be integral to its fabric of meaning, not a snag or a loose end. For instance, when we encounter the following lines in *Childe Harold's Pilgrimage*—

And send'st him, shivering in thy playful spray
And howling, to his Gods, where haply lies

> His petty hope in some near port or bay,
> And dashest him again to earth:—there let him lay.[11]

—it feels unseemly to harp on the final line's solecism. So much good rhyme comes at a price, we tell ourselves; or we appeal to the dictionary, which points out that in the seventeenth and eighteenth centuries, "lay" occasionally has "intransitive uses . . . resembling those of 'lie.' "[12] (Gavin Hopps offers this latter excuse in an essay called "Byron and Grammatical Freedom.")[13] Never mind that Byron was not writing poetry during the seventeenth or eighteenth centuries. Such open-minded attitudes toward mistake were not a given during Byron's own lifetime nor in the decades immediately after, and Matthew Arnold has no qualms in disparaging him on these grounds:

> Byron is so negligent in his poetical style, he is often, to say the truth, so slovenly, slipshod, and infelicitous, he is so little haunted by the true artist's fine passion for the correct use and consummate management of words, that he may be described as having for this artistic gift the insensibility of the barbarian.[14]

Arnold was a pedant susceptible to errors of his own: in his elegy for Charlotte Brontë, for instance, he figures Brontë's grave "[i]n a churchyard high 'mid the moors," whereas in reality Brontë is buried with her sisters inside the church. And his poem describing "The Church of Brou" is famously full of inaccuracies regarding the landscape.[15] These geographical mistakes may not be on par with the "slipshod" style that grieves him in Byron, but they likely would have haunted him nevertheless (we have no reason to believe Arnold incapable of reproaching himself with the same rigor he affords others). The intervening years have softened readers to error, perhaps, or perhaps it is more accurate to say that a critic's appealing to the "true artist's fine passion for the correct use and consummate management of words" is simply too limiting for a contemporary conception of artistry. ("What is *correct* use?" I can already hear myself wondering.) Notions of what is acceptable—morally, politically, aesthetically—are constantly changing.

However, while attitudes toward mistake have tended to shift according to readers' own notions of propriety and its value, the broader question of how to distinguish error from poetic license is nearly as old as poetry itself. Aristotle poses it at length in the *Poetics*:

> [T]here is not the same kind of correctness in poetry as in politics, or indeed any other art. There is, however, within the limits of poetry itself a possibility of two kinds of error, the one directly, the other only accidentally connected with the art. If the poet meant to describe the thing correctly, and failed through a lack of power of expression, his art itself is at fault. But if it was through his having meant to describe it in some incorrect way . . . that the technical error, . . . or impossibilities of whatever kind they may be, have got into his description, his error in that case is not in the essentials of the poetic art. . . . Any impossibilities there may be in his descriptions of things are faults. But from another point of view they are justifiable, if they serve the end of poetry itself—if . . . they make the effect of some portion of the work more astounding. . . . If, however, the poetic end might have been as well or better attained without sacrifice of technical correctness in such matters, the impossibility is not to be justified, since the description should be, if it can, entirely free from error.[16]

The nub for Aristotle seems to lie in whether or not the mistake could have been avoided without laying waste to the work itself. If so, then the poet's art is at fault. But if not, then—what? Shall we simply suspend our disbelief, not only with regard to misrepresented facts and narrative impossibilities but also with regard to grammatical and lexical laws (e.g., *Childe Harold*)? Faced with this uncomfortable dilemma for more than two thousand years, readers have tended to take Aristotle's mandate to "justify" mistakes very seriously. Those like Arnold, who are willing to venture that the poet should have applied himself more strenuously against error, are increasingly the exception. Instead, most critics assume the opposite task of reading error strenuously, which is to say that the burden of justifying errors in poems more often than not falls upon the reader (rather than the poet), who feels a responsibility to determine *how* (not *whether*) the mistake serves to "make the effect of some portion of the work more astounding." And so while it is likely that mistakes in poems are as frequent today as they were in ancient times, our conceiving of them as flaws precipitated by poets is rarer than it used to be.

This change in habit may have something to do with the fact that the word "mistake" has become vexed by its own negative connotations. Joyce's Stephen was willing to concede error ("his errors are volitional") where he would not concede mistake. "Blundering" aggravates, too, but at least enjoys the advantage of comedy: one would occasionally blunder for a laugh. But mistake? Never. "Erring," on the other hand, takes on a scholarly air, meaning literally "to wander" (from the Latin *erro, errare*). Error floats; mistake falls flat. In everyday conversation, we may use these words interchangeably; each implies a misstep, an expectation gone awry. But in literary criticism, mistake is the far more serious crime.[17] "Mistake"—the word having formed in English as a simple compound (i.e., "mis" and "take")—is what remains to the poet when justification fails.[18]

Error has had a special provenance in poetry since Edmund Spenser first punned on "her" at the beginning of *The Faerie Queene*. Aptly hidden in a "wandring wood," the vile monster "Errour" lies waiting to be slain by Spenser's errant Knight, "Her vomit full of bookes and papers" and her progeny "fowle, and blacke as inke."[19] By figuring error with literary attributes, Spenser not only connects his poem's fate with that of his Redcrosse Knight but also acknowledges error to be among the primary encounters for any poet setting out. Poets and knights are necessarily wanderers—often straying in their errancy to the brink of "*Errour's* den."[20] His portrait may draw on error's expanding boundaries as a literary phenomenon during his lifetime; the idea of "error" in early modern literary culture encompassed more than just moral, political, and poetical blunders. The availability of the printing press brought along with it the possibility for printer's errors and mechanical glitches. At the same time, the "errata" list became a standard inclusion in printed books. Seth Lerer notes,

> the errata sheet, in the late fifteenth and early sixteenth centuries, records more than slips of typesetting; it details errors in doctrine, dialect, or usage. At its most complex and self-conscious, the errata sheet stands as the site of humanist erudition and early modern

subjectivity. It is the place where the past is publicly brought in line with the present, where errors of all kinds could be confessed and corrected.[21]

Error had become a natural and expected element of both a poet's encounter with his process and a reader's encounter with the text. The object was nearly always to slay it—by confessing, or correcting, or both—but there was little shame in the confrontation.

The modern errata list still reflects this urge to correct, but its scope for doing so tends to be limited to typographical errors and the occasional mischosen word. Poets' "confessions" of error have been superseded by a sense that error works in tandem with meaning itself. Thus Paul Muldoon writes in the author's note to his collection *Poems, 1968–1998*:

> Other than to correct such factual errors as my having written "painfully" for "painstakingly," "bathyscope" for "bathysphere," "*Ranus ranus*" for "*Rana temporaria*," "jardonelle" for "jargonelle," and "aureoles" for "areolae," I have made scarcely any changes in the texts of the poems, since I'm fairly certain that, after a shortish time, the person through whom a poem was written is no more entitled to make revisions than any other reader.[22]

Exactly how much time must pass, one wonders, before the author loses his rights to revise? Is it as soon as he lays words on the page, or only once they are distributed widely—when the reader has had a chance to make meaning of them? Muldoon self-consciously refers to himself not as the poet but as "the person through whom a poem was written." (Where better than in a list of a book's mistakes to cast doubt on its authorship?) His avoidance allies him with "any other reader" and artfully diminishes his own agency in the writing. We are left to wonder exactly where he draws the line between making "changes in the texts" and correcting "factual errors." One implication of this difference is that factual errors betray an agency that the rest of the text does not.

The nature of Muldoon's errata ("my having written 'painfully' for 'painstakingly'") confirms the possibility of erring during composition, however little agency the poet claims to have in this process after the fact. The Portuguese poet Fernando Pessoa takes the opposite tack, insisting almost to the point of absurdity upon his own correctness:

> While my eyes distractedly watch, I inwardly fashion this aquatic image which is more suitable than any other (in part because I thought it would rain) for this random movements.
>
> As I wrote this last sentence, which for me says exactly what it means, I thought it might be useful to put at the end of my book, when I finally publish it, a few "Non-Errata" after the "Errata," and to note: *the phrase "this random movements," on page so-and-so, is correct as is, with the noun in the plural and the demonstrative in the singular.* But what does this have to do with what I was thinking? Nothing, which is why I let myself think it.[23]

Pessoa's defense suggests the impossibility of ever knowing meaning—"which *for me* says exactly what it means"—while also asserting his having a hand in making it. The error here is not determinable by the reader or grammarian but by the agent who creates it. Regarding this particular passage, Adam Phillips points out that "[t]o presume something is an error is simply to look at it from a point of view that makes it one."[24] Pessoa is testing the limits of his own creative powers, as we can devise from the comment he offers at the end: "But what does this have to do with what I was thinking? Nothing, which is why I let myself think it." "Randomness" is what gives rise to thought here. That is, something more seemingly consistent with his purpose might be deemed "correct" but less worth thinking. And so his "random" error betrays an unexpected, if still wished for, meaning that in turn calls into question its own randomness. The logic may be summed up in Wittgenstein's enigmatic formulation: "There is no sharp distinction between a random mistake and a systematic one. That is, between what you are inclined to call 'random' and what 'systematic.' "[25]

Pessoa explains "this random movements" by pursuing randomness and its relation to literary meaning. Freud, who was writing at the same time as Pessoa, engages with a similar pursuit. His aim in *The Psychopathology of Everyday Life* is not to defend mistakes, exactly, but to uncover the repressions that lead to them. Justification is another thing altogether. Aristotle means, when he writes that certain errors are "justifiable," that their wrongness can be seen as worthwhile. J. L. Austin points out that there is actually a constellation of terms, each of which suggests different kinds of absolution: to "justify," "excuse," "defend," "plea"—is one better than the other when it comes to reading errors in poetry?[26] The simple answer, as will become clear throughout this book, is that different kinds of mistakes inspire different kinds of readerly techniques. For example, one could "justify" Shakespeare's Bohemian shores by pointing out (as Jonathan Bate does) that it was safer for the playwright to conflate the geographies of Sicily and Bohemia than to risk offending members of the court of King James.[27] In Austin's terms, to justify "is to admit that he, [i.e., Shakespeare], did do that very thing, [i.e., give landlocked Bohemia a shore], but to argue that it was a good thing, or the right or sensible thing, or a permissible thing to do, either in the general or at least in the special circumstances of the occasion."[28] On the other hand, in the case of the turkeys, justification becomes nearly impossible—we may only "excuse" Shakespeare of either not recognizing the turkey as a New World bird, or not caring. To "excuse," says Austin, is to "admit that it was bad" but not to "accept full, or even any, responsibility."[29] Freud suggests the possibility of excusing when he writes that "ignorance is the opposite of mistaken memory."[30]

These differences point to an underlying taxonomy of poetic mistaking. Shakespeare's anachronisms relate to matters of fact: there *were* no striking clocks in ancient Rome, no turkeys in England at the turn of the fifteenth century. These errors may be excused on the grounds of carelessness or ignorance—but they are not entirely justifiable. Christopher Ricks explores this complexity in "Literature and the Matter of Fact," recalling a "contractual model in literary understanding" in which it might be possible to accept these sorts of implausibilities (for instance, on account of Shakespeare's energies being willfully devoted elsewhere).[31] But in most cases, he warns against simply "letting the matter pass," citing Ruskin's impassioned statement about truth and the imagination in *The Seven Lamps of Architecture*:[32]

> It is necessary to our rank as spiritual creatures, that we should be able to invent and to behold what is not; and to our rank as moral creatures, that we should know and confess at the same time that it is not.[33]

For Ricks, as for Ruskin, our ability to "know and confess" truth comes as nothing short of a moral responsibility, even when we read or behold imaginative works of art. The severity of such a responsibility may be less when we encounter mistakes like Byron's, which do not pertain to matters of truth or fact so much as propriety. And yet Byron's grammatical mistake leaves him vulnerable to other avenues of attack, its being a technical flaw and therefore a dent in the artistry of the verse. For his part, Byron offers the following justification in *Don Juan*:

> few are slow
> In thinking that their enemy is beat,
> (Or *beaten*, if *you* insist on grammar, though
> I never think about it in a heat).[34]

However, the parenthetical correction here undermines Byron's message— for what is he doing in these lines but thinking about it? He is less defensive in "Hints from Horace," where he wonders more earnestly:

> And must the Bard his glowing thoughts confine?
> Lest Censure hover o'er some faulty line,
> Remove whate'er a Critic may suspect,
> To gain the paltry suffrage of "Correct"!
> Or prune the spirit of each daring phrase
> To fly from Error—not to merit praise?[35]

In these lines, Byron fears the pruning of grammatical shears more than censure itself—and there is indeed something noble in his idea of letting the "spirit" dictate the parameters of the phrase. But an exacting poet like Horace would not actually condone sloppiness—nor does Byron most of the time. If correctness truly amounts to "paltry suffrage" for him (I have my doubts), it certainly means something more to poets like the American A. R. Ammons, who admits to taking great care over poetry's minutiae:

> [T]he rational, critical mind is essential to making poems: it protects the real poem (which is nonrational) from blunders, misconceptions, incompetences; it weeds out the second rate.[36]

Ammons's blend of the "rational, critical mind" and the "nonrational" poem (he carefully avoids calling the poet himself irrational) may be the required equation for producing first-rate verse. Pulling out the weeds of error constitutes an essential part of his process. Byron, drunk on passion, could be rational too—even when he wrote on gin, he revised on soda water.

Grammatical mistakes are not the only kind of technical flaws, though they are certainly the most common. Milton may be charged on a different sort of technicality for the confused chronology in book 10 of *Paradise Lost*, wherein Satan appears to overhear a conversation between Adam and Eve that, according to the logical time sequence of the book, has not yet taken place.[37] His architectural error might, in an extreme case, hamper our ability to follow the book's narrative, but it does little to affect its overall meaning. But Milton's mistake in "Lycidas" is another matter—its being bound up in the sense, rather than the structure, of the lines that contain it:

> *Fame* is the spur that the clear spirit doth raise
> (That last infirmity of Noble mind)
> To scorn delights, and live laborious dayes;
> But the fair Guerdon when we hope to find,
> And think to burst out into sudden blaze,
> Comes the blind *Fury* with th'abhorred shears,
> And slits the thin-spun life.[38]

The hitch here is that Milton seems to be referring not to one of the Furies, who were responsible for punishing mortals on behalf of the gods, but to Atropos, one of the Fates, whose job it was to cut the thread of life with a pair of shears. His mistake has little to do with technique; rather, it comes with the allusion—perhaps a result of some false notion of the mythology, or simply a moment of confusion. Whatever the reason, this kind of mistake requires a different mode of defense from both Shakespeare's and Byron's. And then there are even peskier historical mistakes, like Joseph Warton's confusing Aztecs and Incas in "The Dying Indian" when he first published it in 1755 (he fixes the poem in subsequent editions).[39] The conscientious reader feels responsible not only for determining the nature of the error but also for finding the appropriate method of justifying it.

But why defend such mistakes at all? The answer may simply be that the dangers of *not* doing so seem serious enough to drive a reader toward over-excusing. They include, for instance, the possibility of coming across as too literal or even pedantic. Pointing out grammatical flaws is rarely a flattering pursuit. Similarly, critics who acknowledge mistakes open themselves up to the accusation of "not getting" the poem or poet. (And who but the poet has the right to determine how the poem should be written?) Vanity may not be the only thing at stake: the sensitive reader will also not want to misjudge the extent of a poet's genius. For instance, it is impossible to know for sure that Milton had not read an account of the Furies that equipped one of them with scissors.

But problems arise. Justifying mistakes can be as perilous as not. Keats's poem "On First Looking into Chapman's Homer" furnishes us with the best example. Admirers of the sonnet have been attempting to justify Keats's mistake ever since Tennyson first pointed out, forty-five years after the poem's initial publication, a historical error in line 11, which intro-duces the Spanish explorer Hernando Cortez standing on a mountain in Darien:

> Much have I travell'd in the realms of gold,
>> And many goodly states and kingdoms seen;
>> Round many western islands have I been
> Which bards in fealty to Apollo hold.
> Oft of one wide expanse had I been told
>> That deep-brow'd Homer ruled as his demesne;
>> Yet did I never breathe its pure serene
> Till I heard Chapman speak out loud and bold:
> Then felt I like some watcher of the skies
>> When a new planet swims into his ken;
> Or like stout Cortez when with eagle eyes
>> He star'd at the Pacific—and all his men
> Look'd at each other with a wild surmise—
>> Silent, upon a peak in Darien.[40]

"History would here suggest Balboa," Tennyson writes in the notes to Francis Palgrave's popular anthology *The Golden Treasury* in 1861.[41] And he is right insofar as it was Vasco Nuñez de Balboa—rather than Cortez—who climbed a mountain range on the Isthmus of Darien in present-day Panama and saw the Pacific Ocean for the first time. Cortez, who colonized Mexico soon after, and caught sight of the Pacific from there, never set foot in Darien himself.

But then, Tennyson always was a fussy poet. Meticulously attentive to detail, particularly details relating to fact, he made sure that whatever histories he invoked were as accurate as possible. As Ricks reminds us in "Literature and the Matter of Fact," when Tennyson learned immediately before publishing "The Charge of the Light Brigade" that he may not have been exact in referring to the figure of "six hundred" cavalrymen at the battle of Balaclava (some reports from Crimea gave a number closer to seven hundred), he appended a note to the poem saying so for its December 1854 appearance in the *Examiner*.[42] In fact, Tennyson's poem takes error as one of its subjects:

II
'Forward, the Light Brigade!'
Was there a man dismayed?
Not though the soldier knew
    Some one had blundered:
Their's not to make reply,
Their's not to reason why,
Their's but to do and die:
Into the valley of Death
    Rode the six hundred.[43]

Tennyson's men ride honorably to their death despite knowing that the order telling them to do so is mistaken. The "blunder" he refers to likely came from two ranks up—an absent British commander who erroneously thought that the Russian troops were retreating rather than at the ready. His men followed the order without hesitation, and the poem became hugely popular for its celebration of their valor. But Tennyson's tone is as admonishing of the officer's blunder as it is admiring of the men's sense of duty. The sting of their knowing about the mistake and not saying so is part of the poem's complicated morality.

Perhaps Tennyson's own scruples made him particularly sensitive to Keats's mixing of conquistadors. (He was similarly accused of wrongly thinking that trains run in grooves rather than on rails after writing the phrase "the ringing grooves of change" in "Locksley Hall"—a mistake he chalks up to having taken his first train journey, from Liverpool to Manchester in 1830, in the dark.)[44] John Kandl supposes Tennyson was in one of his "schoolmasterly moods" when pointing out Keats's error, but then Kandl believes that Keats may have intended Cortez all along (his argument being that "it is Cortez's 'first looking' and not Balboa's unprecedented . . . discovery that shapes Keats's analogy").[45] He is one of several recent critics who attempt to rescue the mistake by suggesting that it isn't one. Charles Rzepka offers the most thorough argument of this kind, based on the idea that the sonnet—much like Cortez's view of the Pacific—is an emblem of belatedness more than a celebration of discovery:

> The Darien tableau in which Keats has placed his belated conquistador brilliantly underscores the poignant theme, announced in the very title of his sonnet, of the belatedness of the poet's own sublime ambitions.[46]

For Rzepka, Keats's identification with Cortez is based on their both being stupendous latecomers. The point feels persuasive in light of the accounts from Keats's friend Charles Cowden Clarke noting that Keats had encountered Homer before—in the less inspiring couplets of Pope—and that it was only during this unexpected reading of Chapman's version that he could "breathe its pure serene." Along these lines, it is somewhat plausible that Kandl and Rzepka (and Susan Wolfson, Charles Walcutt, and C. V. Wicker before them)[47] are right that Keats did intend Cortez, with that explorer's second glimpse of the Pacific, rather than Balboa, who saw it first. But if so, then the historical error of placing Cortez in Darien rather than in Mexico still persists. Probably for this reason, Rzepka is careful to refer to these lines as "the Darien tableau"; later in his essay, he justifies Keats's choice of the "wrong" locale with the following ingenious formulation:

> By transporting Cortez to a peak in Darien, Keats represents the contagious effects of his own sublime "transport," collapsing Cortez's

and Balboa's separate encounters with the Pacific into a spatially iden-
tical but diachronically laminated point of exalted awareness, and
investing a scene of belated discovery with the uncanny aura of a first
discoverer whose achievement his successor would both supplant and
appropriate.[48]

Appealing as this proposition is, it neither feels likely nor accounts for other
aspects of Keats's poem that seem to fit Balboa's discovery better than Cortez's—for instance, the fact that Balboa famously asked his men to stand
behind him (perhaps in "wild surmise") so that he could see the ocean
before they could.[49] If Keats did mean Cortez, these inaccuracies are
perplexing.

Questions regarding intentionality and its relation to error lie at the
heart of this debate. One way to begin addressing them is to revisit the
scene of this sonnet's composition, which took place in the early morning
hours of a day in October 1816. Keats had stayed up all night with Clarke
reading and delighting in his friend's borrowed 1616 folio of Chapman.
His enthusiasm for this Elizabethan translation was so great that he drafted
the sonnet immediately after leaving Clarke's home and sent it back to his
friend by messenger only a few hours later. Clarke recollects,

> when I came down to breakfast the next morning, I found upon my
> table a letter with no other inclosure than his famous sonnet, "On
> first looking into Chapman's Homer." We had parted, as I have al-
> ready said, at day-spring; yet he contrived that I should receive the
> poem, from a distance of nearly two miles, before 10, A.M.[50]

Keats presumably began the sonnet while walking home at dawn; he would
have had to put it to paper within an hour or two of arriving home in
Southwark if it was to reach Clarke's table in Clerkenwell before breakfast.
The speed with which Keats wrote the poem was not unusual; many of his
poems were written with what Jack Stillinger has called "spontaneity," usually in the space of a few hours.[51] But these details go some way toward
explaining how it is possible that Keats put Cortez on a mountain in Panama that he had never actually visited. It is doubtful that he composed this
particular poem with history book in hand the way Tennyson composed

"The Charge of the Light Brigade," his fingers still black from the ink of the newspaper report.

What Keats *intended* by situating Cortez in Darien—beyond a portrait of a man gazing at something wonderful that he has never seen before—may of course be read variously. Many early critics considered the poem to be about literary discovery; more recently, it has been read as an initiation into poetic maturity. The sonnet opens with an assertion of experience rendered inadequate: "Much have I travell'd" and "many goodly states and kingdoms seen" and "[o]ft of one wide expanse had I been told." The verbs in this travelogue progress from active to passive across the octave: I have "travell'd," I have "seen," I have "been," I have "been told." Keats does not expound upon "one wide expanse," so we cannot be sure which geographical place this line refers to—only that his speaker was finally able to breathe its "pure serene" via Chapman. Since the wide expanse is also a figure for poetry, it is not a large leap from this inspiration (i.e., breathing in this serenity) to that of the next metaphor, Cortez inhaling his first sight of the new ocean. The word "serene," one of several small revisions Keats makes to the poem later on, connects the described experience of reading in line 7 to the sense of tranquillity suggested by the Pacific in lines 12–14. We can hypothesize that Keats at least means for us to understand that reading, the act of "looking upon" a page, has for him something of the visceral quality of breathing, and that reading something new can feel like gazing upon something never before seen.

I am spelling out these analogies to emphasize the aspects of Keats's conceit that are not specific to Cortez. Many of the comparisons in this poem remain distinct from any likeness between the poem's speaker and that particular conquistador: reading is to breathing as serene is to Pacific as looking upon Chapman's Homer is to seeing an ocean for the first time. It may well be that Cortez's belated looking in relation to Balboa's original discovery is a part of the poem's complicated web of meaning, but there are other metaphors in place too. Working out what Keats *means* by Cortez becomes even trickier if you consider the poet's own idea of how poetry comes to him. His friend Richard Woodhouse quotes him as saying

that he has often not been aware of the beauty of some thought or expression until after he has composed and written it down—It then

has struck him with astonishment—and seemed rather the production of another person than his own—He has wondered how he came
to hit upon it.[52]

It would seem as though Keats often arrives at his meanings ex post facto,
looking upon them with the kind of wonder or "astonishment" ascribed to
the astronomer or the explorer. This sense of chance in composition seems
opposed to the inclusion of historical fact, insofar as once history has occurred—once it is *history*—chance can have little to do with its description.
Keats could not have written about the feeling of seeing the Pacific for the
first time and merely chanced upon Cortez. Or could he have?

Stillinger describes Keats's writing process as one based upon subjects
rather than ideas. The poet, he suggests, sets out to write *about* something
and only comes to the *ideas* of his verse through the act of composition.[53]
We might therefore imagine Keats as having intended to write, for his
friend Clarke, a sonnet about the experience of reading Chapman—with
no more specificity than that. What happened next was subject to chance:
the serenity of the air as the poet made his way back home, perhaps, or the
way it drew his attention to the planets fading above him in the early morning sky. In this sense, the analogy between the reader-as-discoverer and
Cortez was not so much the *intended* force of the poem as it was a by-
product of the original conception. Keats himself describes this phenomenon in Shakespeare's sonnets as "fine things said unintentionally—in the
intensity of working out conceits."[54] Picking up on this notion, Willard
Spiegelman has said that for Keats, "[w]riting seems to be unconscious and
unwilled activity . . . but also an intense 'working out' of and through conceits."[55] If he is right, then it may be better to think of Cortez neither as
intended nor accidental; rather, Keats makes the "unintentional" but suddenly volitional decision as a necessary part of his "working out" of the
sonnet's logic and imagery. He means "Cortez" no more or less than he
means "silent" or "peak" or "Darien."

To separate intended meaning from received meaning is not to diminish
the import of either. On the contrary, what Keats intends, both consciously
and unconsciously, directs his poem in its entirety. However, what we understand his intentions to be becomes a separate inquiry altogether—a
"critical inquiry" that, as W. K. Wimsatt and Monroe C. Beardsley put it

in "The Intentional Fallacy," could not even be "settled by consulting the oracle" himself.[56] Their mandate—that we use as our evidence for meaning what is "internal to the poem" only—has been a useful if provocative one for more than seventy years,[57] as has its more recent antithesis in Stephen Knapp and Walter Benn Michaels's essay "Against Theory," which attempts to dissolve the gap between meaning and authorial intention by treating them as one and the same.[58] Sean Burke has pointed out the convergence of these two seemingly oppositional positions in their shared belief that "it is fruitless to inquire into an author's intention"—either because what the author means "cannot find its way back into his or her text" or because "what the author meant is everything the text means."[59] But we might concede that Keats's historical error puts pressure on both sets of parameters, and that there are other ways of reading around—and for—intention that might better account for poetry's mistakes. For instance, E. D. Hirsch, in arguing for "validity" but not "certainty" in the interpretation of literary texts, has noted that there may be a third possibility for meaning, outside of an author's intention and a reader's supposition, that denies neither but that essentially belongs to the text itself; he labels this idea " 'autonomism'—the doctrine that literary texts belong to a distinct ontological realm where meaning is independent of authorial will."[60] Here at least, between author and reader, mistake may gather some momentum as a driving force, albeit a reckless one, for if mistakes occur somewhere, and indeed some*time*, between an author's intentions for, and a readers' interpretations of, a text, they carry a distinct kind of importance, being neither purely intended by authors nor entirely irrelevant to readerly meanings.

One way mistakes throw extra light on intended meanings is by corrupting them (the *Oxford English Dictionary* [*OED*] defines "mistake" as "[a] misconception of the meaning of something").[61] Thinking about Keats's mistake, in other words, may also shed light on some of the conscious choices he made during the period in which he wrote and revised this poem. But these conscious choices represent only half of the story: mistakes—while often resulting from the difficulties and pressures involved in craft—can also be linked to unconscious desires. Even if we could formulate a reasonable judgment about whether Keats really meant Cortez or whether he in fact meant Balboa, we would have to consider the possibility that, at least unconsciously, he meant Cortez either way. Unlike accidents, which merely happen, mistakes are made—they are born of choice. In the case of this poem, we are forced to acknowledge that Keats both *meant* to write Cortez *and* mistook him for Balboa at the same time.

This inevitable duality makes the fervor with which critics argue on either side of the Cortez-Balboa dilemma particularly fascinating. Apart from Tennyson, who remains agnostic about Keats's intentions, nearly all of the readers who mention the Cortez error display a remarkable amount of creativity in explaining why it must have happened. And what almost all of the critics—both those for and against reading Cortez as a mistake—have in common is a compulsion to justify Keats's decision. It is easy to see how those who favor Cortez as correct make a case for Keats's inalienable rightness. Kandl's appeal to the analogy of second sightings is an obvious plea for taking Keats's poetical choices seriously, and Rzepka's clever justification for his unlikely placing of Cortez in Darien—that he is "investing a scene of belated discovery with the uncanny aura of a first discoverer"—asks that we give precedence to the imaginative and unconscious elements of Keats's process over the details of what Rzepka calls a "negligible" historical error.[62] Susan Wolfson argues similarly, pointing out that

> Cortez was not the first European to view the Pacific, even as Keats himself was not the first to read Homer through Chapman; what they share is the testimony of personal witness and the sensation of expanding possibilities such experience brings.[63]

Yet none of these arguments for the appropriateness of Cortez make much of an attempt to account for the fact that Keats's known historical source—William Robertson's *History of America* (1777)—includes a description of Balboa's discovery that very closely matches the scenario in Keats's poem:

> When, with infinite toil, they had climbed up the greater part of that steep ascent, Balboa commanded his men to halt, and advanced alone to the summit, that he might be the first who should enjoy a spectacle which he had so long desired.[64]

To those critics for whom Keats remains free from mistake, the similarity between the "wild surmise" of Cortez's men and this famous account of

Balboa's men halting behind him so that he could enjoy the first prospect remains a mere coincidence.

Even more provocative than these justifications are the apologies from critics who *do* consider Cortez to be a mistake. Far from simply mentioning Balboa and letting the error be, many of the critics who follow Tennyson's correction to Keats do so while simultaneously excusing him. For example, Claude Finney testifies in his 1936 volume *The Evolution of Keats's Poetry*:

> If Keats had failed to suggest the emotion with which Balboa stared at the Pacific he would have committed a serious artistic error; his mistake in substituting Cortez for Balboa was an historical error which lies outside the art of poetry.[65]

Finney's appeal to an Aristotelian sense of poetry's borders is perhaps the most subtle way of making amends. Marjorie Levinson takes the apology one step further:

> The contained badness of "Chapman's Homer" constitutes its goodness, which is to say, its rhetorical force.[66]

Levinson's accusation becomes a celebration. And in much the same way, no sooner does Jerome McGann remind us of Keats's mistake than he begins to exalt it:

> The crux of this poem involves its infamous "mistake" . . . Cortez standing silent on the peak in Darien: the image is at once ludicrous and wonderful . . . Keats's schoolboy error transforms and redeems the poetical machinery and fine rhetoric he wants to parade. The poem transports us to the most forbidden world of all—the . . . world of adolescence. . . . The poem's absurd error is the sign that it has pledged its allegiance to what would mortally embarrass a grown-up consciousness. . . . If it weren't so naïve—if it lacked that mistake about Cortez, for example—the sonnet might well strike us as less sublime than trumped up and factitious. But in fact it *has* escaped the serious business of Culture. The poem drops us to a place of actual

magic, an embarrassing place that here should not and will not embarrass. That is its magic.[67]

With impassioned defenses like this, it is hard to decide which set of justifications are more creatively ingenious: those that refuse to read Cortez as a mistake or those that do. The irony of these responses is that Keats now enjoys a reputation that almost no flaw could mar; he is among a handful of English poets whose talents are celebrated as innate. We must conclude that the impulse to justify encompasses more than a simple desire to recuperate any specific poet's blunder—it goes beyond, even, the scruples of adhering to historical fact. Something in us wants a poem to be right even when we know its poet is wrong.

When we insist on a poem's inalienable rightness, we risk overemphasizing the extent to which its mistakes derive from unconscious intentions. In arguing for the importance of acknowledging mistake, I do not mean to discount the *possibility* of such intentions—only to limit their purview. Freud's study of mistakes (in the form of accidents, slips, and forgettings) uncovers the ways that seemingly unintentional actions are really volitional and demonstrates how we might produce meanings from them that can be useful in understanding ourselves and our personal histories.[68] Critics of poetry—psychoanalytic and otherwise—have seamlessly appropriated this methodology into their own reading practices. We produce meaning not only from the elements of poems that feel most purposeful but also from poetry's subtler moments of unintended creativity. And we are careful not to (necessarily) attribute such meanings to the poet. It can be satisfactory, even satisfying, for our interpretations to constitute meanings only insofar as they play upon the psyche of the reader, regardless of whether or not we believe them to originate in the psyche of the writer. But Freud's discovery need not blind us to the many instances in the history of poetry where mistakes speak more relevantly to the poet's conscious choices in craft than to their potential unconscious origins in the mind. As Phillips notes, Freud himself "was not an orthodox Freudian."[69] There can be moments in poetry, as in life, when chance intervenes not as a result of our wishes but at the expense of them.

Thinking of certain kinds of mistakes in poems as having no discernible psychically determined origins—and little or no bearing on the production of meaning—may disturb an illusion about poetry and poets upon which we have come to depend. We usually rely on this kind of psychic determinism to show us how our experience is shaped by our own wishes rather than by chance. However, as Phillips has pointed out with regard to Freud, it may also sometimes be the case that chance or contingency (which can masquerade in poetry as mistake) is frightening enough that we treat it as unconscious volition in order "to counter the anxiety that chance is determining our fate and the potential loss of meaning this could entail."[70] When this happens as we read poetry's mistakes, we risk turning psychic determinism on its head. That is, we may occasionally find ourselves making meaning out of things that have little meaning *because* it is reassuring. For the contemporary reader of poems, psychic determinism may not always be an explanation but a desire.

This readerly desire for meaning, coupled with a benevolent wish to give poets the benefit of the doubt, may seem like reason enough to justify mistakes in poems wherever and whenever possible. But we often do so at the cost of understanding the very process of creation we mean to celebrate. When we deny mistakes, or read them as magical—as something that happens within a poem rather than as something made by a poet—we are in danger of making a different kind of error of our own. By interpreting poems with a view toward undoing poets' mistakes, we prioritize the unconscious aspects of poetry-making and, in doing so, indirectly marginalize matters of craft that are so important to poets themselves. Poets make conscious, aesthetic decisions that are subject, as all of our choices are, to both unconscious desires and the contingencies involved in everyday living—which often lead to mistake. Denying mistake places undue weight on the former while trivializing the importance of the latter. Seamus Heaney refers to the balance of these two influences when he writes that "[t]he constant problem, the constant question" for the poet, is "the relationship between the conscious and the unconscious aspects": "If you see too much intention in another person's work," he remarks, "you resist it. [But i]f you see too little, if it's not been brought far enough, you regret it."[71] As readers, we should be careful not to resist the tension between what writers choose to say and what happens to those choices as they become manifest in words on a page. As Anne Ferry's study *By Design: Intention in Poetry* demonstrates, poets' choices are everywhere in a text, revealing the extent to which they are both "self-aware" and "critically adept."[72] Poems have designs—on us, yes, but also in and of themselves as works of art. To relegate the poet's designs for the poem as secondary to its designs on a reader is to strip the art of its origins in the decisions of the self-conscious poet. Poetry's knowledge and meanings are overdetermined: they necessarily reflect a combination of poets' wishes, readers' desires, and the contingent world from which they both inescapably draw.[73]

Austin's account of the difference between accidents, mistakes, and other mishaps that inspire excusing suggests this complexity as it relates to error:

> In an *accident* something befalls: by *mistake* you take the wrong one: in *error* you stray: when you act *deliberately* you act after weighing it up (*not* after thinking out ways and means). It is worth asking ourselves whether we know the etymology of "result" or of "spontaneously," and worth remembering that "unwillingly" and "involuntarily" come from very different sources.[74]

In addition to reminding us of the differences between accident, which occurs despite the will, and mistake, which occurs because of it, his appeal to etymology clarifies an important aspect of intention.[75] The poet may write "involuntarily" but still retain some degree of will: his language can betray the influence of unknown or unidentifiable desires that (in Freudian terms) fulfill a suppressed wish. In such cases, he shows no conscious volition but is nevertheless not un*willing*. In fact, the opposite may be true: when words come involuntarily, they display a pure willingness on the part of the poet to betray the unconscious intentions behind them. As Hirsch explains:

> It is not possible to mean what one does not mean, though it is very possible to mean what one is not conscious of meaning. . . . There is a difference between meaning and consciousness of meaning, and since meaning is an affair of consciousness, one can say more precisely that there is a difference between consciousness and self-consciousness.[76]

It may therefore be the case that in any poem, there are not one but two kinds of intentions. Why prioritize poets' unconscious intentions over their self-conscious choices?[77] They work in concert—offering a productive tension between what Wordsworth calls the "unfathered vapour" of the imagination and the more deliberate elements of poetic craft.[78]

The chapters in this book seek out and appreciate this tension in their effort to show how readers can approach mistakes like any other stylistic element of a poet's work. They are arranged roughly in chronological order and according to the nature of the mistakes they describe. (I say "roughly" because although Robert Browning was born nearly twenty years after John Clare, the poems of theirs under discussion in this book were written during the same period of time.) Chapter 1 attends to Wordsworth's misuse of the present-perfect tense in his famous lines about a boy of Winander—a mistake that implies that the boy is still living when we know from the poem that he is gone, that the episode was in the past.[79] I investigate several possibilities—the poet's ambiguous treatment of death in other poems about children, the prevalence of the present perfect elsewhere in Wordsworth's verse, his own sense of grammatical propriety—before calling a mistake a mistake. This particular error suggests a difference between accident and mistake that will be central to the chapters that follow.

Chapter 2 looks at a rather embarrassing error in the closing section of Browning's *Pippa Passes*, where he casually uses a slang word for female genitalia when meaning to refer to part of a nun's clothing. Like Wordsworth, Browning comes by his mistake honestly, having drawn his definition for the word from his memory of it in a seventeenth-century satirical ballad. Browning's error turns out to be a case of misreading: his source poem actually uses the word correctly—but Browning misses the joke. By exploring his mistake in context, this chapter raises the question of how interpretive mistakes relate to broader questions of meaning and its duplicity, not least in poems that are dramatic. Browning's mistake in reading thus serves as a proxy for the kinds of misinterpretations to which all readers of poetry are susceptible, especially when treating mistakes like his.

Chapters 3, 4, and 5 explore mistakes by poets whose individual styles seem to invite error rather than repel it. Chapter 3 focuses on a word used wrongly by a poet who often took pride in his own wrongness; unlike

Browning and Wordsworth, Clare paid little attention to details like spelling and punctuation: he depended on editors for clean copy. So what should readers make of his writing "wander" with an "o" in one poem and an "a" in another? Or of his invoking both meanings—wondering and wandering—in a single poem, but spelling them the same? Resisting the urge to gloss over this mistake, either by shrugging it off as a careless misspelling or by treating the words as yoked ("wondering is the literary form of wandering"), this chapter disentangles the idea of mistake from carelessness on the one hand and lack of knowledge or education on the other. It calls for the possibility of blundering even amid competing editorial concerns over what constitutes a draft and when to edit for consistency, suggesting that readers have much to gain by distinguishing Clare's feigned errors from his unwilling mistakes.

Like Clare, Emily Dickinson wrote copiously and quickly; her gifts came naturally and in abundance. Mostly unpublished during her lifetime, her poems were first made public after her death and under the influence of a strong editorial hand. In their original form on scraps of paper, in letters, and in hand-sewn "fascicles," they seem to exhibit mistake—grammatical, spelling, and otherwise—at every turn. But because they constitute instances of private expression, these improprieties can seem to belong to a set of personal norms not quite subject to the standards of the day. However, Dickinson herself was cognizant of her breaches, often confessing them in letters and sometimes even within the poems themselves. Chapter 4 seeks to determine how Dickinson's own admissions of "wrongness" complicate our readings of her poetry's mistakes. Does the poet's complicity undo her solecisms, or can awareness coexist with error? I suggest the possibility of reading much of her wrongdoing nevertheless as mistake; the difference between knowing better and doing better may, for Dickinson, be a difference in degree rather than in kind.

Hart Crane loved the freedom inherent in Dickinson's idiom and even dedicates a poem to her. But chapter 5 reads Crane's extreme license with words against stricter conceptions of error. For instance, in the second section of his poem "Voyages," he describes the sea as "Laughing the wrapt inflections of our love"—his odd spelling of "wrapt" here conjuring the sense of both "wrapped" and "rapt" simultaneously, giving "inflections" an appealing physicality.[80] Reading mistake along these lines is particularly

Cranian: his letters make it clear that language's ability to elide, change, and intimate (rather than simply mean) excites and propels him into writing poetry. Accordingly, Crane's admirers tend to focus their praise on the very moments of inexplicability that his critics find most inhospitable. By placing "wrapt" and other neologisms in the context of this long-standing debate about Crane's work, this chapter suggests the benefit of reading his creativity as a form of mistake rather than the other way around.

Chapters 6 and 7 consider historical and factual mistakes in the context of a poet's quest for creative freedom. Elizabeth Bishop was a writer dedicated to a sense of accuracy; her poem "In the Waiting Room" bears the markers of a specific place and time—"Worcester, Massachusetts" and "the fifth / of February, 1918."[81] Descriptive specificity is one of her specialties, and this poem, which refers to real stories in that month's *National Geographic* magazine, gives the impression of combining specificity with objective truth. And yet its facts are muddled: much of the material in the poem actually comes from a different issue of the magazine. Does Bishop's inaccuracy matter given her own adherence to the facts, or is it possible for descriptive poetry to offer its own aesthetic narrative? Focusing on her use and misuse of historical detail in this and other autobiographical poems, chapter 6 highlights what Bishop's readers have to gain by separating her poetry's fictionalized facts from its literal and empirical truths.

Chapter 7 takes this problem as far as it can go in the work of Seamus Heaney, another semiautobiographical poet whose work nevertheless presses on the boundaries of fact. Heaney's poetry often raises the question of whether, or how, remembered experience differs from historical reality. Can memory—and, in particular, memory as revealed through poetry— have a knowledge separate from what happened? Reflecting on conceptions of memory developed by Wordsworth, a poet with whom Heaney identifies on multiple levels but whose poetry he occasionally misremembers, this chapter argues for the necessity of acknowledging mistake even as it pertains to aspects of a remembered life, fictional or not. The act of misremembering emerges as a technique for Heaney—as well as for other poets—to figure the difficulty of mapping the imagination onto a historical world.

My conclusion measures this book's argument about mistake against poems that openly describe the process and feeling of mistaking. Can poets use their own mistakes productively and still be mistaken? What does their trying to do so say about the nature of mistakes in poetry more broadly? I suggest that when poets celebrate the unconscious creativity associated with error, they likewise confirm mistake's inevitability—and the importance of acknowledging it. Touching on the work of several contemporary poets, including John Ashbery, Paul Muldoon, and Geoffrey Hill, this final discussion positions mistake alongside other elements of poetic craft and suggests that the critical urge to deny mistaking is often at odds with the process it means to defend. The closing pages tell a story of making via poets who usually treat their mistakes as flaws worth mentioning, not excusing.

I have limited my examples in these chapters to mistakes made in the last two centuries—after the eighteenth-century standardization of English and during the period in which notions of selfhood became more closely linked with the lyric voice. But it does not follow that the argument could not apply to the mistakes of poets writing before the Romantics. The reception of mistakes, on the other hand, has proven itself to be intellectually distinctive in the post-Freudian era, and so the historical parameters of this book are defined as much by the period of the commentary as by the period of the poetry. In identifying examples for inclusion, I have taken a conservative approach to the definition of mistake in order to avoid letting a small leak sink the entire ship. But there are numerous ways to define this term— each valuable in its own context. For instance, I could imagine an argument for including a chapter about mistakes in judgment (which, like their cousin errors in technique, are doubtlessly influenced by unconscious as well as contingent factors). I could equally see, perhaps as a subsection of such a chapter, an exploration specifically of mistakes in taste. Elaine Scarry speaks to this kind of error in her meditation on beauty—and indeed cites several instances where poets admit to making mistakes of this nature within their poems.[82] The problem with mistakes in judgment and taste is that, by definition, they can only be determined subjectively. Who is to say where such errors begin or end? Errors in judgment, as and with our moods, are always changing. There could likewise be a section on the unpoetical— what Keston Sutherland calls "wrong poetry"—but again, such a discussion would risk eliding error with opinion.[83] The mistakes I include in the following chapters are deemed genuine according to factors that I consider to be empirically determined: mistakes in grammar, mistakes in the use or meaning of words, mistakes in historical fact, and mistakes in reading and interpretation. The mistakes of printers, amanuenses, and publishers are a related matter, and they speak interestingly to the relation between contingency and volition, but I have not included them simply because they are not errors committed by poets themselves. Reading printers' errors would emphasize the aspects of poetry that are external to individual consciousness, treating poems in their capacities as physical objects from which we generate meanings that are produced collaboratively.[84] I am interested here in the avenues mistake opens up for exploring poetry's subjectivity and its interpretation—concerns that are central to twentieth-century criticism as inflected (consciously or unconsciously) by Freud. Poets err as often as printers do—as often, I suggest, as readers and everybody else. Their mistakes in verse may well be volitional, but not to the exclusion of chance. Horace lamented that *quandoque bonus dormitat Homerus*—sometimes even Homer nods.[85] Poetry encompasses error as it does any other contingent element of form. The following pages offer an account of the poet's mistake that reveals it to be a phenomenon well worth defending—and eventually letting go.

CHAPTER I

Wordsworth's Imperfect Perfect

Wordsworth may have been thinking of one of several children when he first scribbled down, in the autumn of 1798, some lines about a boy of Winander hooting at owls. But it is likely that he partly had an experience from his own childhood in mind, since the earliest surviving draft of that poem contains the following inconsistency: after beginning in the third person, "There was a *boy*," Wordsworth suddenly shifts the address, eleven lines down, to the first person. Here are the draft's opening lines:

> There was a boy ye knew him well, ye rocks
> And islands of Winander & ye green
> Peninsulas of Esthwaite many a time
>   when the stars began
> To move along the edges of the hills
> Rising or setting would he stand alone
> Beneath the trees or by the glimmering lakes
> And through his fingers woven in one close knot
> Blow mimic hootings to the silent owls
> And bid them answer him. And they would shout
> Across the watry vale & shout again
> Responsive to *my* call.[1]

Surely Wordsworth means responsive to *his* call—the call of the boy, not the poet. And yet several lines later, he continues in this autobiographical vein:

> when it chanced
> That pauses of deep silence mockd *my* skill
> Then, often, in that silence while *I* hung
> Listening, a sudden shock of mild surprize
> Would carry far into *my* heart the voice
> Of mountain torrents . . .[2]

It is easy enough to justify this incongruity. Wordsworth likely considered his story to be autobiographical from the very beginning, opening retrospectively in the third person about a "boy" in order to emphasize the number of years intervening between then and now. He explains in his "Preface to *Poems*" (1815) that the poem was "Guided by one of my own primary consciousnesses,"[3] and indeed he does occasionally write of the self as though it has multiple versions or consciousnesses, some of which are alien even to him. For instance, of his school days, he muses in *The Prelude*:

> so wide appears
> The vacancy between me and those days
> Which yet have such self-presence in my mind
> That, sometimes, when I think of them, I seem
> Two consciousnesses, conscious of myself
> And of some other Being.[4]

Self-presence without selfhood might be one way to reconcile the difference between "a boy" and the version of Wordsworth that composes his draft. As David Bromwich has noted about the passage I have just quoted, "the work of memory is to associate virtually separate selves and not to recollect the shadows of a self already unified."[5] "There was a boy," as Wordsworth first conceived it, both reconnects the writing man with the boy he recollects while also acknowledging the irreparable distance between them; his shift from third to first person makes such a gulf grammatically explicit. Perhaps he also delays the inward turn to suggest through narrative drama the universality of the hooting game among schoolmates. As he later remarks in a note: "This practice of making an instrument of their own fingers is known to most boys, though some are more skilful at it than others."[6] (He comments elsewhere that the protagonist in the poem represents a blend of himself and a boy named William Raincock, though the grave he is thinking of belongs to a school friend named John Tyson.)[7] By simultaneously observing and being the boy of Winander in this draft, Wordsworth manages to toe that crucially murky line between experience and reflection he valorizes across his work.

But by the time he publishes the poem in the 1800 edition of *Lyrical Ballads*, Wordsworth has cleared up any confusion.[8] Alongside other minor revisions, he changes "my" to "his," "I" to "he," and writes a poignant ending in a churchyard in which the speaking poet stands "Mute" at the boy's grave—a scene that confirms the boy's separateness from Wordsworth once and for all. However, in correcting one mistake, Wordsworth commits another. The newer version of the passage reads like this:

> And they would shout
> Across the wat'ry vale and shout again,
> Responsive to his call, with quivering peals,
> And long halloos, and screams, and echoes loud
> Redoubled and redoubled, a wild scene
> Of mirth and jocund din. And, when it chanced
> That pauses of deep silence mock'd his skill,
> Then, sometimes, in that silence, while he hung
> Listening, a gentle shock of mild surprize
> *Has carried* far into his heart the voice
> Of mountain torrents, or the visible scene
> Would enter unawares into his mind
> With all its solemn imagery, its rocks,
> Its woods, and that uncertain heaven, receiv'd
> Into the bosom of the steady lake.[9]

Describing that "gentle shock," Wordsworth uses the present-perfect verb "has carried," implying that the boy is still living. But his verb in the next phrase, "or the visible scene / *Would enter* unawares into his mind," reminds us that the boy is gone, that the episode occurred in the past.[10] This new present perfect appears in a draft written in Wordsworth's own hand in 1799 and lingers in all subsequent instances, including in both published versions of "There was a boy" (in 1800 and 1815) and in the texts that appear in the 1805 and 1850 *Preludes*.[11] And despite its being a subtler error than the earlier draft's perspectival shift, this mistake is harder to reconcile. How can it be that a gentle shock "[h]as carried" when we are told, only moments later, that the boy is dead?

Let me dally with false surmise before calling a mistake a mistake. For one thing, Wordsworth's story—one of the most suggestively rich in the long poem—may seem richer yet for the ambiguity of "has": there is beauty in the idea that a flirtation between a boy and owls could go on indefinitely, especially if the boy died young. Furthermore, what "carries" here is, strictly speaking, "the gentle shock of mild surprise," and perhaps Wordsworth allows that gentle shocks may resonate not just far into a heart but also far beyond their given temporality. (Trauma theorists have paid special attention to this moment in the poem for this very reason.)[12] Likewise, the present perfect suggests the poet's differentiated senses of sound and sight: voice carries indefinitely, whereas a scene can enter only once. On a more literal level, the lack of response from both boy and owl can also be read as carrying on in death, a state that perpetuates and ensures such silence. The boy's death may thus be understood as prolonging forever that feeling of hanging, listening for an answer that will never come. Wordsworth's second enjambment of the verb "hang" in the last lines of the poem ("the churchyard hangs / Upon a slope above the village school") indeed suggests his interest in conjuring a sense of anticipation. And whereas the first enjambment, "hung / Listening," places the boy squarely in the past, the second instance, "hangs / Upon a slope," rewrites the poem's sense of time, so that the boy's body is still hanging, albeit indirectly and in the grave.[13] Moreover, the word "has" gives the poem a finer music: the "z" sound at the end of "has" follows nicely on the heels of "surprise," and the "h" recalls the sound of "hung" a few lines before it and prepares us for "heart" a few spaces later. "Would carry" has less to offer in this regard; if Wordsworth had used it in the final version (as he does in the draft), the word "would," with its homonym "wood," would occur three times in the space of six lines—not as elegant. Finally, we could imagine that Wordsworth consciously and deliberately chose "has carried" in order to confer a special lastingness to the heart—as if to say the heart remains continually receptive even when the mind cannot.

As I have begun to demonstrate, Wordsworth's problematic verb can help critics read beyond the nostalgia of the passage toward its quieter nuances of meaning. "Has carried" picks up where the errors in the early draft left off: it suggests an ongoing relation between the speaker of the poem and its dead subject. Without mentioning "has carried," Geoffrey Hartman uses other hints of likeness between the boy and the poet to describe how Wordsworth both "solicit[s] and defend[s] against" his maturity in the closing lines.[14] The divided episode, Hartman suggests, of the boy standing first silently below the owls and then the poet himself standing mute above the boy's grave is a way for the poet to rejoin his own "present and past modes of being."[15] During the half hour spent by the boy's grave, writes Hartman, Wordsworth "looks not only at something external" but also "at something within, his former heart."[16] Hartman is in fact responding to one of the earliest criticisms leveled at Wordsworth's poem by the reviewer Francis Jeffrey, who in the April 1808 issue of the *Edinburgh Review* complained:

> all that [Wordsworth] is pleased to communicate of the rustic child
> is that he used to amuse himself with shouting to the owls, and hear-
> ing them answer . . . and for the sake of this one accomplishment, we
> are told, that the author has frequently stood mute, and gazed on his
> grave, for half an hour together![17]

Hartman's belated rebuttal to Jeffrey offers a moving account of what may be at stake for Wordsworth in staring at the grave for so long. Along these lines, we could also allow that what Hartman reads as a "return" of the boy in the form of the poet at the end of the poem is implied earlier through its present perfect. Likewise picking up on the poem's complicated temporality, Susan Wolfson has remarked that Wordsworth's self-reference in the draft "haunts" the lines that he eventually publishes.[18] The finished version has, as she puts it, "autobiographical implication, displaced into third person."[19] What form this implication takes could be under the surface, or explicit, or both—but it needn't take the form of mistake unnecessarily.

To my knowledge, Gavin Hopps is the only critic who actually points out Wordsworth's mistaken verb, but no sooner does he accuse than he exonerates, using a logic similar to Hartman's:

the use of the present perfect allows a dilation of the reference of the verb into the present, which the past tense or habitual form would exclude, thereby extending the effect of the encounter with nature not only beyond the moment of its occurrence but also beyond the death of the child, which is thus robbed of its finality. . . . It might therefore be argued that the poet's choice of grammatical structure serves an ontological purpose, and that it is his view of reality rather than his attitude towards language as such that differs from the norm.[20]

For Hopps, the fact that "has carried" lends credence to the supposed meaning of the lines renders the linguistic construction less mistaken. Later in his argument, he explains that errors like Wordsworth's are "impressionistically correct, in that they accurately represent what seem to be the feelings of the poems' speakers."[21]

Now we are on shaky ground. These dalliances with meaning—mine as well as Hartman's, Wolfson's, and Hopps's—rely on the notion that what Wordsworth wrote is always equivalent to what he meant (if such a thing were knowable). But Wordsworth may also have meant his poem to be grammatical, just as (we may presume) he meant to use matching pronouns when he revised the lines of his draft. A poet can mean several things at once, consciously and unconsciously, as Samuel Taylor Coleridge once suggested to Robert Southey in a letter: "Wordsworth's words always *mean* the whole of their possible Meaning."[22] It is certainly reasonable to think that the poet on some level wished to keep the boy alive in poetical if not literal terms—plausible even that he made, whether knowingly or not, such a contradictory wish manifest in the present-perfect verb "has carried." But does it necessarily follow that such mistaking is itself wished for? William Empson noted that "contradiction is a powerful literary weapon," and indeed what is meaningful in the wording of "has carried" derives its power by defying the acceptance of death Wordsworth exhibits in the rest of his passage—for a moment claiming the opposite of what the poet appears to know to be true.[23] Of a reader's handling such contradictory possibilities in the treatment of literary texts, Empson points out: "any contradiction is likely to have some sensible interpretations; and if you think of interpretations which are not sensible, it puts the blame on you."[24] It might follow then that a reader could identify the literal meaning of "has carried" (that

the boy still lives) as nonsensical and pursue the more sensible meaning—
that the boy's influence lives on in the heart of the poet—without regard
to the contradiction. But to say that the contradiction is not there and that
the sensible interpretation of the line does not in fact rely on a mistake of
grammar is to prioritize ease of reading over complex understanding.
Wordsworth contradicts himself when he writes "has carried"; he does so
perhaps because of his own conflicted feelings about death, memory, and
childhood. We can understand the beauty behind this contradiction while
still noting that it relies on a mistake. The phrase "has carried" is not wrong
because it contradicts the meaning of the lines Wordsworth composes
around it (poems tell untruths all the time); it is wrong because it is grammatically mistaken. What if, rather than receiving "has carried" as a suggestion toward creating meaning, we approached this phrase as a mistake
in the text, as any copyeditor would? Acknowledging mistake need not
diminish our appreciation for the unexpected pathos bound up in the contradiction of these lines, and doing so would allow us to preserve a sense of
Wordsworth's decisions as a craftsman even as we hypothesize about what
he may have meant.

Strictly speaking, there is little any reader can do to justify "has carried"
grammatically. *The Cambridge Grammar of the English Language* describes
the present perfect as involving

> reference to both past and present time: it is concerned with a time-
> span beginning in the past and extending up to now. It is not used in
> contexts where the "now" component of this is explicitly or implicitly
> excluded.[25]

It goes on to explain that the "connection with now" can be

> the potential for occurrence, or recurrence, of the situation at any
> time within the time-span up to now. Thus [the example "His sister
> *has been* up Mont Blanc"] implicates that his sister is still alive.[26]

Wordsworth's present perfect is not mistaken only because it is incongruous
with the verbs that precede and follow it but also because such a phrase
requires the boy to be living.[27] If Wordsworth had written "has carried far

into *my* heart," both the tense of the verb and the pronoun would have seemed strange, but neither would have so clearly constituted a mistake.

And yet "has carried" does not appear in the original first-person draft of Wordsworth's poem. Rather, the original tense of the line neatly matches that of the lines that follow it:

> a *sudden* shock of mild surprise
> *would* carry far into *my* heart the voice
> of mountain torrents[28]

Here, the past conditional "would" clearly indicates a prior action completed—in this case, an action whose receiver, the poet himself, lives to tell of it. Counterintuitively, when Wordsworth prepares these lines for publication, he changes not only the person but also the tense—and in so doing suggests a continuity that he simultaneously negates. One possibility for how this mistake came to be resides in the subject matter itself. As an elegiac poem, "There was a boy" not only celebrates and memorializes the child Wordsworth describes but also performs the work of mourning him, from the initial reassertion of his life ("There was a boy"), to a nostalgic remembrance of him ("he, as through an instrument, / Blew mimic hootings to the silent owls"), to a recognition of his absence and a final expression of grief ("near his grave / A full half-hour together I have stood / Mute—for he died when he was ten years old"). Wordsworth writes in his "Preface" to the second edition of *Lyrical Ballads* that a poet shows "a disposition to be affected more than other men by absent things as if they were present."[29] Perhaps in remembering the boy, Wordsworth became so affected by his absence that he erroneously mistook it for presence. Later in the "Preface," he explains that

> it will be the wish of the Poet to bring his feelings near to those of the persons whose feelings he describes, nay, for short spaces of time, perhaps, to let himself slip into an entire delusion, and even confound and identify his own feelings with theirs;[30]

In blending the poet's mind with the mind of the boy, the poem may well enact the poet's capacity for "slipping" into a mistaken consciousness that is able to suspend, however briefly, its own disbelief at death. In such a suspension, the poet's mistake in language would stem not from an artistic or aesthetic wish to reinscribe the boy in terms of the poet but rather from an unconscious rejection of his mortality. The boy's absence would be re-written as presence in a passionately unwitting defense against death. Our challenge as critics is to separate this possibility from any temptation to think of the grammar as being *right*.

Doing so might allow us to consider whether elegy is a form of poetry that is particularly susceptible to mistakes. As both an artistic representation of loss and an expressive working-through of grief, the elegiac poem encompasses certain fits and passions of the grieving mind that may give way to error more easily than in other kinds of poems. Wordsworth himself touches on this idea in the first of his "Essays upon Epitaphs":

Yet, though the writer who would excite sympathy is bound in this case, more than in any other, to give proof that he himself has been moved, it is to be remembered, that to raise a monument is a sober and a reflective act; that the inscription which it bears is intended to be permanent, and for universal perusal; and that, for this reason, the thoughts and feelings expressed should be permanent also—liberated from that weakness and anguish of sorrow which is in nature transitory, and which with instinctive decency retires from notice. The passions should be subdued, the emotions controlled; strong, indeed, but nothing ungovernable or wholly involuntary. Seemliness requires this, and truth requires it also: for how can the narrator otherwise be trusted? Moreover, a grave is a tranquillising object: resignation in course of time springs up from it as naturally as the wild flowers, besprinkling the turf with which it may be covered, or gathering round the monument by which it is defended. The very form and substance of the monument which has received the inscription, and the appearance of the letters, testifying with what a slow and laborious hand they must have been engraven, might seem to reproach the author who had given way upon this occasion to transports of mind, or to quick turns of conflicting passion; though the same might constitute the life and beauty of a funeral oration or elegiac poem.[31]

In Wordsworth's formulation, the epitaph calls for all "passions" and "emotions" on the part of the writer or engraver to be "subdued" and "controlled." Because they are etched in stone, the very content of the words in an epitaph should speak to their author's "slow and laborious" hand, never "ungovernable" or "wholly involuntary." On the other hand, Wordsworth cautions against what he calls "transports of mind" and "quick turns of conflicting passion," suggesting that these are not qualities of epitaph but of elegy. His admission that these involuntary transports and passions "might constitute the life and beauty" of an elegiac poem may help clarify his susceptibility to mistake in "There was a boy." What's more, Wordsworth's qualification of the word "involuntary" with the adjective "wholly"—the engraver of an epitaph must ensure his emotions are not "*wholly* involuntary"—reveals his own understanding of how stubbornly persistent involuntary emotions can be.

If "has carried" is the result of involuntary emotion given over to mistake, we might look to other poems of Wordsworth's where death is treated in a similarly complicated fashion to see whether the error is the exception or the rule. Is the poet careless in other poems about the death of children? In "She dwelt among th' untrodden ways," he uses only simple tenses to describe Lucy's actions in the past:

She dwelt among th' untrodden ways
     Beside the springs of Dove,
A Maid whom there were none to praise
     And very few to love.

A Violet by a mossy Stone
     Half-hidden from the Eye!
—Fair, as a star when only one
     Is shining in the sky!

She *liv'd* unknown, and few could know
     When Lucy ceas'd to be;
But she is in her Grave, and oh!
     The difference to me.[32]

The actual moment of Lucy's death occupies an unknown place in time—
"few could know / When Lucy ceas'd to be." And yet her life and death are
unequivocally separate when it comes to the poem's grammar. Before Wordsworth announces her death in the second line of the third stanza, she performs simple, past-tense actions: "She dwelt," "she *liv'd*," she "ceas'd." Once
she is pronounced dead, Wordsworth switches to the present tense: "she is
in her Grave." Part of the slowly enunciated "difference" to which the poet
refers in that final line is represented by this linguistic change: from "dwelt"
to "*liv'd*" to "ceas'd" to "is," Lucy effects a transformation from a child who
occupied life actively to one whose sole action is merely being—but only in
the grave. The sequence is similar in "There was a boy," where Wordsworth
depicts the boy at the beginning of the poem in various states of past-tense
play—he "blew," "he hung"—only to give him presence at the end through
"the grave in which he lies." But none of these changes create confusion;
rather, Wordsworth clearly delineates between life and death by ensuring
that all of life's former actions remain in the past tense, while all of death's
current actions (to be, to lie, to slumber) receive everlasting presence. The
verbs associated with the living Lucy never lead continuously forward the
way "has carried" does; only her death is continuous. Wordsworth's grammatical difference forces the reader to feel the sudden shift between life and
death, between "she dwelt" and "she is," all the more acutely.

This "difference to me" is perhaps most prominent in the shortest of the
Lucy poems:

> A slumber did my spirit seal;
>   I had no human fears:
> She seem'd a thing that could not feel
>   The touch of earthly years.
>
> No motion has she now, no force;
>   She neither hears nor sees,
> Roll'd round in earth's diurnal course
>   With rocks and stones and trees![33]

Both the poet and the child in the first stanza are limited to past action: "I
had," "she seemed." Even the inanimate nouns—"a slumber" and "a

thing"—act in the past: "did . . . seal," "could not feel." When Lucy dies between the two stanzas, the language undergoes her change as well. "No motion has she now"—"She neither hears nor sees." But these present-tense actions are negated even as they are performed. Their implied past gives strength to the absent quality of their presence: if Lucy does not *hear*, she must have *heard*; if she cannot *see*, she must have *seen*. The very impossibility of their and Lucy's presence is what makes the poem so effective in its mourning. Far from letting Lucy's tenses confound the reader, Wordsworth uses them to clarify exactly what the difference between life and death really is.

Wordsworth is similarly savvy in "We Are Seven," a poem whose underlying message is predicated on the distinction between "is" and "was," past and present tense. Questioning a "little cottage girl" about the size of her family, the speaker of the poem begins tentatively in the conditional: "Sisters and brothers, little maid, / How many may you be?"[34] The child slyly responds with a verbless answer: "seven in all."[35] But the aggressive questions continue:

> "And where are they, I pray you tell?"
> She answered, "Seven are we,
> "And two of us at Conway dwell,
> "And two are gone to sea.
>
> "Two of us in the church-yard lie,
> "My sister and my brother,
> "And in the church-yard cottage, I
> "Dwell near them with my mother."[36]

The child makes no mistake here but rather follows the pattern Wordsworth develops in his other poems about the death of children. The sister and brother "are," even in death. They "lie" presently in the churchyard, whereas later in the poem, when the girl relates the circumstances of how her siblings died, she uses the past tense: Jane "lay" moaning in bed and finally "went away." Later, John "was forced" to go.[37] The cottage girl, scrupulously attentive to the changes caused by death, modifies her tenses the same way the poet does, subjecting life to the grammar of time's passing while imbuing death with everlasting presence. Nowhere in "We Are Seven" does the child buckle under the scrutinizing questions of her skeptical examiner. Her final assertion in the last line of the poem differs from her earlier answer only in the ordering of the words: "seven are we" becomes the more emphatic "we are seven!"[38] Here, as in the Lucy poems, tense plays a crucial role in Wordsworth's ability to convey the news of death. He uses it not as a tool for ambivalence but as a means for conveying delicately what is otherwise difficult to express.

Even in his letters, where feeling often wins over formality, Wordsworth remains attuned to the grammatical propriety of his verbs at the moments when he is forced to write about the deaths of people he knows and loves. Oliver Clarkson has noted the painstaking clarity with which Wordsworth articulates his grief about the death of his brother John in the following letter:

> For myself I feel that there is something cut out of my life which cannot be restored, I never thought of him but with hope and delight, we looked forward to the time not distant as we thought when he would settle near us when the task of his life would be over and he would have nothing to do but reap his reward.[39]

Wordsworth takes great liberty with his punctuation here—enacting what Clarkson calls "the vagabond rhythms of a grieving mind which finds no place in time to 'settle.'"[40] The run-on nature of this sentence surely does have its roots in grief and helps bring such a feeling to fulfillment. But even more interesting is Wordsworth's deft handling of present and past subjunctives as he sets into motion a series of events (John's residing near them) that would have, but never will, occur. Clarkson writes:

> Wordsworth's prose shivers at the prospect of succumbing to a categorical past tense. "He would settle" and "he would have nothing to do" manage to dodge the sadder finality of he would have settled and he would have had nothing to do, but they do so with an eye cast tremblingly on what "cannot be restored." And although the scarcer form of "would," used to express a wish . . . , does not fit grammati-

cally, that does not stop it from loitering in the revivifying doggedness of "he would settle . . . his life would be . . . he would have." The beauty of Wordsworth's syntax lies in its way of keeping an earlier dream on life support, while knowing that "hope and delight" will never reawaken and breathe for themselves again.[41]

Wordsworth ultimately recognizes in his letter that John will never again be near, and despite the lingeringly hopeful syntax, he remains true to that reality even as his verbs glance otherwise. The syntax must eventually acknowledge the loss; "would-as-wish" loiters but cannot stick. "The disappointed mind eludes rationality without debunking it," Clarkson points out—which is one reason that the irrational verb in "There was a boy" feels so strange.[42]

If his poems and letters about death offer any glimpse into Wordsworth's process of composition, they give no indication that an anomalous phrase like "has carried" constitutes anything more than a momentary lapse in clarity. The present perfect is in fact a common Wordsworthian grammatical construction, especially in poems about memory, and one that he uses correctly and with assurance throughout his poetry.[43] Reading "has carried" as a mistake is the simplest way to read the line—and it has the happy consequence of inviting further consideration of one of the poet's most difficult and recurring themes (the death of children). Doing so need not constitute a disappointment; in fact, we have much to gain by responding to Wordsworth's error in this way without attempting to justify it. To develop within "There was a boy" meanings suggested primarily by its slip would be to celebrate his involuntary passions at the expense of his technique. But as I have just suggested, Wordsworth was deliberate in his poetic handling of death; denying him this purposefulness undermines the delicacy of his craft. More likely than not, the poet would have corrected his present perfect had it been brought to his attention—just as he corrected his personal pronouns in revising that original draft.

Thomas De Quincey, who had read his friend's poem in manuscript, may offer a closer view toward the poet's disposition in this regard. In an essay published in *Tait's Edinburgh Magazine* in 1839, he records an evening spent outdoors with Wordsworth in which the two men were waiting on the road for the midnight post. De Quincey recalls that the poet was so eager to discern any sound of the oncoming carrier that he literally put his ear to the ground in anticipation of hearing the wheels of the postman making their approach. But after lying and listening there for a period and hearing nothing, Wordsworth rose, De Quincey writes, looked up at the stars for a minute, and spoke the following words:

> I have remarked, from my earliest days, that, if under any circumstance, the attention is energetically braced up to an act of steady observation, or of steady expectation, then, if this intense condition of vigilance should suddenly relax, at that moment any beautiful . . . object, or collection of objects, falling upon the eye, *is carried to the heart* with a power not known under other circumstances. Just now, my ear was placed upon the stretch in order to catch any sound of wheels . . . ; at the very instant when I raised my head from the ground . . . when the organs of attention were all at once relaxing from their tension, the bright star hanging in the air . . . fell suddenly upon my eye and penetrated my capacity of apprehension.[44]

De Quincey's remembrance of Wordsworth's account of how a star "is carried to the heart" immediately links it to the narrative of "There was a boy," not just because of Wordsworth's pose, listening in silent anticipation like the boy waiting below the owls for an answer, but also because of his language: "any object . . . falling upon the eye *is carried to the heart* with a power not known under other circumstances." Here the poet uses the simple present tense to describe the way sensation enters the heart. Of course we cannot be completely sure what tense Wordsworth actually used, since De Quincey is quoting him from memory, but what follows is equally interesting: De Quincey goes on to say that the poet, upon finishing his proclamation about the star, immediately likens his experience of waiting to the scenario that he wrote about in "There was a boy." In the essay, De Quincey is remembering all of this with great excitement—so much so that after relating to his readers what Wordsworth said to him that night, he begins to quote from "There was a boy" directly. And here is what he writes:

Then, in that instant, the scene actually before him, the visible scene, would enter unawares—

"With all its solemn imagery"—

This complex scenery was—What?

"Was carried *far* into his heart
With all its pomp, and that uncertain heav'n received
Into the bosom of the steady lake."[45]

De Quincey's quotation takes extreme license: the lines are out of order as well as incomplete. Nevertheless the question of tense persists—and De Quincey, after having paraphrased Wordsworth before in the present tense, using "is carried," now misquotes the published lines. He does so by, among other things, offering a revision of the mistake in the poem itself. De Quincey's "fix" is itself flawed, since the actual text requires "would" instead of "was," but the thrust of his correction remains: rather than questioning or complicating Wordsworth's sudden shift in tense, he internalizes a version of the poem that is error-free. De Quincey doesn't creatively interpret Wordsworth's mistake for the readers of *Tait's*—he simply corrects it and moves on.

Silently noting the mistake does not preclude considering the moment to be a psychically determined one, and doing so may help throw into relief one of the crucial arguments Wordsworth tries to make within the lines. "There was a boy" happens to be a poem that celebrates the power of the accidental. Wordsworth writes at the very moment in question:

And when it *chanced*
That pauses of deep silence mock'd his skill,
Then, sometimes, in that silence, while he hung
Listening, a gentle shock of mild surprize
Has carried far into his heart the voice
Of mountain torrents, or the visible scene
Would enter unawares into his mind[46]

That is to say, when listening intently for one sound, sometimes, by chance, you hear another. And not just that, but what sound you hear by acci-dent—the unlistened-for or mistaken sound—is often far more powerful and lasting than whatever it was you were originally trying to hear.

Robert Frost picks up on this element of Wordsworth's meaning when he writes his own version of "There was a boy"—another poem on call, response, and expectation titled "The Most of It":

> He thought he kept the universe alone;
> For all the voice in answer he could wake
> Was but the mocking echo of his own
> From some tree-hidden cliff across the lake.
> Some morning from the boulder-broken beach
> He would cry out on life, that what it wants
> Is not its own love back in copy speech,
> But counter-love, original response.
> And nothing ever came of what he cried
> Unless it was the embodiment that crashed
> In the cliff's talus on the other side,
> And then in the far distant water splashed,
> But after a time allowed for it to swim,
> Instead of proving human when it neared
> And someone else additional to him,
> As a great buck it powerfully appeared,
> Pushing the crumpled water up ahead,
> And landed pouring like a waterfall,
> And stumbled through the rocks with horny tread,
> And forced the underbrush—and that was all.[47]

Like the boy of Winander, Frost's subject, who inhabits a landscape simi-larly filled with cliffs, lakes, rocks, and woods, hangs listening for a sign that his shouts have been received. And like Wordsworth's boy, the response does not come in the form that he or the reader expects. Instead, what Words-worth deems "external accident" comes into play: not as voice or "counter-love," but "as a great buck it powerfully appeared," suddenly rewriting the subject's expectations and forcing him into a different kind of sublimity.

Frost ends his account with an enigmatic statement—the tonally ambiguous "and that was all"—offering no context, as Wordsworth does, about the life or death of his subject. But the pleasure of serendipity is there, connecting his poem to Wordsworth's and acting out the response for which both his character and Wordsworth's boy call. The very thing that alerts both of these boys to nature's splendor is "chance"—that "mild surprize" at *not* receiving the expected sound. In his "Preface" to the *Poems of 1815*, Wordsworth writes the following about "There was a boy":

> I have represented a commutation and transfer of internal feelings, co-operating with external accidents, to plant, for immortality, images of sound and sight, in the celestial soil of the Imagination.[48]

Wordsworth describes what happens to the boy at the very moment that his poem is affected by a grammatical slip as an extraordinary communion with nature caused, in part, by "external accident." Wordsworth's own narrative, then, in both its content and its form, lays bare the very process by which unintended creativity takes hold of the imagination and distinguishes itself from more purposeful poetic craft (as is represented in the poem by the boy's careful mimicry of the owls). In this way, Wordsworth seems to be writing in the manner of his critics, who give as much weight to the unintentional aspects of the poem as to the intentional ones. Or perhaps it is fairer to say that his critics have internalized the poet's own pleasure in cooperating with accidents in their willingness to bring unintended meanings to light.

But accident—at least of the kind Wordsworth describes—and mistake are not one and the same. What the poet celebrates in "There was a boy" is the coming together of a heightened sensibility and an *external* accident: a young boy eager to receive, and the unexpected silence of the owls, which leaves him suddenly susceptible to the beauty that surrounds him. Wordsworth's own mistake is not exactly of this kind, insofar as it is neither external nor beyond his control. Accidents, like the owl's lack of response, or Frost's buck, happen *to* people. (J. L. Austin uses the term "befall," and Edward Eigen in his book *On Accident* similarly points to the lack of volition associated with that word.)[49] Mistakes, on the other hand, are *made*, no matter how unconsciously. They are like the "involuntary" cries of the elegiac poet who cannot help but lose himself in the process. Though un-intentional, mistakes are still born of intention. In using Wordsworth's error to shape our own meanings for the poem, we celebrate the unintentional aspects of Wordsworth's verse, but when we recognize his mistake as a mistake, we acknowledge his conscious choices too. Both come into play here. Together they suggest that the contingency Wordsworth ascribes to the voice of the boy has carried to the voice of the poet too.

CHAPTER 2

Robert Browning's Bad Habit

> And just as we should, if we took Browning seriously as a poet, see
> that he had made many noble literary forms, so we should also see
> that he did make from time to time certain definite literary mis-
> takes. There is one of them, a glaring one, in *Pippa Passes*; and, as far
> as I know, no critic has ever thought enough of Browning as an art-
> ist to point it out.
>
> —G. K. CHESTERTON IN *Robert Browning* (1903)

Chesterton's remark strikes a deliciously rare note. Here is a critic willing
to call a poet out on his mistakes in the name of praising what is noble
elsewhere in the work. But Chesterton's gripe with *Pippa Passes*, Browning's
early verse drama about a working-class Italian girl whose sweet singing in
the streets of Asolo unintentionally affects the activities of various Italians
listening through windows, turns out to be less about an error in craft than
an error in judgment. He takes issue with Browning's decision at the end
of the play to connect Pippa's own life with the people influenced by her
song. "The central and whole splendid idea of the drama," he comments,
"is the fact that Pippa is utterly remote from the grand folk whose lives she
troubles and transforms. To make her in the end turn out to be the niece
of one of them, is like a whiff from an Adelphi melodrama, an excellent
thing in its place, but destructive of the entire conception of Pippa."[1] This
quibble about the plot is reasonable, but it registers as "mistake" rather
tenuously: Browning surely had his reasons for "mak[ing] the Monsignor
and his brother's accomplice in the last act discuss a plan touching the fate

of Pippa herself," and whatever those reasons were—moral, spiritual, dramatic, or otherwise—is not necessarily for Chesterton, or any other of Browning's readers, to decide.[2]

In fact there is a much more "glaring" mistake in *Pippa* that Chesterton doesn't mention at all. It occurs in the play's final act, as night descends on the young girl's holiday:

> Day's turn is over, now arrives the night's.
> Oh lark, be day's apostle
> To mavis, merle and throstle,
> Bid them their betters jostle
> From day and its delights!
> But at night, brother howlet, over the woods,
> Toll the world to thy chantry;
> Sing to the bat's sleek sisterhoods
> Full complines with gallantry:
> Then, owls and bats,
> Cowls and twats,
> Monks and nuns, in a cloister's moods,
> Adjourn to the oak-stump pantry![3]

Pippa's closing song could be accused of several stylistic misdemeanors; in fact many of the supposed technical defects in Browning's play, which was not well received when he first published it in 1841, can be found here if one is inclined to niggle. As one anonymous reviewer for the *Athenaeum* warns:

> Our faith in [Browning], however, is not yet extinct,—but our patience *is*. . . . [W]e yet find his texts nearly as obscure as ever—getting, nevertheless, a glimpse, every now and then, at meanings which it might have been well worth his while to put into English.[4]

Another says:

> Let no one look into [Browning's inventions] who merely cares for easy-going verse, with the sense on the surface. . . . Here, almost every phrase or figure is suggestive; the metre is full of broken and sus-

pended cadences, and the store of allusions collected from sources remote and recondite.[5]

Thomas Powell writes:

> [I]f Mr. Browning wishes to make a simile, and illustrate redness, he will not take the rose, but select some out of the way flower equally red, but of whose name not one in a thousand has ever heard: this added to a style so condensed and clipt of all aids as to sometimes be unintelligible, has sealed Mr. Browning's works to the many.[6]

It is true that "mavis" and "merle" are unusual names for rather common birds, and the rhyming triplet of "apostle," "throstle," and "jostle" perhaps makes the whole thing feel a little loose at the joints. Rhyming "chantry" with "gallantry" and "pantry" imposes an odd stress on the second word's middle syllable—rarely, if ever, pronounced gall*ant*ry. But a reader less troubled by obscurity could just as easily praise the poet for his originality, as Browning's admirers have always done. And the rhymes, never quite Hudibrastic, have a certain flair. None of these quirks seem to me like much more of a defect than Chesterton's complaint about the contrivance in the plot. But it *is* puzzling how all of Browning's detractors, as well as many of his admirers, fail to ask what surely presents itself as the most urgent question of all: How does one take the word "twats" in line 96?

> Then, owls and bats
> cowls and *twats*

Here is a word so singularly unexpected from innocent Pippa's mouth as to render her whole song preposterous. What could this slang and vulgar term for female genitalia be doing alongside owls, bats, and especially a monk's cloak? Only a few lines earlier, Pippa has demurely refrained from saying a much cleaner word:

> Suppose there's a king of the flowers
> And a girl-show held in his bowers—
> "Look ye, buds, this growth of ours,"

Says he, "Zanze from the Brenta,
I have made her gorge polenta
Till both cheeks are near as bouncing
As her . . . name there's no pronouncing!"[7]

If Pippa cannot bring herself to say the word "breasts" at this point in the play, then it seems awfully unlikely that moments later she should have no qualms referring openly to a twat.

And yet as far as we know, not a single reader questioned Browning on this point until the philologist Frederick J. Furnivall, a friend and admirer of the poet's and also one of the cocreators of the *OED*, wrote him about it nearly thirty years after the play's publication. Browning's reply reveals an astonishing mistake:

> In the Royalist rhymes entitled "Vanity of Vanities, or Sir Harry Vane's Picture"—wherein Vane is charged with being a Jesuit—occur these lines " 'Tis said they will give him a Cardinal's hat: / They sooner will give him an old nun's twat!" The ballad is partly quoted in the Appendix to Forster's Life of Vane, but the above lines are left out—I remember them, however, and the word struck me as a distinctive part of a nun's attire that might fitly pair off with the cowl appropriated to a monk.[8]

Browning's letter appeals to lines from an anonymous poem first published in 1660. It is striking that he is able to recall the lines and the word at all. (Donald Hair has noted that Browning "had a remarkably retentive memory," which Chesterton compares to "the British Museum library."[9]) But Browning's powers of recollection do not serve him well here; never mind that the original lines actually read a little different from how he remembers them—

They talkt of his having a Cardinalls Hat,
They'd send him as soon an Old Nuns Twat[10]

—the gist is the same either way. The raunchy jibe launched by the seventeenth-century balladeer appears to have flown straight past him.

Whether Browning realizes his mistake by the time he responds to Furnivall is less clear, but if he does, his letter is certainly very coy. Nor does he make any effort to emend the poem in subsequent printings as he does with minor mistakes elsewhere. We must assume that the vulgarity in "Vanity of Vanities" was simply lost on Browning, at least initially, and that the falsely phrased nun's habit in his own poem is an extreme case of reading gone awry.

Among the mistakes discussed in this book, Browning's is particularly distinguished by its stemming from such a worthy cause. Any poet can get a word wrong, but "twats" is not so much a miswriting as it is a misreading: when Browning actually uses the word "twats" in Pippa's song, he very much consciously means to do so. He may even have been extra pleased to have thought up such an unexpected word to rhyme with "bats" that simultaneously complemented his analogies between owls and monks, bats and nuns. His mistake occurred not at the moment of composition through carelessness or ignorance but rather much earlier, at the time of his reading the royalist rhymes—and as a result of his voracious appetite for verse. Poets rarely consider their reading habits to be an occupational risk. The habit of reading poetry is in fact so closely associated with the practice of writing it that many a good poet has confused his own work with that of another— has unwittingly incorporated somebody else's word or turn of phrase into his own poem simply for having read and remembered it from elsewhere. Doing so does not necessarily make for inauthentic poetry. Rather, the opposite: internalizing other poets' language is often the mark of a strong, readerly poet—one who exhibits, in the best way, his own anxiety of influence. Allusion can work similarly; it codifies this unconscious art of internalization into a trope. When poets allude, they write by reading and, in doing so, promote the good habit of reading to other poets.

But reading wrongly is a different matter altogether—and I do not mean in the Bloomian sense, wherein all poems are "misreadings," but more literally, when a reader engages in the accidental practice of erroneously taking this for that, of supposing one thing to mean another.[11] This is the fate of the mistaken poet-as-critic. The subtle difference between Browning's error of interpretation and more palatable poetic tropes that derive from what Bloom calls "influence-relation" comes down to the question of will. Mistake in the case of "twats" involves an unwittingly false grafting of meaning onto a word. A trope is necessarily more calculated, even when it originates in the unconscious. As Bloom describes it in his own formulation about misreadings,

> a trope is a *willing error*, a turn from literal meaning in which a word or phrase is used in an improper sense, wandering from its rightful place.[12]

Browning's mistake involves a turn from literal meaning that results in an improper sense—but it is not a "willing *error*," despite his having willingly chosen the word. Tropes allow poets to stretch and complicate language in a controlled and artistic way. As Bloom says, they "[defend] ultimately against the deathly dangers of literal meaning, and more immediately against all other tropes that intervene between literal meaning and the fresh opening to discourse."[13] Yet it is not likely that Pippa's song defends against the literal at this moment. Rather, she sings about twats in spite of Browning's choices, and the discourse her words open into is not pleasingly "fresh" but embarrassing and unrelated to the play's subject matter. It would be a stretch to celebrate the unintended meaning of "twats," not because unintended meanings are irrelevant but because the relation between the actual meaning of this word and Browning's falsification comes as the direct result of misguided understanding rather than artistic freedom or unconscious creativity.

Reading wrongly has obvious downsides, but for a poet it is an especially precarious thing to do. By the end of his career, Browning had come to understand the dangers of haphazard reading as well as writing, and he was—at least publicly—as scrupulous about the accuracy of his work after the fact as he may have been carefree while writing it. Browning actually revised *Pippa Passes* several years after its first publication—unfortunately keeping "twats"—and wrote to his publisher:

> the point which decided me to wish to get printed over again was the real good I thought I could do to *Paracelsus, Pippa*, and some others; good, not obtained by cutting them up and reconstructing them, but by affording just the proper revisions they ought to have had before they were printed at all.[14]

His careful distinction between revisions that ought to be made and those that ought not to be is telling. The "good" that comes of revision does not involve "cutting . . . up and reconstructing" old poems in an attempt to change the subject matter or manner of the verse. Rather, he revises well who would fix what should never have been printed in the first place. Browning is not a poet who prioritizes the original poem, true to its first breaths, no matter what his opinion of it later. His feeling for the poem takes into account a greater and longer-lasting sense of its overall propriety. Christopher Ricks finds Browning's particular susceptibility to compunction "endearing" and points to a fascinating example of the poet's revising a mistake—not of misreading but of fact—in the poem "Prince Hohenstiel-Schwangau," where he mistakenly "yokes" a particular temple with a "tradition of sacrifice which was really based elsewhere"; upon learning of the mistake, he not only tells his friend—the critic Alexandra Sutherland Orr—"to give notice of it in her *Handbook* to his poetry" but then also revises the poem to have the prince himself discover the mistake within the verse and account for it on his own terms:[15]

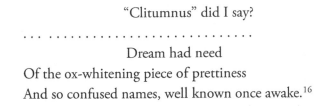

> "Clitumnus" did I say?
>
> . . . .
>   Dream had need
> Of the ox-whitening piece of prettiness
> And so confused names, well known once awake.[16]

Browning's scruples suggest an impulse not just to get his facts right but also more generally to be open with his reader about the nature of the errors to which even poets find themselves susceptible. The prince's mistake (and, by proxy, Browning's) was one of unconscious desire—the need of our dreams to make words into tropes. But what would Browning have had Pippa say about *her* mistake? Nothing, of course—not only because Pippa would consider the word "twat" to be "a name there's no pronouncing," but also because nowhere does the mistake in her song as neatly transpose itself into a representation of Browning's. Browning's mistake was made as a reader, not as a writer, and Pippa, his proxy-singer, is no reader of seventeenth-century royalist verse—rightly or wrongly. The mistake is all his own.

And yet Browning's critics rarely mention this error in studies of his work. (His editors occasionally do—the Longman edition, for instance, footnotes the actual meaning of "twat" along with Browning's letter to Furnivall.)[17] The only published comment I have been able to find, apart from notes in several editions of Browning's poetry and a brief remark in John Fuller's recent book on puzzles in poems, appears in a journal during the poet's own lifetime.[18] H. W. Fay, an American reader, takes the blunder public in a letter to the *Academy* in 1888:

> In a recently published volume of *Selections from Browning* . . . there is a note upon the phrase "cowls and twats." . . . [The editor] Mr. Rolfe says: "*Twats* is in no dictionary. We now have it from the poet (through Dr. Furnivall) that he got the word from the Royalist rhymes, entitled 'Vanity of Vanities'" . . . It would seem that Mr. Browning and Dr. Furnivall and Mr. Rolfe have, all three of them, made a distressing blunder. . . . The word in question is probably still in provincial use, and may be found in its place in Wright's Dictionary.[19]

Fay's account makes clear that he believes the "distressing" word was Browning's error initially, though he indicts the poet's editors as well as Furnivall for condoning and propagating it. Unmoved by the excuse of the royalist rhymes, Fay presumably wishes Mr. Rolfe had been clearer about Browning's misreading of the earlier text when annotating the poem. The editors of the *Academy* appear to agree: they wryly append a note to Fay's letter explaining that "Like other provincialisms, ['twat'] is also in use in London."[20] But Browning's admirers, then and now, have generally preferred to stay quiet about the whole thing. There could be a number of reasons for their reticence beyond the notion that such a misreading simply does not matter, and I will pursue a few of them.

An obvious risk to accusing Browning (or indeed any "dramatist") of mistake relates to the complicated distinction between character and poet. The murky but crucial line that distinguishes Browning's oddball personae from his own voice has been a subject of debate since his first plays and poems appeared. John Ruskin responded to Browning's early works in a letter to the poet in December 1855, and among the many limitations he perceived in them (obscurity and difficulty were his main concerns) was a sense that the consistency of the voice occasionally wavered:

> I entirely deny that a poet of your real dramatic power ought to let *himself* come up, as you constantly do, through all manner of characters, so that every now and then poor Pippa herself shall speak a long piece of Robert Browning.[21]

Ruskin unfortunately does not elaborate on how he distinguishes passages of pure "Robert Browning" from Pippa's song. But his complaint was important to Browning, who responded a week later:

> —The last charge,—I cannot answer, for you may be right in preferring it, however unwitting I am of the fact. I *may* put Robert Browning into Pippa & other men & maids—if so, *peccavi*: but I don't see myself in them, at all events.[22]

To "put Robert Browning into Pippa" is indeed a sin for a poet who painstakingly tries to keep his own personality out of his poems.[23] The enforced separation between himself and his "men and maids" goes beyond the dramatic principle; it also allows him to pursue philosophical, spiritual, and moral issues free from judgment. The objectivity that coincides with such compartmentalized subjectivity gives Browning room to conjure up material and debate that is not available to poets whose reputations more closely rely on their lyric speakers.

Browning had little time for readers who mistook his characters' opinions for his own. Accused at one point of being "against Darwin, rejecting the truths of science and regretting its advance," he responded that "it came, I suppose, of Hohenstiel-Schwangau's expressing the notion which was the popular one at the appearance of Darwin's book—and you might as well charge Shakespeare with holding that there were men whose heads grew beneath their shoulders, because Othello told Desdemona that he had seen such."[24] Browning regretted such conflations but made his stance very clear to friends as well as to critics and editors, the latter of whom often questioned him on potential snags in the poems prior to publication. For instance, he had to defend similar charges in "The Bishop Orders His Tomb at Saint Praxed's Church": when asked in 1886 by the editors of his forth-coming volume of selected poems about what they thought was a factual mistake in line 95—the bishop refers to the female "Saint Praxed" as a man, seemingly confusing her with Christ—Browning explains that "the blunder as to the sermon is the result of the dying man's haziness; he would not reveal himself as he does but for that."[25]

His annoyance is particularly striking in another letter to Furnivall in February 1888. In it he responds to a comment made at a Browning Society meeting, where a man named Edward Berdoe spoke up after listening to a paper titled "Browning's Jews and Shakespeare's Jew":

> I was looking over the account of that paper concerning my treatment of the Jews. It was remarked that I mistook a Rabbi for a High Priest! This comes of forgetting that one writes dramatically. The speaker, Baldinucci, is a typically ignorant Tuscan, and makes the gross mis-take already noted in Arbuthnot's Martinus Scriblerus—of whom it is said, at the very beginning: "Those who had never seen a Jesuit took him for one, while others thought him rather to be some High Priest of the Jews." Somebody objected to a Jewish burying-ground being in the neighbourhood of any habitation, but Baldinucci tells the story, and describes the locality as he knew it—and I follow him, of course.[26]

Browning's notion of "following" his characters (rather than the other way around) is both convincing and counterintuitive. Baldinucci is a product of his own imagination, but the character's knowledge (and propensity for mistake) still guides the poem. One sees the trap ahead: in light of such a defense, how can a reader impugn Browning for a "twat" that Pippa speaks? Perhaps this is one reason why no one apart from Fay does. Yet it would be absurd, as I have already pointed out, to attribute such a vulgar slip to the imagination of an impoverished young girl working in the silk mills of northern Italy. Browning's excuse to Furnivall in his earlier letter makes this impossible: no one could reasonably believe that Pippa herself had read the obscure poem "Vanity of Vanities" or had any particular interest in Henry Vane.

Still, the slippery nature of dramatic poems may seem like a strong reason to avoid commenting on "twats," even if it does not fully exonerate Browning on this occasion. But the dramatic monologue—as Ruskin suspected—has always been a complicated mode. As Yopie Prins has remarked, "Much depends on how to read the mediating figure of voice, always a complex issue in Browning's poetry."[27] Scholars of the form as it developed in the nineteenth century consistently note its permeability and collusions. Matthew Campbell points out that a "[d]ramatic monologue must allow its speakers to reveal themselves, and then draw back; its writers must move in and out of their role as anonymous impersonator."[28] The specificity of circumstance—the time and the place in which the words are spoken—contributes to the speaker's primacy as well. Herbert Tucker calls this phenomenon "the historical contextualization that is the generic privilege of the dramatic monologue."[29] The history *in* the poem sits above the history outside of the poem for the purposes of reading it, so whatever the circumstances in the poem consider to be factual takes on greater importance than it would in other poetical modes. Prins elaborates that "mediation is what Victorian poems are made of, their aesthetic glitter. And these mediating figures are not discourses outside the poems but how the poetry works from the inside out."[30] Browning's poetry at its best and most dramatic takes advantage of such mediations, making it especially difficult to differentiate between circumstance and reality, fact and fiction. In his "Essay on Shelley," Browning writes of the value in "efficacious knowledge," which amounts to knowing something to be untrue but nevertheless believing in it for some good purpose or reason (he cites as an example believing in Thomas Chatterton's fictive "Rowley").[31] Fiction, as developed historically and through character, may become its own desired version of fact. Prins's commitment to "a historical poetics that works recursively as a loop, reading simultaneously from the inside out and from the outside in" prioritizes this approach to poetry, meaning that what is historical about the circumstances of a work such as *Pippa Passes* becomes part of the poem itself.[32] To read Browning's language ("twats") outside of its context in the poem is partly to rewrite the poem and partly to dismantle it. Because a word belongs to a text that is historically situated, contributing to a reading experience that is likewise historically embedded, it becomes difficult to give "twats" any other meaning than the one for which it was chosen and through which it was—at least for most of Browning's lifetime—read.[33]

Even readers who are reluctant to subscribe to such a historically inflected view of what belongs to and becomes a poem have to reckon with the dramatic monologue's resistance to complaints about the counterfactual in its words or meanings since those very words and meanings are intrinsic to its dramatic scenario. Before Prins and other scholars of nineteenth-century poetry turned toward the concept of "historicity,"[34] Robert Langbaum introduced similar issues related to contextualization in order to tease out the moral implications of reading Browning's work:

> [I]t [is] characteristically the style of the dramatic monologue to present its material empirically, as a fact existing before and apart from moral judgment which remains always secondary and problematical. Even where the speaker is specifically concerned with a moral question, he arrives at his answer empirically, as a necessary outcome of conditions within the poem and not through an appeal to an outside moral code. Since there conditions are always psychological and sometimes historical as well—since the answer is determined, in other words, by the speaker's nature and the time he inhabits—the moral meaning is of limited application but enjoys within the limiting conditions of the poem a validity which no subsequent differences in judgment can disturb.[35]

According to Langbaum, a reader of Browning's historically situated poetry is both at liberty to judge and at liberty not to: the conditions within the poem preside over its morality to such an extent that even when a reader disagrees with a character's decisions or actions, those aspects of the poem (for the purposes of its appeal to the reader) remain safely distinct from "real-world" moral codes. What happens in the poem stays in the poem. In the case of *Pippa*, it may also be the case that problems of meaning ("twats") are likewise better determined by conditions within the poem than without. Since Pippa herself speaks the word, and indeed apparently believes the word to mean the female equivalent of a monk's cowl, her intended meaning may seem to hold more value than the meaning of the word as it stands outside of the poem. As such, the poem's dramatic form, its closed circumstance, would take precedence, and intrapoetic empiricism would rule over extrapoetic fact. But for readers who prefer to keep one foot in and one foot out of the poem, this wholehearted susceptibility to fictionality is hard to accept.

Isobel Armstrong similarly acknowledges the primacy of character in dramatic poetry but questions its validity:

> The derangement of these monologues comes from Browning's remorseless understanding of the structural problems which arise from the expressive poet's abolition of externality, of agency and action, time, and above all the obliteration of the reader. The characters obsessively read themselves, and if we understand the poems in terms of expressive psychological moments, they effectively suppress the fact that they are being read or "heard." They obliterate the active, critical presence of the reader because they obliterate their status as *texts*.[36]

For Armstrong, the "presence" of a reader and the external world within which such a reader lives is denied by Browning's poems; this is to their credit, but also to their "derangement." Browning's subtle and "remorseless" capacity for contextualizing fact makes it very difficult for a reader or critic to exert any pressure on the verse—to ask of it anything beyond what it already contains.[37] Langbaum relatedly argues that within these poems "judgment is largely psychologized and historicized . . . [it] must be perpetually checked against fact, which comes before judgment and remains always more certain."[38] The trouble when applying this argument to the problem of "twats"—which I see as a problem of language, not of judgment—is that for Langbaum, fact can only be established in the empirical underpinnings of the poem itself: psychological and historical fact belong to the verse. What happens when such empirical foundations are themselves shaky—when the historical conditions of the poem's composition, which should be factual, are indeed not?

Tucker's description of the lyric aspects of Victorian dramatic monologues may begin to supply an answer. As history is "dramatically replayed" in these poems, he writes, "[t]he charmed circle of lyric finds itself included by the kind of historical particularity that lyric genres [normally] exclude by design, and in the process readers find themselves unsettlingly histori-cized and contextualized as well."[39] He diagnoses the problem thus: "The extremity of each monologist's authoritative assertion awakens in us with great force the counter-authority of communal norms."[40] In other words, the reader becomes trapped—first historicized by the dramatic position of the character, and then forced into believing as fact something that propri-ety tells him isn't so. The tension created by this poetical strong-arming is part of the impact, if not the enjoyment, of the poem. A reader can know and understand the historical circumstance while also resisting the material it imposes. The less it conforms to our own norms, the more suspect it is—but also the more interesting. Tucker goes on to say that "[d]ramatic monologue in the Browning tradition is, in a word, anything but mono-logical. It represents modern character as a quotient, a ratio of history and desire, a function of the division of the modern mind against itself."[41] But what is the correct ratio of historical fact to desire? Put another way, how important is the context of a poem versus our own understanding of how things really are, or should be? These questions can be asked equally of a poem's moral issues and its features of language and meaning. "[T]o assume in advance that a poetic text proceeds from a dramatically situated speaker is," Tucker explains,

> to risk missing the play of verbal implication whereby character is engendered in the first place through colliding modes of signification; it is to read so belatedly as to arrive only when the party is over. At the same time, however, the guest the party convenes to honor, the ghost conjured by the textual machine, remains the articulate phe-nomenon we call character: a literary effect we neglect at our peril.[42]

Tucker is putting pressure here on Browning's own assertion that the poet necessarily "follows" his character. His challenge raises pertinent questions: To what extent should critics and readers separate their respect for character and contextualization from their nuanced understanding of language and its complex way of signifying? What are the various ways that language comes to mean things for Browning? Browning himself seems on the brink of addressing these questions in appending the poem "One Word More" to the end of his collection *Men and Women* where, for a brief moment, he willingly steps outside of the contingent reality constituted by his characters to address his wife Elizabeth directly:

> There they are, my fifty men and women
> Naming me the fifty poems finished!
> Take them, Love, the book and me together:
> Where the heart lies, let the brain lie also.[43]

It would seem as though Browning is finally lifting the mask to speak truly: no dramatic voice can intercede between man and wife. And yet, with one punning sleight of hand, he also simultaneously concedes that all is a "lie."

These hermeneutic complexities provide yet another reason for Browning's critics to avoid the problem of "twats": it is certainly easier to argue that Browning's word, in its place, means what he believes it to mean than to prove otherwise—both because he is the poet and also because meaning is always contextual. If Browning uses "twats" to refer to an article of clothing—chooses the word expressly for that purpose, as we know from his letter to Furnivall—why shouldn't we let it be? Poets use language idiosyncratically, and a good part of a poem's pleasure comes from a reader's knowing that many of its words bear secondary and tertiary meanings as well as nuances drawn from etymological, historical, and poetical sources. Yet in the case of "twat," this extra freight arrives on the wings of misinterpretation, not through an act of will. Misreading and trope—error and allusion—are not one and the same.

One could argue that Browning thought of words and their meanings rather loosely compared to other poets. For instance, in his study of Browning's language, Hair has explored the poet's avid interest in Samuel Johnson's *Dictionary*—a source to which Browning often appealed in his conversations and letters. Browning "would gain from Johnson," Hair writes, "a sense of language as a living form which is modified, subtly but inevitably, by every speaker of it, the changes being the result not so much of broad historical or social or cultural forces as of individual decisions."[44] His interest in language's malleability widens tremendously the possibilities for meaning and interpretation in his poems—it is one of the reasons his speakers so often feel authentic but hard to grasp. In the same letter in which he accuses Browning of stepping into Pippa's shoes, Ruskin also challenges him on the accuracy of his words:

> "Depths—sublimed." I don't know what you mean by "sublimed." Made sublime?—if so—it is not English. To sublime means to evaporate dryly, I believe[,] and has participle "Sublimated."[45]

Ruskin is naughty and pedantic here, especially given the cultural baggage attached to a word like "sublime," but his point brings into relief the fundamentally colloquial nature of Browning's language—its basis in, as Hair says, "individual decisions." Part of Browning's interest in the *Dictionary* surely stems from his excitement about the sociological way words come into and out of being. (Even "twat," as Fuller points out, has evolved since Browning's day, now also meaning an idiot as well as serving as an acronym for the "The War against Terror.")[46] Their arrivals and departures happen at the level of human exchange and are tied, as such, to personal need. Replying to Ruskin on this point, he takes the poetical high ground: "I *know* that I don't make out my conception by my language—all poetry being a putting the infinite within the finite."[47] It is hard to argue with such a retort.

But if poetry's conceptions are infinite—limited only by the language a poet grudgingly squeezes them into—a single word's possibilities cannot be. Browning ties his own poems' meanings most often, as we have seen, to the intentions of his historically situated and internally motivated characters. Hair writes:

> For the purposes of practical criticism, the reader must bring to the words of the text the understanding that embedded in them are the multiple meanings that represent choices or judgments made by the speakers of the language, some or all of which may be reiterated by the dramatic character. . . . The status of words as obsolete or archaic or dialect, for instance—their history, in short, as opposed to current use—seems less important to Browning, though sometimes the diction of a monologue does require a diachronic reading. . . . For

Browning, that which is stored up in language is the record of spiritual development, upon which every speaker draws in making his or her own choices.[48]

Hair is partly accounting here for Browning's inconsistencies. Archaisms, formalities, and slang coexist in his poems in ways that other nineteenth-century poets would balk at; even Wordsworth's professed "real language of men" could not accommodate half of the freedom and eclecticism of Browning's men and women.[49] But what is "infinite" about Browning's poetry is ultimately tied to the depth of these characters, not their words. Even his arch response to Ruskin shows a belief that poets, as craftsmen, must do their best to work with the "finite" tools given them. The word "sublime" in particular may have flexible properties—or at least the character who utters the term may be allowed to think so—but that small liberty in word-shaping is, for example, not comparable with substituting, in the mouth of a young girl, a slang word meaning genitalia for a nun's headpiece. The former could reasonably be called license, the latter only ignorance—or else good sense run amok.

As philologists compiled the first edition of what they called the *New English Dictionary* (now the *OED*) toward the end of Browning's life, they were already reckoning with his obscure usage. James Murray, its first editor, noted that "Browning constantly used words without regard to their proper meaning. He has added greatly to the difficulties of the Dictionary."[50] Murray, Furnivall, and others often wrote to Browning questioning his language—and indeed Furnivall's (now lost) query about "twats" may be but one example of their attending to him. These editors were looking for concrete answers in order to supply readers with examples. But Browning's words were rarely suited to black-and-white definitions. In his book on Browning, Tucker fortifies the poet's sense of the give and finesse of language with his own take on Derridean *différance*:

> The rhetorical troping of figurative language represents the absent object by re-presenting it, making it present in a different way. In such a process, which is essential to poetic language itself, Browning finds one of his surest defenses against the semantic or metaphysical foreclosure of meaning.[51]

Tucker supplies here a deconstructionist's excuse for Browning's mistake without mentioning it explicitly. For what can "twats" signify in absolute terms? Like all words, it signifies continuously and differently, deferring its own meanings and defending against the fixity of definition:

> Now representation, as Browning conspicuously and tirelessly teaches, forever betrays its incapacity to do anything more than represent, mediate, or substitute. It reveals, if it does not proclaim, an ineradicable, incurable difference between what represents and what is represented. Through an inevitable dissimulation, a figure of speech unsettles and supplants what it is intended to render; because as a representation it differs from the irreducibly other thing (object or idea or person) to which it points, it can only display that thing by displacing it. Precisely because it means, it can never simply be. This fundamental difference between image and truth, fancy and fact, opens an interminable process of reference—one that is indeed cognate with the process of deference in Browning and that from a temporal perspective may be considered as identical with it. Insofar as meaning is a temporal phenomenon, figurative language defers what it refers to. Permanently transitory, it intends an ungraspable future that it also postpones.
>
> Under Browning's hands this seemingly gloomy account of imagination's guilty involvement with language glows with promise. . . . representational language lights Browning's way by concealing what it pretends to reflect: the terminus of original meaning.[52]

Tucker enfolds Browning's habits of language within a broader sense of the poet's willful obscurity. Just as Browning's characters conceal and reflect their own messages (sometimes even from themselves), so the language of this poetry in particular—though of all poetry, to some degree—fends off concrete or absolute meanings by never quite managing to represent what it intends. Far from being a flaw, this "interminable process of reference" gives Browning's poetry the "glowing" depth that even his detractors so often seem to revere. In this regard, the poet who misuses "twats" simply takes on the habit of one of his strangest and most beloved characters, Bishop Blougram, who, as Browning writes in the epilogue to that poem, "said true things, but called them by wrong names."[53]

Browning certainly liked using slang words and even made-up ones. In abstract terms, he is not the sort of poet above putting the so-called provincialism "twat" to use. Philip Drew comments that unlike Gray and Wordsworth before him, Browning

> leaves himself free to choose any word he feels necessary for his poetic effects, even though it would have been too mean for Gray or too exotic for Wordsworth. He claims for himself in other words the rights of a man in ordinary conversation to use the *mot juste*, where it happens to be vulgar (e.g. *pully-hauly*) or technical (e.g. *monostich* or *abductor*), newly-coined (e.g. *calotypist*) or oldfashioned (e.g. *quoth* or *terquisition*), familiar (e.g. *dirt-cheap*) or unfamiliar (e.g. *acromia* "shoulderblades"), prosaic (e.g. *bunghole* or *ginger-pop*) or fanciful (e.g. *rose-jacynth*).[54]

So how can we be sure "twats" is not Pippa's *mot juste*? Or that Browning isn't simply having a little fun? At a stretch, one *could* believe that he vaguely knew what the word meant and that his spirited love for "wrong" and bad words convinced him to slip one into Pippa's mouth. As Chesterton points out, "[Browning] was clever enough to understand his own poetry," though he adds, a moment later, that "he was also entirely unconscious and impulsive."[55] Barbara Melchiori has pointed to an interesting example in *The Ring and the Book*, in which Guido, Browning's speaker, makes and then realizes his own Freudian slip:

> His Altitude the Referendary,—
> Robed right, and ready for the usher's word
> To pay devoir,—is, of all times, just then
> 'Ware of a master-stroke of argument
> Will cut the spinal cord . . . ugh, ugh! . . . I mean,
> Paralyse Molinism for evermore![56]

Here Guido's parapraxis—saying "cut the spinal cord" instead of "Paralyse"—registers as an unwonted confession, something to take back ("ugh,

ugh!"). Browning here and elsewhere plays with the idea of the unconscious; as Melchiori says of this moment: "Written long before Freud, in
The Psychopathology of Everyday Life, had drawn attention to the import of
this kind of verbal slip, it is a striking example of Browning's intuition."[57]
To have written these lines, the poet of *The Ring and the Book* must indeed
have been familiar with the sensation of discovering one's own mistake as
soon as it leaves the mouth. But does it follow that we should read "twats"
as a veiled confession—Browning's own personal "ugh, ugh!" moment? It
seems unlikely. One might just as easily argue that his innate sense of errors'
revelations and their value as truth-telling devices reminds us how common
mistakes can be, even for poets.

And yet it is still difficult for critics to talk about "twats." Perhaps their
silence also stems from the mistake's coincidental connection to the plot of
Pippa Passes itself. After all, the entire premise of the play rests on the notion
of innocent words having unintended effects. Pippa's lovely song presides
and spreads over her world; her singing changes the lives of those around
her in what we can only read as a happy allegory for poetry itself. (At the
time of writing the play, Browning would have been familiar with Mill's
dictum that "eloquence is *heard*, poetry is *over*-heard.")[58] Francis Russell
notes the "the accidental appropriateness" of Pippa's song, Roma King
points out that "[c]ertainly, the good she accomplishes is the result of unconscious rather than conscious action," and Chesterton refers to the play's
"beautiful deification of unconscious influence."[59] Pippa's own "over-heard"
song works upon different characters unknowingly, allowing Browning to
showcase the unintended consequences of words. As Jacob Korg writes:

> [T]he world, as it is seen in *Pippa Passes*, is intricate, deceptive, and
> full of concealed meanings. Browning has gone to exceptional lengths
> to show that every event in the daily life of Asolo is charged with
> unperceived significance. . . . [E]verything is encoded and disguised,
> heavy with sinister latent meaning. Pippa's parentage, Bluphocks'
> identity, the forged love letters written to Jules, the students hidden
> outside his window, Lutwyche's poem, the secret signs in the signature
> on Luigi's passport, the code of A and B which Luigi and his mother
> use in their conversation, and Pippa's songs themselves form parts of

this context. The world of *Pippa Passes* is a cryptogram; its people cannot read the book of their experiences.[60]

The more one begins to notice *Pippa*'s subtleties and concealments, its codes and "latent meaning," the easier it becomes to think of its embarrassing word as a part of the overall conception.[61] Might "twats" constitute another layer of deception—a wink from the author of a play that indeed brims with content intended to be barely perceptible?

Along these lines, a closer look at the opening section of Pippa's song reveals similarly sexual undertones. Pippa herself may not hear them, but Browning's reader certainly can:

Day!
Faster and more fast,
O'er night's brim, day boils at last:
Boils, pure gold, o'er the cloud-cup's brim
Where spurting and suppressed it lay,[62]

Spurting and suppressed? Pippa's girlish innocence surely belies a poet's snicker at the words he puts in her mouth to describe a hot sun boiling over. And a few lines down, Pippa does indeed use the word "breast," even if she shies away from doing so later:

Till the whole sunrise, not to be suppressed,
Rose, reddened, and its seething breast
Flickered in bounds, grew gold, then overflowed the world.[63]

These words, which Pippa sings in her bedchamber before she takes to the streets, already hint at doubled meanings and repressions. One could even suppose that Browning sets up here a dynamic between poet and reader that mirrors the dynamic between Pippa and her listeners. When we finally get to "twats," who is to say how it should be heard? As Drew has pointed out more generally, "Pippa's songs have throughout the play been used as instruments of dramatic irony."[64] Her final speech "reflects on the events of the day in terms deliberately designed to call into question the imagery of her carefree song."[65] Perhaps taking her at her word—literally—was never the point.

One of the things Browning's play seems to teach us is that it is not Pippa's words but their effects that matter. If we were to apply this logic to "twats," we might likewise conclude that the word itself, with its prior or intrinsic meanings, is less important than the context of its appearance in the play. The characters in the play are moved by Pippa's words not according to how she meant them but rather according to the ways in which they apply to their own troubled lives. The plot thus presents a series of misreadings that on one level seem to correspond to Browning's own when he first encountered the word "twat" in the royalist rhymes. And so one of the extraordinary coincidences surrounding this particular mistake is the way in which Browning inadvertently reinscribes his own ignorance about the word in Pippa, who no more suspects the intentions of the people listening to her song than he suspected the intentions behind the royalist verses from which her word sprung.

The idea that "twats" reinvests the innocence Browning had when he read "Vanity of Vanities" into the song of his main character is an appealing one. But yoking the play's broad focus on unconscious meanings to the circumstances of its slip brings a different sort of trouble, since elsewhere in the play, Browning also shows himself to be attentive to the subtleties of will versus accident. So does his little singer, who in her opening song, cognizant of the rarity of her holiday, reminds herself not to "squander" any of the day's "choices or . . . chances."[66] Browning takes his first opportunity to make choice (along with chance) one of his play's thematic touchstones; his character Jules in part 2 also champions choice, remarking that "One may do whate'er one likes / In Art."[67] To excuse Browning's "twats" on the grounds that unconscious meanings take precedence in this play over conscious ones would be to overlook the play's lesson about the importance of what people choose over what they are given. Tucker describes this aspect of the play's message most succinctly when he writes that

> [T]he difference between what one is given and what one chooses
> makes all the difference in Browning's world. Innocence is often con-
> ceived as a state anterior to significant choice, a state in which every

alternative is equally valid . . . *Pippa Passes*, Browning's songbook of innocence, questions this relation of innocence to choice. For the figures of this play, the state of innocence is a state of their own choosing: not a prelude to the necessity of choice, but its result.[68]

If the characters in Browning's play celebrate the *choice* of their innocence, then would it not be misguided to read Browning's own innocence as a main force driving the text unbeknownst to him? *Pippa Passes* offers a reading of the will in its capacity for using innocence as a way to make good—to correct or make right. It would hardly be in keeping with the subject matter of the play to proclaim that Browning's unconscious error of innocence overrides his artistic decisions. Browning was in many ways a scrupulous and deliberate craftsman: justifying his mistake by denying him these qualities would be our own version of a misreading.

In appealing to Browning's sense of propriety here, I am suggesting that we respect the difference between the unconscious errors of a reader-poet and the more purposed determinations of his craft, no matter how intertwined the two may be. Chesterton also suggests this way of thinking when he points out, in the opening quote to this chapter, that only by identifying the weakness of the verse can we truly celebrate its merits. Ricks makes a similar point when he reminds us that "it would be condescending to murmur that, come now, such an error would not matter to us, as enlightened readers, even though it would assuredly have mattered to the author."[69] By acknowledging Browning's mistake as a mistake, we respect his conscious choices as a craftsman and poet along with his unconscious ones as a reader and interpreter of text. Both matter—and mattered to him.

Would we approach Browning's mistake differently if it had merely been a mistake in his language rather than in his reading? For instance, what could we say about "twats" if Browning had been *right* in his interpretation of "Vanity of Vanities," and it was actually that anonymous seventeenth-century poet who had used the word wrongly? Let me answer by way of another example. At the very end of "Childe Roland to the Dark Tower Came," Browning puts the following words into the mouth of his strange, unyielding protagonist:

> I saw them and I knew them all. And yet
> Dauntless the slug-horn to my lips I set,
>   And blew. "Childe Roland to the Dark Tower came."[70]

The horn's triumphant blow announces the utter persistence of Browning's speaker at the very end. It is a winning manifestation of the impenetrability of the human spirit—an act comparable to that of Tennyson's own "[d]auntless" and unyielding Ulysses—except for one little problem: there is no such instrument as a "slug-horn." The word is an archaic form of "slogan" meaning a battle cry. Where did Browning get the mistaken idea that a slug-horn was a horn, rather than a sound? From his extensive reading, of course. "Slug-horn" does not appear in Johnson's *Dictionary* (nor does "slogan," for that matter),[71] but Thomas Chatterton uses it, erroneously, in his poem "Battle of Hastings." Bloom sees significance in this mistaken borrowing, since Chatterton was, for Browning, a forerunner in the art of poetic ventriloquism:

> Chatterton . . . enters Childe Roland at the close with the slug-horn . . . As a cry-to-battle by a crazed, self-defeated poet, its appropriateness is overwhelming at Child Roland's end. [Browning's "Essay on Chatterton"] is essentially a defense of Chatterton's assumption of the mask of Rowley, anticipating Browning's extraordinary essay on Shelley, with its implicit defense of Browning's assumption of the many masks of his mature poetry.[72]

Bloom suggests here that Chatterton's voice—heard, or overheard, through the medium of the fictive "Rowley"—was particularly important to Browning as he experimented with masks of his own. But as we have seen in the case of *Pippa*, such ventriloquizing raises difficult questions when a poem's historical circumstances, with their attendant empirical meanings and facts, collide with the more subjective and interpretive aspects of its characters and readers—as they do when Browning encounters Chatterton's slug-horn. Daniel Karlin has noted the way in which "Childe Roland," the poem, "takes place in a psychological present dramatized as a historical past."[73] Its main character both does and does not subscribe to the factual-ness of his own history; in this one respect, Roland is both speaker and poet at once.

Browning particularly admired the ingenuity of Chatterton's language. In his essay on the poet—one of the few substantive pieces of literary criticism he ever wrote—he praises Chatterton for his ability to make word "acquisitions" that always seem "but a little out of more in reserve":[74]

> If only a foreign word clung to his memory, he was sure to reproduce it as if a whole language lay close behind—setting sometimes to work with the poorest materials; like any painter a fathom below the ground in the Inquisition, who in his penury of colour turns the weather-stains on his dungeon wall into effects of light and shade, or outlines of objects, and makes the single sputter of red paint in his possession go far indeed! Not that we consider the mere fabrication of old poetry so difficult a matter. For what *is* poetry, whether old or new, will have its full flow in such a scheme; and any difficulty or uncouthness of phrase that elsewhere would stop its course at once, here not only passes with it, but confers the advantage of authenticity on what, in other circumstances, it deforms: the uncouthness will be set down to our time, and whatever significancy may lurk in it will expand to an original meaning of unlimited magnitude.[75]

This extraordinary defense of Chatterton's ability to make a "foreign" or "uncouth" word "go far" and even take on a new "original meaning" is deeply ironic given Browning's appropriation of "slug-horn," not to mention "twats." (It may also be worth noting that Browning misattributes his moral of a painter who, out of necessity, creates effects from stains on a dungeon wall to an imprisoned artist of the Inquisition, when in fact the anecdote is lifted from the notebooks of Leonardo da Vinci.)[76] The stamp of authenticity Browning gives "slug-horn" feels especially pronounced in "Child Roland" because of the overall message of that particular monologue; as King suggests, "The poem is a negation of external meaning. . . . It depicts the paradox of man's . . . need to create meaning when no meaning exists."[77] Just as *Pippa*, a play about innocence and the unconscious effects of language, seems to anticipate Browning's own mistake at its end, so Roland seems to encapsulate Browning's belief in "original," if deformed, meaning through his willful denial of external circumstance. The "unlimited" power of a deformity such as "slug-horn" is what Browning's newer poem celebrates when it recommits Chatterton's mistake—but presumably without knowing so.

Mistakes are passed on this way, by reading, from poet to poet. For instance, Seamus Heaney, probably with Browning's poem in mind, erroneously pairs his own "slug-horn" with a "slow chanter," or pipe, in the sequence he calls "Glanmore Sonnets."[78] Heaney takes Browning at his word, just as Browning does of Chatterton. And so one of the benefits of acknowledging mistakes like Browning's is to nip them in the bud before they can multiply. Identifying mistakes also helps tease out complex questions about genre, voice, history, reception, and interpretation—in other words, the myriad factors that make up poems. Mistakes may not be where meaning lies, but they provide opportunities for reading ourselves reading; they are places in poems where we can look inward and reflect upon the meaning of our own acts of interpretation.

Thomas Carlyle wrote Browning about *Pippa Passes* after receiving a copy of it and another of Browning's plays. In his somewhat patronizing letter, he encourages the poet to "fight on" toward "what best light you can attain to," pointing out that "[t]he light we ourselves gain, by our very errors if not otherwise, is the only precious light."[79] By "errors" Carlyle was not referring to "twats" or any other particular instance in the poetry, but his sentiment gives value to error as worthy of attention and recognition. If Browning can no longer learn from his mistakes, his readers might. When confronted with the temptation to create meaning where no prior meaning exists, we might think twice about prioritizing our own interpretive ingenuity at the expense of Browning's authorial intentions, however elusive they seem to be.

And yet I cannot resist asking, finally, whether there might be something to the fact that "twats" and "slug-horn" both occur in the final moments of their respective poems. Tucker's excellent book *Browning's Beginnings* also makes a salient point about his endings:

Often at the ends of these works the expected deed remains uncommitted, the complex issue unresolved, so as to suggest a residue of action exceeding the formal and temporal limits of the plot. In Browning's lyric poems, likewise, the traditional weight of closure feels less like exhaustive aplomb than like a force temporarily compressing a spring that remains tensed for further speech.[80]

"Twats" and "slug-horn," both of which cap off long dramatic pieces, are not narrative or moral incompletions; but they are artistic lags, and they wreak a different sort of havoc on closure's satisfaction. One begins to suspect that part of Browning's unconscious genius—his artist's knack for sensing what a well-made thing requires—may consist in his ability to allow mistake to creep in where it might be felt or desired most. We do him more of a disservice when we ignore his frayed ends than when we pick at and unravel them. As Browning himself once said of Shelley, the poet he most admired: "Let the whole truth be told of his worst mistake."[81] I have tried my best to do so.

CHAPTER 3

Wondering about John Clare

"Blundering" is one of John Clare's favorite words. He uses it to describe the hapless path of sleepy shepherds "Blundering off to fold their sheep."[1] He uses it to describe the woodman "Wi hasty blundering step & folded arm."[2] In one poem, he celebrates the "rage of the blundering plough";[3] in another, the ploughman, "blundering on robust & strong."[4] He writes of the horseboy who whips his horse into a "blundering trot."[5] He writes of "blundering pheasants" startled by noise and "blundering beetles" taking wing.[6] Nor does Clare consign "blunder" to the domain of the physical: he satirizes a "Learned lecturer" who astonishes ignorant crowds with "Each thoughtless pause—& helpless blunder," and elsewhere, he uses "worthles' blunder" to describe an ill-fated, embarrassing love letter.[7] Far from haphazard himself, Clare exposes blunder's manifold meanings—"to confuse, confound," "to move blindly or stupidly," "to stumble," "to utter thoughtlessly . . . to blurt out," "to make a stupid and gross mistake in doing anything."[8] And yet blundering is clearly not all bad. He might even have his reader believe *him* to be the consummate blunderer. In his daily occupation as a field laborer, he could "blunder" through furrow, hedgerow, and farm with the best of them. And as a poet, he makes beauty out of "thoughtless" utterance even as he blunders through language more conventionally, frequently misspelling words and sometimes using them ungrammatically—often to great, if mistaken, effect.

But Clare's poetic blundering is sometimes willed and sometimes unwilling, making it difficult for readers to distinguish unintended mistakes from blundering more generally. His poems often have the mark of a fine Persian rug: rigged with a deliberate mistake, they slyly suggest the impossibility of perfection (of which only Allah is capable). And like the weavers of such rugs, he knows the value afforded by obvious signs of the down-home and handmade. Such complicity on his part vexes a reader who would try to discern the unforced errors from the affected ones, the staged mistakes from the flaws. A sonnet Clare writes about mist suggests this dilemma on multiple levels:

> The shepherds almost wonder where they dwell
> & the old dog for his night journey stares
> The path leads somewhere but they cannot tell
> & neighbour meets with neighbour unawares
> The maiden passes close beside her cow
> & wonders on & think her far away
> The ploughman goes unseen behind his plough
> & seems to loose his horses half the day
> The lazy mist creeps on in journey slow
> The maidens shout & wonder where they go
> So dull & dark are the november days
> The lazy mist high up the evening curled
> & now the morn quite hides in smokey haze
> The place we occupy seems all the world[9]

Clare composes these lines sometime between 1832 and 1837, during the period many scholars now consider to be his most fruitful and mature as a poet. Its descriptions of the disorienting effects of November mist mirror the alienation the poet felt in leaving his native town, Helpston, to live in the nearby village of Northborough, whose cottage, fields, and forests never quite felt like home despite their being less than three miles away. Sarah Guyer has noted the "microcosmic meaning of home for one whose sense of knowledge and observation is intense, and for whom displacement can occur at an almost imperceptible scale."[10] In his biography, Jonathan Bate points out "Clare's sense" during these unhappy but productive years "of his own status as a perpetual outsider, a man who did not fully belong in either the world of landed property or that of literary propriety."[11] For this reason, Bate suggests, "so many of the Northborough poems have an eerily detached tone."[12] In the sonnet I have just quoted, detachment is figured both in the mode of the verse—the poem, though not quite first person, features a universalizing "we" at the end—as well as in its story or narrative. The plot consists of foggy bloopers: the shepherds are lost, the ploughman has disappeared, neighbors fail to see one another despite staring each other in the face, and the poor maiden cannot locate her cow no matter how many times she passes it by. It is a special kind of detachment Clare understood well. But it is also blundering at its finest—physically depicted, and also thematic. Clare puts human fallibility on show and blames it on the weather. It would be comic if it weren't so sad; the final line—"The place we occupy seems all the world"—almost gestures toward the fullness of the pastoral scene but ultimately points to its enclosure and provinciality.[13] Seeing beyond oneself in these conditions is impossible.

Clare's usual linguistic mistakes cooperate in these lines with his visual portraits of mist-induced error. "Think" should be singular rather than plural, "loose" should be "lose," "november" should be capitalized, and "smokey" shouldn't have an "e." As in all of the sonnets he wrote at Northborough, Clare leaves out punctuation and employs ampersands, and as Stephanie Weiner notes, his "central syntactic strategy during these years" is "parataxis."[14] He structures his sonnet by accrual rather than any kind of argumentative or geographical logic. Simon Kövesi has pointed out the way this poem's eight ampersands link its images together at the same time that "the poem describes the disjunctures of human bewilderment and wonder,"[15] and indeed part of the "wonder" of this scene is that the blundering happens to everyone equally. "We" in line 14 comes to represent everyone under the mist- and cloud-blotted sun.

But "wonder" is a complicated word here, not only because it appears three times, but also because one of these instances appears to be a mistake. In lines 5 and 6:

The maiden passes close beside her cow
& wonders on & think her far away

Never mind the disagreement in number between the singular noun "maiden" and the plural verb "think" (this is the kind of obvious solecism readers find all over Clare's poems and learn to ignore in an effort to appreciate the rest). Much more unusual is his use of the phrase "wonders on" rather than the expected, arguably physical verb "wander." He seems to have conflated "wonder" and "wander" here despite using "wonder" without any ambiguity or confusion in lines 1 and 10. It isn't a major blunder—to "wonder on" is certainly plausible contextually—but it isn't exactly right either. Wandering is surely what he is actually describing.

In fact, "wonder," as both a noun and a verb, appears frequently throughout Clare's writing—as it does in the verse of other Romantics. Wordsworth, who uses it often, along with its cousin "wander," deems wonder the "natural product of ignorance."[16] (For a poet who sets the innocent unknowing of childhood above most else, this is not necessarily a bad thing.) Peter Swaab, in a lovely essay on the word, points to a passage in Coleridge's *Aids to Reflection* that celebrates its trajectory in philosophical terms:[17]

> In Wonder all Philosophy began: in Wonder it ends: and Admiration fills up the interspace. But the first Wonder is the Offspring of Ignorance: the last is the Parent of Adoration. The First is the birth-throe of our knowledge: the Last is its euthanasy or apotheosis.[18]

Coleridge illustrates "wonder" at its two poles: the original site of inquiry and the place where inquiry necessarily comes to an end. We wonder *about* things until we wonder *at* them. Clare also understands these modes and uses both. In his autobiography, he exclaims, "I had often read of the world's seven wonders . . . but I found in London alone thousands."[19] In another Northborough sonnet, he writes:

> The passing traveler with *wonder* sees
> A deep & ancient stone pit full of trees
> So deep & very deep the place has been
> The church might stand within & not be seen
> The passing stranger oft with *wonder* stops
> & thinks he een could walk upon their tops[20]

Here and in his prose, Clare uses "wonder'" as the "parent of Adoration." Being in a state of "wonder" is a favorite occupation for him, which is perhaps another reason he identifies so readily, in these Northborough

poems, with strangers. During Clare's lifetime, churches, with their tall
steeples, would have been a crucial navigational tool helping orient locals
and visitors alike; imagining a pit so deep the church's steeple could not be
seen would be wondrous indeed. In the following lines, also about strangers, he uses "wonder" more simply:

> The stranger *wondering* where the village lay
> The path goes on & guesses all the way[21]

"Wondering" here is synonymous with "guessing" rather than being in awe.
And in the following lines about a mouse's nest, Clare manages to combine
both senses of the word:

> I found a ball of grass among the hay
> & proged it as I passed & went away
> & when I looked I fancied something stirred
> & turned agen & hoped to catch the bird
> When out an old mouse bolted in the wheat
> With all her young ones hanging at her teats
> She looked so odd and so grotesque to me
> I ran & *wondered* what the thing could be[22]

In this sonnet, "wonder" puns on itself: the initial questioning and the
consequent awe happen simultaneously. (Clare might as well be saying, "I
wondered *that* the thing could be.") In lines 1 and 10 of his "november"
sonnet, Clare writes with similar nuance. He offers the word in its primary
sense—"wonder" as the opposite of knowing—but accounts for its other
meaning too. The shepherds and maiden do not know where they are, to
be sure, but the awe of it plays upon the poem's surface as well. Wonder's
secondary implication may help answer the question Kövesi poses of the
poem's first line: "What is it to *almost* wonder?"[23] How *wonder*ful, and *awe*-
ful, to be somewhere you know and yet not to know where you are: the
place you occupy seems all the world!

But the "wonder" in line 6 is a different matter. Clare uses the term there
to connote movement, to suggest the nearness of the maiden to her cow as
she fumbles or blunders blindly through the pasture. In light of the word's

capaciousness, it is tempting to accept the phrase "wonders on" as a kind of enhanced proxy for "wander," wherein the poor maiden, while physically searching, is also nodding her head in ignorant, wondrous disbelief. In this case, "wondering" and "wandering" would be productively yoked—as they often are. Discussing a different Northborough sonnet that uses both words, Andrew Hodgson thinks through them together and suggests the ways in which Clare consciously plays them against one another:

> The homophone [of wonder and wander] is a fertile one for Clare, because it allows him to accomplish quicksilver shifts between casual indirection and intense imaginative engagement. Here it mobilizes the poetry's openness to the value of accident.[24]

Wonder and wander are not homophones exactly, though they may have sounded very similar in Clare's Northamptonshire dialect. But to wander aimlessly in a physical sense could indeed be a metaphor for wondering. And Clare himself suggests this wordplay in an early prose passage from his autobiography, which describes a day spent wandering in childish wonder:

> I lovd this solitary disposition from a boy & felt a curiosity to *wander* about spots were I had never been before I remember one incident of this feeling when I was very young . . . it was summer & I started off in the morning to get rotten sticks from the woods but I had a feeling to *wander* about the fields & I indulged it I had often seen the large heath calld Emmonsales . . . & my curiosity urgd me to steal an opportunity to explore it that morning I had imagind that the world's end was at the orizon & that a days journey was able to find it so I went on with my heart full of hope's pleasures & discoverys expecting when I got to the brink of the world that I could look down like looking into a large pit & see into its secrets the same as I believd I could see heaven by looking into the water So I eagerly *wanderd* on . . . I felt no fear my *wonder*-seeking happiness had no room for it I was finding new *wonders* every minute & was walking in a new world & expecting the world's end bye & bye but it never came often *wondering* to myself that I had not found the edge of the old one the

sky still touchd the ground in the distance & my childish wisdom was puzzld in perplexitys[25]

In this extraordinary anecdote, Clare describes the childhood feeling of leaving home; Guyer has suggested the passage "simultaneously remembers and anticipates . . . his other experiences of displacement, including those tied not to childhood curiosity, but to enclosure."[26] Despite his casual prose, Clare carefully depicts the feeling of trying to reach the end of the world, by which he partially means any place just beyond his knowing, and which he will necessarily never reach because "the destination is always at a distance."[27] The three "wanders" in the first part of this sketch seem almost deliberately matched with the three "wonders" in the second. By keeping both of these words in play and making them parallel, Clare not only celebrates wandering and wondering as emblematic acts but also links them, suggesting the latter to be a consequence of the former. David Higgins points out: "There is a powerful pun at the heart of this passage: to *wander* is also to *wonder*."[28]

Perhaps. But to return to the sonnet and question at hand, are the two words actually interchangeable for Clare? His poem would seem to suggest so at the moment it conflates them. When Kövesi encounters the second instance of "wonder" in his long and careful treatment of the poem, he feels compelled to make the connection explicit:

Wondering—meaning surprise, astonishment or marvel—carries with it the activity of "wandering," and this poem is particularly directed towards sauntering, uncertain direction, roaming and rambling, or, as the *OED* has it, moving "hither and thither without fixed course or certain aim" . . . This is an overall effect brought about by this poem.[29]

And yet this reading of "wonders on" may take the interpretive act too far for a poet so famously terrible at spelling, even if the poem does enact the sense of both words simultaneously. Lest it seem as though I am unnecessarily pointing fingers, let me impugn myself: in writing about the "november" sonnet in an essay I published in 2011, I briefly suspended my argument about Clare and nature in order to make the very same claim about wonder and wander at which I now raise my eyebrows. "[I]t would be a mistake," I then feverishly wrote of line 6, "simply to assume the poet has gotten the spelling wrong here, as we might be inclined to do with Clare, who so often spells words phonetically or according to their vernacular usage."[30] Instead, I suggested "wonders on" was not an error at all, pointing to the "similarity, even the deliberateness, of ['wonder' and 'wander'], particularly for a poet whose very sense of seeing is defined by the wonderment of that act."[31] Because we naturally assume that the maiden is physically wandering, I argued, the poem asks us to understand further that she is also wondering. (Never mind that the word "think" performs this same work only moments later.) Then I devolved into what I now suspect may have been passionate silliness: "the speaker surely wonders where to wander poetically, just as the characters do spatially."[32] It was the old content-matches-form/form-matches-content logic: perfect for getting out of a scrape.

My defense of Clare's spelling was well-meaning. After all, "wonders on," while odd, is not ungrammatical, and anyway, why should we concede yet one more mistake when the poem dedicates itself so assiduously to describing the very feeling of confusion and disorientation that gives rise to error itself? What's more, the two words in question are particularly evocative in this context. "Wonder" is the state of ignorance out of which error learns to correct itself; before Coleridge wrote of it, "this feeling of wonder" was "only the beginning of philosophy" for Plato,[33] and Aristotle noted that "all men begin . . . by wondering."[34] And as for the missing "wander," what better word to err upon than the one that defines error in its most literal sense? As I have noted elsewhere, to err *is* to wander, from the Latin verb *erro, errare*.[35] Clare's poetic errancy, which on this occasion concerns itself with the very term that prefigures it, belongs to a long tradition of poetical erring that originates in Spenser, who began his own epic journey in the *The Faerie Queene* by putting an errant, or wandering, knight in the den of the monster "Errour" herself.

But there I go doing it again. This kind of literary meditation is a long way from the fields of Northborough and from Clare, who did not study Latin and rarely punned on etymologies. (Though he *was* a reader and admirer of Spenser.) His poem may admit to confusion, but it claims no purposeful confusion of rhetoric. And as Hodgson reminds us, these fourteen lines are not the only ones written at Northborough in which Clare places wonder against the backdrop of wandering. Among numerous sonnets about wondering wanderers, here is one that to my ear shows no sign of confusion between the two:

> One day when all the woods where bare & blea
> I wandered out to take a pleasant walk
> & saw a strange formed nest on stoven tree
> Where startled piegon buzzed from bouncing hawk
> I wondered strangley what the nest could be
> & thought besure it was some foreign bird
> So up I scrambled in the highest glee
> & my heart jumpt at every thing that stirred
> Twas oval shaped strange wonder filled my breast
> I hoped to catch the old one on the nest
> When somthing bolted out I turned to see
> & a brown squirrel pattered up the tree
> Twas lined with moss & leaves compact & strong
> I sluthered down & wondering went along[36]

In this sonnet, Clare develops a story of accidental encounter that characterizes his sense of "wandering" in the second line. The woodland walk involves keeping an eye out for the unexpected: the prospect of "a strange formed nest" causes him to "wonder[ ] strangely" at the "foreign bird," and its ovoid shape fills him with "strange wonder." Clare's surprise—"twas" no bird but a squirrel!—leads him again to "wondering" in the final line, the contemplative act here replacing the earlier physical one, which he transfers to the verb "went." Clare's trajectory from wandering to wondering fulfills the ambition bound up in that initial word—the *point* of wandering *is* wondering. The poem demonstrates on a semantic level his complicated impulse to turn the physical experience of exploring into a psychological and poetic act. It also, I might add, confirms the poet's understanding of the spelling distinction between these two words, for those of us who briefly had our doubts. "Wandering" and "wondering" may be connected—but they are different enough, even for Clare, to warrant separate usage. He actually clarifies the distinction here.

In fact, Clare uses "wonder" and "wander" more than fifteen times in the Northborough sonnets alone; and in every case except the "november" poem, he uses the word with an "a" to denote physical movement and the word with an "o" to imply thought. Even if these two words sounded exactly the same to his ear, I think it very unlikely that he had trouble discerning the difference semantically. (The handwritten draft of the "november" poem in the Peterborough archives shows a definitive "o" in "wonder" that looks sufficiently different from his "a" in other words—to clear up any suspicion that the mistake belongs to his editors.)[37] As it happens, throughout his writing, Clare rhymes "wonder" squarely with "blunder" and "thunder,"[38] whereas "wander" finds such disparate-sounding companions as "slander," "meander," and—at quite a stretch—"defend her."[39] No confusion there. Clare marks these two words as discrete most obviously in his lines about "Lolham Bridges":

> Sketch Lolham brigs where strangers come & go
> & boys sit fishing in the floods below
> Where strangers loiter till the cart is gone
> & look below awhile & soodle on
> & swordy well where many gipseys lie
> & groups of outlaws daily wander bye
> Where travellers wander to the waters brim
> & dash the rushy well till leaches swim
> & langly bush where cowboys lie & sing
> & lonely day shines on the ravens wing
> Where strangers often stand till wonder tires
> & counts the peeping mills & many spires
> Stand by that aged tree where nature smil[e]s
> & map the prospect of a hundred miles[40]

Again Clare celebrates the wandering and wondering of strangers—boys, gypsies, outlaws, and tourists. The characters in this poem "come & go" specifically by wandering in lines 6 and 7. By line 11, such haphazard movements bear fruit: in these environs, people can "stand till wonder tires." And then Clare repeats himself: "stand by that aged tree . . . / & map the prospect of a hundred miles." Wandering means coming and going—"soodling" here and there. Wondering happens when you stand and look.

All this worrying over a single letter may seem like splitting hairs. But in a body of work full of different categories of error (spelling, grammatical, and otherwise), it can be fruitful to discover where Clare would have considered himself to be wrong rather than simply informal or haphazard. Identifying genuine lexical errors in Clare's poetry is a task complicated by the fact that his manuscripts are dotted everywhere with obvious blunders, not to mention colloquialisms and dialect words that he deliberately includes. Clare's editors and scholars have, since the early days, debated over the extent to which this poet consciously uses the *trope* of stylistic sloppiness to express something authentic about the landscape of the English countryside and the people who inhabit it. In many cases, they are working from the poet's own cues; as Clare explains in one of his letters: "Putting the Correct Language of the Gentleman into the mouth of a Simple Shepherd or Vulgar Ploughman is far from Natural."[41] Clare's first editor, John Taylor, in his introduction to *Poems Descriptive of Rural Life and Scenery (1820)*, primed the poet's first readers to accept what he calls "deficiencies" as effects:

> From the want of a due supply of [words that can fully declare his meaning], and from his ignorance of grammar, he seems to labour under great disadvantages. On the other hand, his want forces him to an extraordinary exertion of his native powers, in order to supply the deficiency.[42]

Taylor's logic highlights error's silver linings and paves the way for critics to appreciate one of the most distinctive elements of Clare's style. But it also glosses over the complexity of his errors and exacerbates the difficulty of distinguishing between so-called native mistakes that denote Clare's vernacular and more pesky mistakes in technique. It seems to me there *is* a difference between the errors permissible under Clare's own terms for himself as an authentic peasant poet pursuing natural description and those that would surely embarrass him. Celebrating the unusual craftsmanship of his work involves maintaining, rather than ignoring, that distinction.

But for the past thirty or so years, readers of Clare have tended to treat all of his inconsistencies in spelling and usage—like that plural verb "think" with a singular noun—as features rather than flaws. John Barrell remarks that it is "in the language of his poems, and . . . in the syntax of them, that Clare finds the specifically local quality that he is seeking."[43] Accordingly, the recent editors of the new Oxford edition of Clare's poems make a point of reproducing his work exactly as it exists in its original form—regardless of whether such poems were subsequently "corrected"—so as to dissolve the mask of editorial polish laid on by editors during the poet's own lifetime. They explain:

> What we decided *not* to do, was to publish corrected versions of Clare . . . We do not accept the argument that, because Clare had sometimes passed proof for Taylor and Hessey, we should accept the corrected readings. We believe that Clare's genius is rooted in his language—in his vocabulary, his spelling, his syntax; his idiom, his tone and his use of dialect. . . . We believe that to change Clare's language is to alter his social and economic status and to destroy his local culture.[44]

Clare's modern editors take a hands-off approach not because of the usual difficulty of determining the "right" or "fair" copy, but from a proactive determination not to inflict editorial standards on a poet whose idiom resists the very notion of standards. Their decision offers a portrait of a decidedly "local" Clare, free from any pretensions imposed on his work by former editors (who were equally as anxious about his reception, just in a different way). Clare probably would have welcomed this good-hearted posturing. Mina Gorji's recent study points out several ways in which he actually played up his own persona as a local-yokel poet. "Clare wanted to maintain the appearance of clownishness," Gorji points out, "mindful that this was part of his literary appeal."[45] She suggests that in "confessing a lack of learning, he was staking a claim to genius."[46] Reproducing a letter in which Clare parodies a rustic "specimen" of a poem, full of grammatical and spelling errors, Gorji notes how he

> was mindful that this kind of "mistake" was expected from someone in his cultural position, and that coming from the pen of a peasant poet it might be seen as an authenticating feature, "revealing" a lack of education which could, in turn, be read as a mark of sincerity and

originality. Examples of genuine rather than artful error are numerous in Clare. . . . In Clare's case, it can be difficult to distinguish between accident and art. And yet he knew that, like all literary models, peasant poetry had codes and conventions which could be imitated. One of these was incorrectness; another was being unlettered and unread. Both could be interpreted as signs of original genius, both could be feigned.[47]

Gorji's reading of Clare's purposefulness in mistakes accounts for some of the difficulty in distinguishing between "accident and art." Clare, she points out, makes artful as well as genuine errors. And this distinction is even murkier than she spells out, since genuine errors, too, can be artful. Error's link to unconscious desire means that feigned error and genuine error often occupy two sides of the same coin. It is likely that many of Clare's genuine errors are both involuntary *and* volitional.

But since Clare is a poet whose incorrectness also constitutes an effect, we must tread extra carefully. Not all mistakes in his poetry are created equal. Some errors result from a poetical effort that includes, or accounts for, carelessness. In these instances, the poet is like the blundering ploughman. But others appear *in spite* of such an effort. Clare codifies the former kind of slip in lines that describe his laborers' errancy: for instance, he writes, "I often turn / A *careless* look at things as I go on,"[48] and of course there is that "ploughman *blundering* on robust & strong."[49] But the other kind of mistake—to which "wonder" likely belongs—happens beyond the poet's knowing jurisdiction. It does not conform to his usual practice of erring as Gorji and other critics aptly describe it. Its strangeness tempts the reader to make excuses beyond simply that Clare is a bad speller or that his diction celebrates the language of laborers rather than Londoners—excuses that read past the poet's conscious intentions and, in so doing, compromise our sense of his technique. Such excuses, while generous and related to poetry's connection to the unconscious mind, can blind readers to the elements of poems most important to poets themselves. When we overinterpret error, we underestimate craft.

Clare's readers must keep their own creativity in check in approaching poems that are open-ended and themselves outside of the box. He would likely have chuckled at my and others' readings of "wonder" *as* "wander":

I think so not only because of his meticulous spelling of both words throughout the rest of his many books and manuscripts, but also because I detect, in the very lines that immediately follow his error, an indirect and probably unconscious move toward self-correction. Here are the lines again:

> The maiden passes close beside her cow
> & *wonders on* & think her far away
> The ploughman goes unseen behind his plough
> & seems to loose his horses half the day
> The lazy mist creeps on in journey slow
> The maidens shout and wonder where they go[50]

One of the most charming aspects of this sonnet is the way its Shakespearean form gives way to apropos pathlessness after the second quatrain. Clare suddenly breaks into his couplet four lines too soon. (In the manuscript, this is the moment when Clare seems to run out of space on the page and turns the sheet sideways to continue.) In doing so, he returns to the maiden, reinscribing her as the plural "maidens," a change that retroactively justifies the ungrammatical "think." Unlike the first maiden, who redundantly "wonders" and "thinks" (two mental acts), these second maidens "wonder" and "go." Pairing "wonder" with the physical verb "go" faithfully connects the imaginative act to a distinct—if complementary—sense of movement. The effect is the same as with "wondering" and "went" in the squirrel sonnet. And though it is unlikely that Clare consciously makes this adjustment, its appearance in the poem, and his repetition of the maiden more generally, suggests to me a feeling on the part of an uncommonly intuitive poet that something has been amiss.

Clare is not one of the great Romantic revisers. "I always wrote my poems in great haste," he said, adding that "what corrections I made I always made them while writing the poem and never coud do anything with them after wards."[51] And yet he may well have unconsciously revised his error in the second half of his sonnet in the same manner that he spontaneously wrote all of his poems. Each phrase in the poem gives way to the next through an authentic inner logic, which includes the logic of words as well as the sights and sounds they describe. As Alan Vardy has pointed out, Clare understood his own use and misuse of grammatical conventions to be a political act—a "defence of vernacular speech."[52] We know, for instance, that he abhorred Lindley Murray's standard English grammar of the period, and likewise that he admired the much more forgiving one published by William Cobbett, which was intended "especially for the Use of Soldiers, Sailors, Apprentices, and Plough-boys" like him.[53] It is incumbent upon us as readers to distinguish the incorrectness associated with such politics from the solecisms Clare himself would have gladly corrected had someone pointed them out. Even though most of Clare's errors stem from his special vernacular, not all of them support his wish be authentic, nor are they all political. John Goodridge has even suggested that Clare occasionally errs in order to defend himself against charges of forgery.[54] In other words, Clare's errors are overdetermined; they are liberal, stylish, purposeful, and careless. And the fact that there are so many should not blind us to the possibility that Clare—like every poet before and after him—could blunder conventionally, even spectacularly, without conscious volition. Clare read prodigiously, owned the most important English grammars and dictionaries available in his day, and lived in the years immediately following "the eighteenth-century standardization of English," which, as Andrew Elfenbein has noted, "focused not only on grammar, spelling, and pronunciation, but also on punctuation."[55] Some of his mistakes in this regard belong to the same category as mistakes by his more polished contemporaries, including Keats, Wordsworth, and Byron.

In suggesting that Clare's "november" sonnet contains an unfeigned and perhaps even regrettable mistake (as opposed to a characteristic and charming one), I do not mean to assume the fussy helm of a critic like Matthew Arnold, nor to discount the possibility of unconscious intentions or associations making their way into this and other poems in ways that can be productive. For instance, Kövesi's reading of the "loose lostness, lost looseness" of this misty landscape, as suggested by the spelling mistake on the word "loose" (i.e., "lose") in line 8, makes use of "wordplay" that could certainly stem from unconscious but associatively productive intentions:[56]

[T]he doubling of the meaning of "lose" through the given "loose" (a common appearance in Clare) is central to the meaning of the poem: all of these characters, human and animal alike, have lost their way and have had their grip on their locations, directions and associations loosened.[57]

In this act of interpretation, which follows closely on the heels of Kövesi's reading of the wonder/wander double, "the meaning of the poem" belongs as much to the reader as to the poet. If the language of the sonnet is, as Kövesi contends, "relaxed, unforced . . . non-standard, unfixed," as would seem fitting to reflect its outward scenario, then using the mistakes within it as a way into such an interpretation is indeed useful, as long as we remember whose associations are whose, and which conscious, which not. Kövesi goes on to declare that " 'loose' is not simply Clare's poor spelling of 'lose' that editors should correct" (in the same manner as I originally did with "wonders on" in my 2011 essay), but what he does not explicitly say—and might—is that the main reason editors should not correct it in editions is so that mistakes like these can remain suggestive for *readers*, regardless of whether or not they were intended by, or productive for, the poet.[58]

If Clare's subconscious did lead him to write the word wander with an "o" rather than an "a," that psychological phenomenon need not preclude our considering the word to be a mistake—nor should it cloud our ability to see Clare's more conscious wish for clarity as suggested by his subsequent correction and as exemplified by his proper spelling of "wonder" and "wander" everywhere else. That is to say, we can both register the plausible unconscious design of his mistake and still feel it to be a flaw in technique. Clare was a poet intensely devoted to a poetic craft that both celebrated and encompassed spontaneous, unexpected turns. To "wander" is to move intentionally, but without intention. His mistake on "wonder" is important not only because it is related to this very quality in his own writing, but also because it reminds us of the dangers of our own critical impulses in this regard. With Clare, the dangers of underinterpreting and overinterpreting are equally strong. Sometimes the best way to handle his mistakes is to ignore them. Other times we should read them and celebrate. And still other times, it is our duty as readers to point them out—even if only to wonder on.

CHAPTER 4

Emily Dickinson's Eloquent Lies

Some poets manage to be wrong nearly as often as they are right. Is it possible for mistakes to characterize a poetry rather than to defeat it? Like Clare, Emily Dickinson makes her fair share of grammar, spelling, punctuation, and other kinds of mistakes, but her style sometimes masquerades as error too: metaphors so private or metonymically coded that they initially seem wrongheaded or impossible, tantalizingly knotted syntax, words boldly ill-fitted to their use ("Amethyst remembrance," "disc of snow").[1] In an environment so free and figurative, it can be difficult to tell wrong from wrong. Take, for example, this short stanza Dickinson incorporated into a letter to her friend Mary Higginson, who was suffering from a prolonged illness in the summer of 1876:

> The Flake the Wind exasperate
> More eloquently lie
> Than if escorted to it's Down
> By Arm of Chivalry.[2]

Even the most admiring, lenient reader finds trouble here. Of course "Flake" requires singular verbs—exasperates, lies—or else "exasperate" and "lie" call for multiple flakes and the plural pronoun "their." And "it's" should technically carry no apostrophe—a punctuation misdemeanor that most of Dickinson's editors silently correct while assiduously respecting her dashes and other personalized pointing marks. (She was not alone in this mistake—"it's" was often still used as a neuter possessive during the nineteenth century.) But beyond these superficial problems, deeper questions take root: "Down" in line 3 is a strange adverbial substitute for a noun phrase meaning "resting place" or "spot on the ground," and the metonymic noun "Chivalry" comes in lieu of the expected adjectival form of that word (i.e., "Chivalrous Arm," or even "Arm of Chivalrous Man"). It is easy to understand why Dickinson chooses the abstract noun here: closing her stanza with "Arm" or "Man" would have ruined the rhyme; "Chivalry" works better metrically, and "chivalrous" would have implied a human subject—preposterous given the flake. Yet nothing else is standard about these lines. "Flake" is as unlikely an object for the transitive verb "exasperate" as "Wind" is for its subject. And how to square those uninflected verbs? And what does "eloquence"—which is usually heard rather than seen— have to do with this otherwise visual picture? Something isn't quite right. But whose place is it to say?

Dickinson's early readers were more comfortable dealing in questions of quality and correctness than her recent critics have been. Yvor Winters was able to quip in 1938 that "no poet of comparable reputation has been guilty of so much unpardonable writing."[3] But her now-established genius along with a further developed sense of the editorial and interpretive cruxes associated with reading her verse in print form make it difficult to be persnickety. As David Porter writes, "values associated with printed poetry—a tradition and a self-conscious artist—apply to [Dickinson] only in a special way."[4] To criticize her poetry on the grounds of its irregular grammar, odd punctuation, or ambiguous syntax is to quibble over supper before it has been served. Moreover, doing so perhaps unfairly constrains Dickinson's "fugitive identity" since, at least as Porter sees it, those "renunciations, evasions, and defects" are the places where she "inserts her freedom in the resistant medium of language."[5] Sharon Cameron similarly notes that "[Dickinson's] language marks rupture . . . for the sake of italicizing the arbitrariness of units of sense understood as conclusive."[6] Cristanne Miller puts the defense more bluntly:

> The question of correctness is generally irrelevant as a criterion for judgment in reading Dickinson's work. If one could identify grammaticality with skillful use of language and ungrammaticality with flawed or careless use (as one does in the speech of children), then

there would be some point in advocating grammaticality for its own sake. With Dickinson, however, ungrammatical and grammatical uses of language are equally intentional and manipulated with equal precision and skill.[7]

The license Miller retroactively grants Dickinson here paves the way for new readers to approach the poems unarmed and with open minds. But her dismissal of certain ways of reading as "irrelevant" should raise eyebrows as well as some questions: Who decides what language in Dickinson is skillful and what careless? How can we know for sure which of Dickinson's ungrammatical constructions are intentional and which are not? Is intention always conscious?

Strong defenses of Dickinson's errors from nearly all of her admiring critics make it clear that there are many good reasons not to discount the poems simply because they contain what might initially seem to be flaws. But an attentive reader must still grapple with difficult questions regarding what to do with them. "A Flake the Wind exasperate" is the sort of poem Dickinson's critics have tended to coax into acceptability by pointing out, persuasively, that "to see the characteristics of Dickinson's poetry is to see its deviance from those characteristics we customarily identify with poetic utterances."[8] For instance, addressing the complicated matter of punctuation, Miller contends that Dickinson's misplaced apostrophes ("it's") are "meaningless" since they alter "neither the tone nor the content of the poems."[9] And Porter concludes that most if not all of the uninflected verbs "are among the points where she exercised her freedom, separated her voice from others of the age, and inaugurated the audacious attitude we have come to see as postmodernist."[10] Calling the lines I quote above a "minute morality play," Porter celebrates the mismatch between the nonhuman nouns "Flake" and "Wind" and personifying words like "exasperate," "eloquently," and "escort" by suggesting that the asymmetry of Dickinson's "hidden metaphor . . . helps readers to tolerance and then to investigation of her abstract allegories."[11] For him, the greatness is indistinguishable from the problem—and perhaps this is especially true of this poem in particular, since its subject matter pits organic freedom against artificial composure (wrongness here—in the form of exasperation—represents authenticity in the end). Dickinson expresses her preference in these lines for messy, natural arrangements: Who would prefer a flake carefully placed to one blown around? But does her point excuse the errors with which she delivers it? It is not the first time this poet has celebrated the chanciness of snow. An earlier, less convoluted poem demonstrates a similar predilection on her part for the wayward pleasures of happenstance:

SNOW FLAKES.

I counted till they danced so
Their slippers leaped the town –
And then I took a pencil
To note the rebels down –
And then they grew so jolly
I did resign the prig –
And ten of my once stately toes
Are marshalled for a jig![12]

These rebel "flakes" have more agency than the single flake in the poem she sent to her friend, but the "moral" (to use Porter's term) they suggest remains unchanged. Here Dickinson enlists the flakes in her own process of loosening up. The difference between a priggish, stately dance and a jolly jig becomes, in those later lines to Mary, the difference between a chivalrous escort and eloquent exasperation, health's boredom and sickness's nobility.

Critics less sympathetic to Dickinson's thematic and verbal rebellions (or simply less tolerant of solecism) might still be able to excuse the difficulties of the later stanza simply on the grounds that it was produced within the casual and private confines of a letter sent in a specific context. Mary Higginson was surely exasperated by her illness that summer, and her poet friend, by way of an odd metaphor, tries to offer some form of (albeit dubious) consolation: recovery—or death—she suggests, may feel better for the suffering. (Dickinson had once before conceived of flakes as a beautiful symbol for death: in an earlier poem, she uses the phrase "They dropped like Flakes –" to describe fallen Civil War soldiers.)[13] Under these private conditions, Dickinson's short poem resists and defends against evaluative judgment because it comes to being in a setting that exempts it from interpretive scrutiny. Why should verses never meant for publication, not "printed" or published during the poet's lifetime and never pronounced complete, be subject to a critic's microscopic gaze? Dickinson did not sew these lines about the flake into the "fascicles" where she preserved much of her poetry, nor did she retain—as far as we know—a separate fair copy. The poem can barely be called finished—or even a poem.

With this kind of view in mind, Virginia Jackson asks larger generic questions about Dickinson's writing: "[H]ow do we know that lyrics are what Dickinson wrote? What definition of the lyric turns words on an envelope into a poem?"[14] These questions would seem to absolve the poems of any perceived insufficiencies; and yet, perhaps counterintuitively, Jackson's criticism also opens up new ways of reading Dickinson's mistakes that may increase their value for readers (if we can measure the value of mistakes in terms of their productiveness or suggestiveness). Whereas most readers find the errors in Dickinson's poems forgivable either because they contribute to her idiosyncratic style or because they constitute the poet's rebellion against convention, many of these same mistakes also undermine lyric "finish" in ways that help fully recategorize the poetic event as something time-stamped and historically specific while still inherently "other." Here both new critical and historicist accounts of Dickinson's poems work in concert. That is, for reasons both historical and formal, the temptation to disregard "correctness" as a criterion in Dickinson's writing persists.

Putting correctness aside has for most readers had an appealingly prismatic effect on interpretation: suddenly it becomes possible, even preferable, for a reader to take Dickinson's poems in multiple directions. Miller finds in the poet's ungrammatical constructions an invitation to read with total interpretive freedom:

> Unusual uses of language foreground themselves and their effects on the surrounding text. By speculating about these effects, a reader only follows a writer's cue. Consequently, even when a conventional explanation of apparently ungrammatical syntax is convincing, the reader should not be limited by its restrictive view of the poet's intentions from interpreting the construction in other ways, using the context of the poem and the rarity of the construction as guides.[15]

Thus Dickinson's mistakes (her "unusual uses of language") not only lead to particularized readings but also encourage wider, freer speculation. For Miller, the poet's intentions, especially when she writes in error, are only a starting point. The reader of these poems can of course benefit from what Miller calls the "writer's cue" but should never feel limited by it. Such liberty in interpretation sounds appealing indeed! Dickinson's editor R. W. Franklin probably had this kind of critical freedom in mind when he wryly commented that,

> [c]ritically, we say that a work of art is not commensurate with its author's intentions, yet the basic text is recovered, edited, and printed on the basis of authorial intention (so that the critic can then go to work with the theory that it is not commensurate with those intentions). It is an anomaly within our discipline and one that is not always recognized.[16]

Put another way, Dickinson's reader must believe in intention—and even look for it—while simultaneously disregarding it at the same time in order both to make sense of the mistakes throughout the poetry and to use them as a launching pad.

Miller goes some way toward demonstrating this double capacity in her systematic reading of the poem "Essential Oils – are wrung –":

Essential Oils – are wrung –
The Attar from the Rose
Be not expressed by Suns – alone –
It is the gift of Screws –

The General Rose – decay –
But this – in Lady's Drawer
Make Summer – When the Lady lie
In Ceaseless Rosemary –[17]

Here is a poem about the hard, deliberate work involved in making—a kind of *ars poetica*—that puts craft at the fore. Dickinson celebrates the poet's labor of writing even as she shares the credit with nature (i.e., "Suns").

And she does so in a poem that is itself belabored: "Be not expressed," "Rose – decay," "Make Summer," "Lady lie"—each of these ungrammatical phrases itself feels wrung, or screwed, out of the language. Miller takes this idea and runs with it:

> Expression is not natural . . . it entails the application of screws to the "Rose" of language as much as to the experience or life. . . . Although Dickinson uses uninflected verbs in various ways, in "Essential Oils" this ungrammatical form helps create a sense of timeless essence. Leaving a verb uninflected returns it to its basic stem or root form, giving it the flavor of primary or essential activity. In their substitution of an essential or root for a historical form, these verbs embody the process of transformation from General Rose to Attar that is the subject of the poem. Further, and more typical, evidence of the "Screws" of expression in this poem are its lack of standardized punctuation, frequent dashes, lack of clear antecedent for the pronouns "it" and "this," and the uncertain identity and role of the Lady.[18]

Miller carefully points out how each kind of error in Dickinson's language harks back to the poem's thematic touchstones of essence and expression. Hers is a deft handling of the poem's multivalenced metaphor, neatly yoking the scenario of these verses to her larger general argument about Dickinson's formal rebellions. This is a particularly convenient poem for sympathetic readers to land on because it is about distillation—a poem about purity—that offers up a neat context within which to align mistake with symbol. Just as Miller claims the uninflected verbs help Dickinson give power to "essence," so Thomas Johnson defends them on the grounds that they "universalize her thought."[19] Porter points out how they allow her to move "from all particularity . . . into the Absolute; she attempts a verbal, and indeed a visual (for the inflections are visibly pared away), correlative for the insight into essences at the core of meaning and experience."[20] In this context, mistakes are indeed essential—but figuratively so. Miller, Johnson, and Porter thus account for mistake thematically, using one loose end to tie up another (i.e., reading grammar for meaning when grammar is glaring but meaning is not).

And yet there are many other poems where verbs without inflections only call attention to themselves as outliers. Even Miller quietly acknowledges this fact when she mentions that in other poems, Dickinson "uses uninflected verbs in various ways." The same goes for dashes and unattached pronouns: these effects seem to have clear analogues in the conceptual framework of this specific poem, but when they appear throughout the rest of Dickinson's verse, they often feel much less deliberate, less intentionally employed. If something smells fishy about all of this excusing, perhaps it is because poets' intentions are slippery; often they are impossible to grasp. Miller assumes the ungrammatical elements in this poem and others are "equally intentional and manipulated with equal precision and skill" compared to those elements that more easily conform to linguistic and poetical norms. And she may not be entirely wrong, given the prevalence of grammatical and punctuation errors across the poems and especially the consistency of their types. Examples abound: in F61B, "Flinging the problem back / At you and I" (ll. 14–15); in F334, "inner than the bone" (l. 14); in F338A, "Myself – was beggared – too" (l. 24); in F418, "It's distance – to behold" (l. 28); in F449, "Dreams – are well – but Waking's better" (l. 1); in F653, "Circumference be full –" (l. 5); in F762, "Promise This – When You be Dying –" (l. 1); in F800, "And what a Billow be –" (l. 4); in F1012, "Germ's Germ be where?" (l. 8); in F1353B, "To pile like Thunder to it's close" (l. 1); and dozens more. But how do we know that some of these mistakes are not simply careless or wrongheaded? Or, conversely, if they are indeed equally deliberate, equally skillful, should we not still categorize them as mistakes and feel them as defects? If these are all cases where Dickinson errs with some kind of purpose (conscious or not), wouldn't wrongness be part of her point?

Although it is convenient—even comforting—to conclude that the ungrammatical moments in Dickinson's poems are always executed with the same degree of intentionality, precision, and skill, it may also be disingenuous. There is certainly some evidence that Dickinson had a nuanced understanding of her own mistakes—that she was conscious of, if not necessarily pleased by, many of them. (We can only guess at whether such cognizance developed before or after she committed them.) But there are also situations where she seems to mistake with no inkling of purpose or awareness. The portrait of Dickinson as a rebel poet is appealingly convincing in retrospect, but we should not underestimate or ignore her strong sense of propriety. It is clear from her letters that she was attentive to matters of right and wrong and could easily distinguish between adherence to and breaches in convention. For instance, in one of the first letters she sent to Thomas Wentworth Higginson, her longtime "preceptor" and husband of the ailing Mary, in July 1862, she encloses a poem that begins "Of Tribulation, these are They" and ends with the following lines:

> Surrender – is a sort unknown –
> On this superior soil –
> Defeat – an outgrown Anguish –
> Remembered, as the Mile
>
> Our panting Ancle barely passed –
> When Night devoured the Road –
> But we – stood whispering in the House –
> And all we said – was "Saved"![21]

The poem is sophisticated grammatically and syntactically; its opening line even appropriately uses the nominative form "They"; all verbs are inflected according to standard use. But Dickinson catches in her letter a different sort of slip: in a note she appends to the bottom of the page, she writes, "I spelled Ankle – wrong."[22] Higginson, perhaps charmed by the admission, or emboldened by its suggestiveness, retains the misspelling and includes Dickinson's personal note when he publishes the poem in the *Atlantic Monthly* in 1891 after her death. In fact, much of her letter is itself concerned with what Dickinson calls "faults" in her verse: "Will you tell me my fault, frankly as to yourself, for I had rather wince, than die. Men do not call the surgeon, to commend – the Bone, but to set it, Sir, and fracture within, is more critical."[23] These sentences, themselves fractured in various ways that may constitute a degree of posturing, convey not only Dickinson's belief in the possibility of real mistake in her poetry but also her determination to fix error in at least some of its forms. Of course, one must reasonably ask why, if she was so concerned with error, she did not correct the spelling of "Ancle" before sending the letter, unless she secretly preferred the fracture of the word to its setting.[24] And her failure to do so surely influenced Higginson's decision to publish both the mistake and its correction. But this particular misspelling at the very least reflects Dickinson's keen understanding of the subtleties of propriety even as she resists being wholly subject to it. A poet may enjoy the freedom, the carelessness, of mistake while still feeling vulnerable to its censure—at least in polite society.

Dickinson was in general more open about misspellings than she was about other kinds of errors in her poems. As Brita Lindberg Seyersted has pointed out, several letters acknowledge mistakes in spelling, whereas mistakes in grammar and punctuation are rarely mentioned.[25] An early letter to her brother Austin includes a postscript with the following clarification: "I spelt a word wrong in this letter, but I know better, so you need'nt think you have caught me."[26] It is a coy note, all the more so for Dickinson's apparent lack of inclination to identify, fix, or apologize for the error. Indeed this reader cannot locate an error in the letter if there is one, nor can the critic Willis J. Buckingham in his excellent essay on Dickinson's spelling. He goes as far as to suggest that there must be no error at all—that "the postscript is a ruse."[27] Either way, the possibility of Austin's catching her mistake seems to be, for Dickinson, the rub, rather than the fact of her making one. Dickinson was apparently anxious not to appear philistine in her brother's eyes, as becomes clear in another letter she writes while he was studying law at Harvard: "I'm so tired now, that I write just as it happens, so you must'nt expect any style. This is truly extempore, Austin—I have no notes in my pocket."[28] These letters, written when Dickinson was in her twenties, show her to be an already-thoughtful stylist who was both attentive to her readers' expectations regarding correctness but also willing to frustrate them.

Her later letters demonstrate less defensiveness over perceived flaws. Having, in one letter to her friend Mrs. Holland, mistaken the last name of a Mr. Van Wagenen for Mr. Van "Wagner," Dickinson apologizes in the next installment with more verve than actual shame:

> Orthography always baffled me, and to "Ns" I had an especial aversion, as they always seemed unfinished *M*s. Will dear Mrs "Van Wagenen" excuse me for taking her portentous name in vain?

> I can best express my contrition in the words of the Prayer of a
> Clergyman I heard when a Child – "Oh thou who sittest upon the
> Apex of the Cherubim, look down upon this, thine unworthy
> Terrapin"![29]

The excuse here is obviously unrelated to the error—but the poet delights
in her explanation while also managing to convey the seriousness with
which she takes the science of "Orthography." She may get things wrong,
but she cannot be accused of ignoring the look and feel of words. Another
letter to Mrs. Holland two months later brings up the matter of misspelling
once again, this time with even fewer scruples:

> The Birds are very bold this Morning, and sing without a
> Crumb . . . I used to spell the one by that name "*Fee Bee*" when a
> Child, and have seen no need to improve! Should I spell all the things
> as they sounded to me, and say all the facts as I saw them, it would
> send consternation among more than the "*Fee Bees*"![30]

How much consternation Dickinson actually wishes to unleash upon her
readers is hard to say. But the longer she wrote, the less diffident she became
about her spellings.

Whether this growing confidence in her own rebellious disposition was
accompanied by a conscious sense of the uses and pleasures of error is a
question Buckingham raises in his study. Indeed Dickinson's misspellings
can often be hard to identify because so many of them are silently emended
by the poet's modern editors, even when her mistakes in grammar and
punctuation are not. The underlying message of these kinds of editorial
decisions is that, unlike other kinds of error, misspellings are "insignificant
mistakes that warrant continued routine correction," rather than a part of
her "characteristic presence on the page" and thus connected to "her artistry."[31] But isn't there a middle ground—where the misspellings are both
important enough to retain and also not equated with artistry? Perhaps
Dickinson's readers are not yet prepared to treat mistakes in shades of gray.
For instance, if editors were to adopt this compromise and allow seemingly
casual spelling errors to stand, would such mistakes attract the same atten-

tion afforded to other problems in Dickinson's work? And would such attention be warranted?

As is the case with most instances of error in Dickinson, some misspellings seem to matter more than others. For example, both Seyersted and Buckingham note that Dickinson begins her writing life spelling the word "woe" without an "e" (as had once been acceptable in previous centuries) before eventually adopting the silent vowel in her later years—her correction apparently stemming from a simple realization that the "e" had become, by the middle of the nineteenth century, entirely standard in English. But other obsolete spellings linger in Dickinson's verse and throw her seeming adherence to convention into question. Buckingham brings up the example of "vail," a word Dickinson continually misspells despite the likelihood of her knowing that the "a" should really be an "e":

> The last of Summer is Delight
> Deterred by Retrospect –
> 'Tis Ecstasy's revealed Review –
> Enchantment's Syndicate.
>
> To meet it – nameless as it is
> Without celestial Mail –
> Audacious as without a knock
> To walk within the Vail.[32]

This seasonal poem delights in final fruits; it celebrates the fullness of a summer not yet longed for because of its lingering presence. The second stanza hints at ecstatic overload: the unexpected phrase "Without celestial Mail" suggests a naked encounter (but is it the sun or the poet who lacks armor?), and the "Audacious" pleasure of walking "within" a veil without knocking is surely a forbidden one. In other words, Dickinson enacts a fantasy figured in the trespasses of those final lines. Her sense of "Vail" may actually be twofold: its primary meaning is likely the usual one—a thinly woven cloth or covering of some kind. Entering "within" such a space, particularly without a knock, would be akin to lifting the veil from a bride's face (or, more dramatically, breaking into the bedchamber). But the context also enlists the second sense of "vale," a valley, since practically speaking, one would be more likely to walk within a "vale" than within a "veil," especially during summer (there may be a hint of the biblical "walk through the valley of the shadow of death" here too). Buckingham considers the misspelling of the poem's last word a kind of playful yoking of two anachronisms—archaic "Mail" and obsolete "Vail"—the latter spelling of which ceased to be in use after the eighteenth century. If he is right, Dickinson probably adopted this spelling at the suggestion of her American dictionary, compiled by Noah Webster, which listed "veil" as correct while still suggesting that the now out-of-use "vail" was truer to its etymological root (*velum*): "for e, in Latin is our a."[33] Buckingham explains, "What this evidence begins to suggest is that Dickinson was not a poor speller; she was on the contrary an alert, sensitive, and careful one. She was a student of orthography, and in relation to her philologist-preceptor and fellow townsman Noah Webster, she was almost touchingly faithful and attentive."[34] One can see the power of this argument, especially given the visual rhyme with "Mail" and the fact that the poem takes as its subject the delights of lingering pleasures and breaking the rules. On the other hand, Dickinson uses the incorrect spelling "vail" in every instance across her poems—not just in those poems where there appears to be a thematic or formal reason to do so. Maybe she simply forgot how to spell the word?

A second example may throw some light on the issue—or send us further down a hole:

> A Charm invests a face
> Imperfectly beheld –
> The Lady dare not lift her Vail
> For fear it be dispelled –
>
> But peers beyond her mesh –
> And wishes – and denies –
> Lest Interview – annul a want
> That Image – satisfies –[35]

As with the other lines, most editors silently emend "Vail" to "Veil" here. It is clearly a poem exploring the symbolism and suggestions of a woman wearing a veil over her face. But with the misspelled "Vail" intact, lines 3 and 4 take on a secondary life. As Buckingham gleefully points out, "[w]ithout Dickinson's manuscript spelling, the pun on dispelled is defeated."[36] Is this wordplay over a poet's "dispelling" so blatant that it is irresistible to assign intentionality to Dickinson's mistake? Or are we prioritizing our own cleverness over hers by reading too far, too much? If considered part and parcel of the poem, the pun on "dispelled" adds an appealing layer of metaphor to an otherwise conventional flirtation. Just as a full interview—seeing behind or beyond the veil—may ruin the "image" that a veil both creates and hides (that is, the veil creates an "image" by hiding the truth), so spelling a word correctly would dispel its charm. The phrase "Imperfectly beheld" comes to life in this context too. Such a neat reading of error takes the poem further than it could go without the misspelling. And it is not unprecedented for Dickinson to make metaphorical claims regarding the artifice and subterfuge behind her poetry's evasions and devices: "Tell all the truth but tell it slant —"[37] and "My Business is Circumference —"[38] are but two better-known ways of Dickinson's saying what may also be this poem's point. It is extremely tempting to find intention behind such vexing errors—even the following egregious misspelling of "crash":

> Crumbling is not an instant's Act
> A fundamental pause
> Dilapidation's processes
> Are organized Decays –
>
> 'Tis first a Cobweb on the Soul
> A Cuticle of Dust
> A Borer in the Axis
> An Elemental Rust –
>
> Ruin is formal – Devil's work
> Consecutive and slow –
> Fail in an instant, no man did
> Slipping – is Crashe's law —[39]

What is a pedant to do? More often than not, Dickinson's editors emend "Crashe's" to "Crash's" since Dickinson spells the word without an "e" everywhere else. Yet this very justification might give us pause. Could it mean the "e" in this poem was in fact designed? After all, here is a poem about "organized Decays," about how "Ruin is formal"—a poem very openly about "Slipping." Buckingham, already an avid and skilled apologist, takes this opportunity to go wild:

> Is it possible that Dickinson preferred the rhythm of "Slipping—is Crashe's law" . . . and inserted the unnatural e to insure it? *Crash's*, after all, doesn't sound as much like it is slipping as *Crashe's*. [The misspelling] also makes the word look more like a person's name than it does without an e: if we were to be introduced to a Mr. Crashe we would not be surprised to find that he spelled his name with an e, especially someone important enough to have a law named after him—Newton's Law, Murphy's Law, Crashe's Law.[40]

If this is the kind of freedom Miller envisioned when she suggested that readers only use Dickinson's intentions (as far as they can be discerned) as a starting point, it may signal the end of critical fair dealing.

The absurdity of such an argument notwithstanding, Buckingham still manages to demonstrate convincingly that many of Dickinson's spelling errors are at least as provocative as her grammatical ones, and that editors should be wary of correcting them. Even if some of these errors are simply careless, others could plausibly be read as deliberate. As we know from her methods of preserving her poems (and her lack of interest in publishing them), Dickinson was keen to retain control over the details of her verse. For instance, although her letter to Higginson suggesting that a surgeon's job is not to "commend – the Bone, but to set it" might embolden a modern editor to set things right without asking (as was the norm during Dickinson's lifetime, when most writers relied on their editors to comb out any fleas), her reactions on the rare occasions her poems did appear in print suggest otherwise. She was exceedingly anxious that any published lines accurately reflect the versions she originally wrote. When her now famous snake poem "A Narrow fellow in the Grass" first appeared in the *Springfield Republican* in February 1866, she was appalled at the editors, who, in addition to normalizing capitalizations and other pointing marks, decided to end her first sentence at the close of line 3:

A narrow fellow in the grass
Occasionally rides;
You may have met him – did you not?
His notice instant is,[41]

Her own version of the syntax differs slightly, but importantly:

A narrow Fellow in the Grass
Occasionally rides –
You may have met him? Did you not
His notice instant is –[42]

To this sensitive poet, publication of the altered poem felt like a scandal. Later that year, in an effort to convince Higginson that she remained opposed to publishing, Dickinson explains in a letter to him that, "Lest you meet my Snake and suppose I deceive[,] it was robbed of me – defeated too of the third line by the punctuation. The third and fourth were one – I had told you I did not print –."[43] The "robbery" Dickinson describes here and the "defeat" over her own sense of the punctuation and syntax speak volumes about her interest in seemingly small matters. Such a reaction should naturally make any editor think twice about assuming that a misplaced apostrophe, a misspelled word, or an uninflected verb should simply be elided or emended. Her punctuation, spelling, and grammar may not always have produced polished results, but they do suggest a poet who fiddled over details, who was often excited and spurred on by deviations despite— or perhaps because of—an awareness of propriety, and who valued poetry's rough edges as much as its smoothness.

So how much mistaking in Dickinson's poetry is deliberate? There may still be a way of distinguishing right from wrong, even in poems that wear their wrongness loosely. Without some way of discerning style from error, Dickinson's best and most richly suggestive poems (in terms of their interpretive possibilities) are at risk of being tainted by those that are poorly executed. One of the first problems arising from readings that unilaterally assign value to Dickinson's difficulties is that not all of them are—or should be treated as—equal. Placing grammatical, spelling, and punctuation errors in the same bucket with thematic or figurative cruxes only creates

confusion. In order to determine which mistakes likely stem from carelessness and which ones show signs of intention, one must first distinguish
between actual mistakes (whether intentional or not) and elements of style
that may appear similarly difficult or strange but are not technically errors.
Misspellings, uninflected verbs, and mispunctuated contractions, I would
contend, fall into a separate category from Dickinson's characteristically
difficult metaphors, ambiguous pronouns, and abstract handling of ideas.
The former violate laws of linguistic propriety (as determined both socially
and by grammarians). The latter—though they may sometimes seem to
draw from the same well as error—are features of the verse that much more
obviously reflect Dickinson's interest in expressing complex thought (a poet
is allowed to be difficult, after all). Even the most extreme moments of
compression or difficulty still figure Dickinson as an artful, elusive poet in
the act, as Cameron puts it, of "representing interior experience."[44] It is
unfortunate that so many well-meaning readers, in trying to discern sense
and order among mystery and ambiguity, collapse mistakes and artful id-
iosyncrasy into one. But disentangling the difficult or nonsensical from the
mispunctuated or misspelled is critical to understanding where Dickinson
came closest to achieving her own ambitions for her work and where she
failed to adhere not only to her critics' standards for what constitutes good
poetry but also her own.

For instance, there are a number of possible difficulties among the following eight lines of description about a hummingbird, but very little
about the poem should be considered defective:

> A Route of Evanescence
> With a revolving Wheel –
> A Resonance of Emerald
> A Rush of Cochineal –
> And every Blossom on the Bush
> Adjusts it's tumbled Head –
> The Mail from Tunis – probably,
> An easy Morning's Ride –[45]

Dickinson was especially fond of these lines; she sent them to no fewer than
five different friends over the course of four years—meaning, among other

things, that there are several existing variants.[46] All versions use more or less the same words (apart from a fair copy she kept, which substitutes "delusive" for "revolving").[47] But the punctuation varies considerably: some copies contain commas where others employ hyphens or dashes; others use both kinds of marks sparingly, only punctuating the final three lines. The apostrophe in the word "it's" occurs in most but not all versions. These differences speak, on the one hand, to the haphazard manner in which Dickinson often treated the more empirical elements of language (i.e., its notation, spelling, and grammatical laws). On the other hand, to this poem's more thematic, conceptual, and symbolic elements—in particular its words and their meanings—she was always unwaveringly attentive.

Dickinson's "Humming Bird" (as she refers to the poem in her letters) is a poem that purposefully styles difficulty to its advantage. Some scholars see in it an appealing resistance to sense that is not exactly defective but is still comparable to the rebellion they read in her lapses of grammar or punctuation elsewhere.[48] And yet the richness of these particular lines comes less from the fact that the words she uses in them are in certain ways illogical or indeterminate than from the poem's subtle manner of defending against this charge by offering what initially sound like strong, confident descriptors: "Evanescence," "Emerald," "Cochineal." How could the subject elude us in a poem that claims the specificity of "Emerald" (rather than "green") or "Cochineal" (rather than "red")? Never mind that these adjectives are actually functioning as nouns.

The interpretive possibility created by Dickinson's particularized vocabulary relies, counterintuitively, on the very qualities of her writing that seem to deny us freedom in favor of clarity, control, and precision. Her words point to, but then throw a shade over, their referents. In so doing, they offer nuance at moments when readers most expect fullness. For instance, because the opening noun phrases cling to no obvious verb, the word "Cochineal" may at first appear to describe the "tumbled head[s]" of blossoms rather than the throat of the bird. Despite the fact that the image is fleeting, the word that Dickinson uses to describe the color of the "Rush" is far from unstudied. "Cochineal" is not just red but the shade of scarlet extracted from an insect that goes by the same name; its precision as an adjective belies what must have been a very imprecise perception (which is one reason why so many critics feel this poem must not be about a hummingbird but sensation itself, despite the poet's insistence). Dickinson describes the bird as though she had hours to analyze with exactitude its movements and its color, even as the poem's form suggests the opposite: with truncated phrases and internal as well as end rhymes (in addition to "wheel" and "Cochineal," there is also "Evanescence" and "Resonance," "Bush" and "Rush," and perhaps even "Emerald" and "tumbled Head"), the structure emphasizes the hurry of the bird rather than the speaker's rumination. "Cochineal" is both crucial and out of place. Even if, as William Howard points out, the word would have felt more commonplace to Dickinson's nineteenth-century correspondents, it still offers a gradation of color that the speedy impression could hardly have produced.[49]

But inconsistency did not matter to Dickinson. Her strategy of transforming a dim impression into a particularized (if abstract) image is a form of denial—a poet's resistance to unknowing. This technique makes her poetry difficult but not mistaken or defective. Her technical or scientific words often turn what should be simple images or clear ideas into ones that are hard to understand. And in this way, they both conceal her subject matter and at the same time reveal its particular import (as a thing worth denying). Along these lines, "Tunis" is both enlightening in its specificity but also confusing in terms of the poem's primary meaning. She uses the place-name as a way of comparing the speed and scope of the humming-bird's flight to the path of the sun (as in the lines to which she alludes in *The Tempest*), but the word, with its connection to Shakespeare's play, ends up moving the poem away from the image of the bird and opening it to a broader set of ideas and texts.[50] "Tunis" no better describes the distance traveled by the bird than would "China" or even "New York." Rather, the name removes the poem's subject—a bird—from its context, dropping it into a literary tradition that turns the central metaphor into a celestial event. Words like "Cochineal" and "Tunis" are red herrings: they promise, in their specificity, an accuracy of description but behave as departure points toward meanings previously concealed.

The crystalline adjective "Emerald" is similarly strange and Dickinsonian: a critic who thinks too hard will get stuck trying to figure out how a green rock can modify an abstract sensation like "resonance." But impossible descriptors are part of the game. In a different poem, she uses a similar strategy to figure—or reconfigure—a sunset:

I'll tell you how the Sun rose –
A Ribbon at a time –
The Steeples swam in Amethyst –
The news, like Squirrels, ran –[51]

The horizon in line 3 takes on a particular hue—and Dickinson expects her reader to translate the metonymic noun "Amethyst" into some shade of purple. But an "Amethyst" sky, as precise as that word may seem, could actually appear as pale as violet or as dark as eggplant. By choosing a word that sounds precise—and what could be more precise-sounding than a crystal with its exact proportions and sharp edges?—but isn't, Dickinson appears to offer more clarity than she does. When pushed beyond its initial implications, the word refracts its meaning rather than driving it to a point. And maybe "Amethyst" even hides within it a semivisible pun on "Amherst," where the steeples of Dickinson's poem literally stood.

Dickinson uses "Amethyst" in another poem to produce a seemingly clearer effect:

I held a Jewel in my fingers –
And went to sleep –
The day was warm, and winds were prosy –
I said, "'Twill keep" –

I woke – and chid my honest fingers,
The Gem was gone –
And now, an Amethyst remembrance
Is all I own –[52]

She may be referring to a poem (or the germ of one) in her first stanza, or to the setting sun, or even possibly to a real gem; it hardly matters by the time we reach the difficult phrase "Amethyst remembrance" in the poem's penultimate line, since this pairing overshadows the rest of the poem and brings to the fore the subtle idea she introduced in line 3 about the "winds." By describing them as "prosy"—we can only imagine she means dull, normal, tedious, safe (in another poem she refers to "paragraphs of Wind"[53])—Dickinson transforms her poem into a particular exemplar of *un*prosiness.

The jewel of poetry is linked to its unpredictability: it never "keep[s]." Her "Amethyst remembrance" suggests such an idea and at the same time defies it. Of course we understand her to mean, literally, that all she has left upon waking is the recollection of the amethyst she once held; but the word, in the poet's able and flexible syntax, turns adjectival: "Amethyst remembrance" as opposed to some other kind. It is another example of style winning over error, despite Archibald MacLeish's complaint that the phrase, along with a similarly outlandish one in a different poem ("Some Polar Expiation –"),[54] doesn't "[exit] upon the retina."[55] Most readers will hear "Amethyst" and imagine a crystal clear act of recall—an idea that is more suggestive than precise (and anything but "prosy"). This habit of switching between nouns and adjectives, concrete images and abstract ideas, makes her poetry difficult, but it does not make it wrong.

Beyond these sudden syntactical switches and layered metaphors, Dickinson also uses punctuation in ways that seem counterintuitively vague. As readers, we are used to taking grammatical cues from periods and commas since, in the hands of most writers, they are a guide to clarity, helping denote how and where subordinate clauses attach themselves to subjects and main verbs. But for Dickinson, punctuation often served as an elocutionary device—allowing her to give rhythm or musical design to language with some kind of physical notation. Her use of dashes (and other incomprehensible marks on the page) to signal pauses is not without precedent. As Seyersted has noted:

> During [Dickinson's] formative years, punctuation practice was still unfixed and wildly debated among theoreticians. The classical tradition of regarding punctuation as a guide to expressive oral delivery was breaking down under the pressure of grammarians advocating a syntactical basis for all punctuation. . . . Although punctuation along syntactical lines was being prescribed by many grammarians, in the majority of cases the two theories appeared side by side. There were numerous complaints of the lack of principle and the chaotic state of actual practice, especially from the printers, who had to bear the brunt of the confusion. . . . In this too, the fanciful sprinkling of the page with inconsistently used marks, Emily Dickinson was, to some extent, a product of her age.[56]

It was clearly a conscious choice for Dickinson to use dashes the way she did, even if the specific use fluctuated from poem to poem (she was never systematic). Her family owned grammars and dictionaries, and she was certainly familiar with the rules of syntax, having studied both Latin and English grammar first at Amherst Academy and then at the seminary at Mount Holyoke.[57] When assessing her poetry in terms of its anomalies of syntax and punctuation, we should neither assume total ignorance on her part nor consider her an expert or pioneer. Dickinson was likely testing out the limits of her tools as any poet would—feeling her way into the right idiom and music. Just as we must be careful not to equate the conceptual difficulty embedded in Dickinson's metaphors and figures with her occasionally flagrant grammatical errors, so we must also distinguish between her idiosyncratic use of dashes that is grounded in personal expression and other instances of punctuation that are simply misguided. Just as omitting words from a syntactical frame for special effect is not the same thing as ignoring tense and number in relation to verbs—the former might be called compression while the latter teeters between willed malfunction and careless mistake—so there is a difference between forgoing commas or periods in favor of dashes and using punctuation marks in ways that work against the sense of her language and thought. Both may be considered deliberate, but surely only the former is poetical.

These distinctions begin to lay the groundwork for a tentative evaluation of error in Dickinson. Although not everything that is anomalous in her writing should be considered flawed, some of her poetry's anomalies reveal themselves to be mistakes even when they are purposeful. This difference is similar to the difference between not knowing something and thinking something to be true when it is not (i.e., between not knowing and knowing wrongly). In such cases, the ignorant are not nearly as dangerous as the misinformed. When Dickinson is unsure, she dwells in possibility. But when she is either careless or wrong, her poems are marred by their own defects.

Perhaps it will be easier to swallow the idea of mistake if we start by appealing to a few occasions when Dickinson showed herself to be misinformed about matters of fact. Unlike elements of language, which perhaps too easily find recourse in poetic license, facts—as we know from the Cortez/Balboa mix-up in Keats—have a way of making even the most poetical-seeming problems appear black and white. Dickinson generally had a scientist's eye for detail—she was a connoisseur of color ("Cochineal," "Amethyst")—but she was not infallible. And her flair for the exotic and the foreign made it difficult for her to know everything regarding the subjects about which she wrote. For instance, she seems to have had a particular interest in volcanoes, writing about them multiple times during her later years:

> When Etna basks and purrs
> Naples is more afraid
> Than when she shows her Garnet Tooth –
> Security is loud –[58]

The stanza offers a brief disquisition on the nature of anxiety with a memorable final line—except that nineteenth-century Neapolitans would have been no more afraid of Mount Etna than Mount St. Helens or Mount Fuji, living, as they did, hundreds of miles away from Etna's Sicilian slopes. The implicit moral of this poem coincidentally sums up the effects of its geographical error: what you don't know can't hurt you, but what you mistakenly think you know certainly can.

Dickinson was not unaware of the existence of Vesuvius (which indeed basks and purrs on Naples's outer skirts); rather, she seems to have gotten the two volcanoes mixed up:

> Volcanoes be in Sicily
> And South America
> I judge from my Geography
> Volcano nearer here
> A Lava step at any time
> Am I inclined to climb
> A Crater I may contemplate
> Vesuvius at Home[59]

As Miller writes in a note to this poem, "Vesuvius erupted several times during ED's lifetime: in 1834, 1839, 1850, 1855, 1861, 1868, and 1872; Sicily's Mount Etna, the tallest active volcano in Europe, was especially active from 1878 to 1886. ED's geography textbooks at Amherst Academy indicated that there were local volcanoes, in the Mount Holyoke range."[60] The confusion between the poems—pairing Etna with Naples and Vesuvius with Sicily—matters not a whit to the meaning of either of these verses, but the mistake does distract a reader from their impact. Dickinson had likely learned the names of both volcanoes in her copy of Professor Hitchcock's *Elementary Geology* (one of her Mount Holyoke texts), which includes a table that lists them thus: "Vesuvius, Etna, Popocatapetl, Teneriffe."[61] And it may be worth noting that in 1861, several years before she wrote either of these poems, she composed a letter that includes the following sentences:

> Vesuvius dont talk – Etna – don't – [Thy] one of them – said a syllable – a thousand years ago, and Pompeii heard it, and hid forever – She could'nt look the world in the face, afterward – I suppose – Bashfull Pompeii![62]

Her likely pun on "Bashfull"—Pompeii was indeed blanketed in ash—suggests that her initial appetite for the details, despite her failure to remember them all, had been keen. But errors in fact, even when they show signs of deliberation or care, are still errors. To number the elusive and abstract qualities of Dickinson's poetry along with its moments of carelessness or error is to celebrate the wrong at the expense of the right.

So when should we read her mistakes as purposeful as opposed to unconscious, haphazard, or ignorant? Her little stanza on the flake may again prove helpful:

> The Flake the Wind exasperate
> More eloquently lie
> Than if escorted to it's Down
> By Arm of Chivalry.[63]

As we have seen, the uninflected verbs are more problematic than, or problematic in a different way to, the syntactical inversions and metonymic difficulty here. But as it turns out, the primary subject matter of this poem—Mary Higginson's illness and Dickinson's provocative metaphor for it—does not tell the entire story. A "Flake" of snow blown in the wind may land with eloquence of a kind, but Dickinson would have known from her lexicon that the word itself is etymologically related to the word "flaw." Even in its current usage, a "flake" can mean "a small fracture or 'chip.' "[64] In this stanza, the underlying root of the word is important—for it brings out a secondary meaning in "lie." Eloquent lying (that is, to cover or account for one's flaws) may be exactly what the poet is doing both here and in many of the poems that give the "lie" of incorrectness despite her knowing better. When a poet feigns mistake, she turns the unacceptable into a feature. This may exasperate her reader, but it is also a form of eloquence. This particular flake, which "lie[s]" in two ways, proves it.

Dickinson often wrote two poems in one. She was also known to reuse the same poem in radically different contexts—mailing lines to one friend for a specific occasion only to repurpose them years later for another.[65] Such appropriation may have been economical, but it likewise speaks to the freedom she afforded her own intentions. Poetry can lie because its meanings are movable. Dickinson enjoyed this freedom in language even as she worried over it. Her ambivalence shows in a poem such as this one:

A Word dropped careless on a Page
May stimulate an Eye
When folded in perpetual seam
The Wrinkled Maker lie

Infection in the sentence breeds
We may inhale Despair
At distances of Centuries
From the Malaria —[66]

Dickinson predicts her own immortality here, but with great irony—through the concept of disease. Her lines invite us, at the distance of more than a century, to perform the interpretive freedoms that a maker's carelessness "stimulate[s]." And indeed, her twentieth- and twenty-first-century audience has complied. But in doing so we should also note that Dickinson frames a careless poet's lastingness in terms of perpetual "Infection." Of course, not all poems show signs of "Infection in the sentence," but she was well aware of the dangers caused by carelessness and the kinds of meanings it propounds. Such have become the reader's—rather than the poet's—affliction.

The afflicted reader should now pause at the line she hangs at the end of her first stanza: "The Wrinkled Maker lie." Dickinson was scrupulous about certain things—but as we know from her stanza about the flake, she held a good stretcher in high regard if it was carried off well. As she wrote in one letter, "Ned tells that the Clock purrs and the Kitten ticks. He inherits his Uncle Emily's ardor for the lie."[67] Uncle Emily also takes "the lie" for her subject in the following poem about fraudulent weather:

These are the days when Birds come back –
A very few – a Bird or two,
To take a final look –

These are the days when skies resume
The old – old sophistries of June –
A blue and gold mistake.

Oh fraud that cannot cheat the Bee –
Almost thy plausibility
Induces my belief,

Till ranks of seeds their witness bear,
And swiftly thro' the altered air
Hurries a timid leaf –

Oh Sacrament of summer days!
Oh last Communion in the Haze –
Permit a Child to join –

Thy sacred emblems to partake –
Thy consecrated bread to take –
And thine immortal wine –[68]

Not unlike her lines beginning "The last of Summer is Delight," Dickinson's poem finds pleasure in the rebellious falsity of rogue sunshine. Probably first sent to Susan Dickinson in the autumn of 1859, this poem celebrates the "blue and gold mistake" of thinking it a summer's day past its season. "[S]ophistries" claiming June's warmth can be enjoyed as eloquent lies when faced with the realities of cold to come. The idea moves in several directions; what begins as an ode to summer develops into a metaphor for false belief—hastily likened in the second half of the poem to taking the sacrament. But Dickinson's handling of error here is complicatedly subtle: "Almost thy plausibility / Induces my belief" does not fully vouch for the deception even if it wishes to. That is, the lie is not quite successful because it is found out. Mistake is welcome here, but not swallowed whole: the "altered air" eventually blows in to set things right.

Cameron, in arguing for the power of error in Dickinson, points out that "[a]ll poetry is characterized by problems; put differently, its characteristics, those properties that individuate and distinguish it, also define the specific form of its difficulty."[69] This idea raises the question of whether Dickinson's cognizance of her own poetry's problems ultimately makes them less problematic. Cameron helpfully describes the way in which errors—even careless ones—redemptively magnify the elements of poems that make them poetic. The work of the critic, she contends, involves exploring poetry's "deviations" in order to discern its norms:

> Seeing the shape of the problem, might we see double the shape of the form that the problem displaces? The conception here is admittedly Platonic, and if it is exaggerated in its suggestion that good poems conform to one shape, it is useful in its reminder that certain forms of deviation are, for reasons that require investigation, intolerable.[70]

Even those errors we may find intolerable in Dickinson thus also define the shape of her verse—at least in the reader's eye. But what about the poet's? Does a flaw acknowledged cease to be a flaw to the poet herself? Let us settle the inquiry once and for all with the following late poem she sent to Susan in 1873:

I saw that the Flake was on it
But plotted with Time to dispute –
"Unchanged" I urged with a candor
That cost me my honest Heart –

But "you" – she returned with valor
Sagacious of my mistake
"Have altered – Accept the pillage
For the progress' sake" –[71]

There are several possible scenarios at play: Should we read the poem as a conversation between two aging women?

"You haven't changed a bit!" says one generous old lady to another.
"Well you certainly have," replies her scrupulous friend.

Or is Dickinson writing another disquisition on the seasons? Perhaps the mistake here is of the "blue and gold" kind: a false belief in the plausibility of summer's remaining "unchanged" all the while knowing that autumn descends. Or does the poem describe a willing suspension of disbelief regarding ill health? To "Accept the pillage / For the progress' sake" would be a hard pillage to swallow indeed.

Whatever the "flake" and whatever the "it," surely these lines are as near an admission of guilt as Dickinson ever makes. To see the flake is to commit the error knowingly: to allow oneself to be deceived. Here the heart says one thing, the head another, and the poet knows her "honest Heart" is at risk. Sometimes flaws lie about their flawedness, but, as Dickinson acknowledges in the second stanza, that doesn't make them right. Flakes record "progress"—but they also register as "pillage." It is a dilemma Dickinson figures but never resolves. And so when her critics justify her errors as deliberate effects, they only account for half of the poet's intentions. Dickinson may have owned her mistakes—some of them, at least—but it should not follow that when she was wrong, she was actually right. In fact, her persistence in making certain mistakes and her complicated feelings about fixing them may more accurately prove that when she was wrong, she was emphatically wrong. Whether all of her mistakes mean something is impossible to know—and not necessarily because intentionality can never be certain, but rather because Dickinson herself could not decide. She may have intended her flaws more often than not, as her advocates have pointed out in persuasive ways. But Dickinson demonstrates that a poet can act deliberately and also be wrong. Hers is the exceptional case where she both knew the mistake and made it. Accidents and mistakes are not the same thing, after all.

CHAPTER 5

Hart Crane's Wrapture

Harold Hart Crane might have been an excellent speller. A letter from the ten-year-old "Harold" to his father makes that clear: "I just came home from the Library with a new book called Mr. Wind and Madm. Rain The day before yesterday I had my test in Spelling, and stood 100."[1] But by the time Crane reached sixteen, he was a fair student at best. "Examination time is *on* now," Crane writes to his grandmother, "and I am kept completely occupied in the preparation for them. We had *English* today and Latin and Geometry are due tomorrow. They are my hoodooes [Crane misspells this word with an "e"] and so I am not a little worried tonight about the outcome."[2] Poetry, rather than more traditional subjects, had already become Crane's main preoccupation—constantly at odds with the discipline required of him at school. He explains in the same letter:

> My writing has suffered neglect lately due to study for examinations, but I am intensely, grippingly interested in a new balled [*sic*] I am writing of six hundred lines. I have resolved to become a *good* student even if I have to sit up all night to become one. You will undoubtedly wink when you read this stale declaration so often made but his [*sic*] time it is in earnest.[3]

If Crane was earnest, it was mainly in the Wildean sense. By the end of the year, he had dropped out of Cleveland's East High School and moved to New York City, resolved to become a poet. He continued to "study" there perfunctorily under the pretense of enrolling at Columbia within a year or two; but those plans petered out before long ("algebra doesn't help any in versifying," he writes to his father—a successful businessman and the inventor of Life Savers candy—in a letter also asking him for more money so as "not to have to eat in some of the sloppy places").[4] By the following spring, full of himself and the literary atmosphere of the big city, Crane declares: "I shall really without a doubt be one of the foremost poets in America if I am enabled to devote enough time to my art. This prediction has come from more than one writer of established merit, whom I have met since my arrival."[5] Crane and his supporters were right, of course, though many of the "writer[s] of established merit" he met in subsequent years also wished for Crane a more studious and disciplined life. His alcoholism and attendant belligerence notwithstanding, Crane's lack of formal education and its effects on his poetry were often a source of embarrassment among his admirers both during and after his life. Allen Tate, who introduced Crane's first collection, *White Buildings*, felt the need to remark on the poetry's "faults" even as he praised its virtues; after Crane's suicide, he went as far as to call the poet "an ignorant man" in order to account for the poetry's "defects of surface."[6] Yvor Winters—also friendly with Crane—nevertheless described "the flaws in Mr Crane's genius" as being "almost of the nature of a public catastrophe."[7] And this was while Crane was still alive.

What flaws and defects of surface are these friends referring to, exactly—and how important are they? Both men give few specific examples, pointing more generally to a failure of "vision" they see as partially mitigated by the value of Crane's overall achievement ("he has given us," Winters says, "several charming minor lyrics and several magnificent fragments").[8] So allow me to harp on just one of the details, which, after all, may matter some to the growing number of Crane scholars still burdened with the responsibility of weighing the poet's merits against his faults. (Crane has as many detractors as champions, even today, as the "controversy" around the publication of the Library of America edition of his work in 2007 made clear).[9] The "defect" occurs in the second poem of the sequence "Voyages," about the sea ("they are also love poems," he provocatively tells his mother), which begins with the following two stanzas:

—And yet this great wink of eternity,
Of rimless floods, unfettered leewardings,

Samite sheeted and processioned where
Her undinal vast belly moonward bends,
Laughing the wrapt inflections of our love;

Take this Sea, whose diapason knells
On scrolls of silver snowy sentences,
The sceptred terror of whose sessions rends
As her demeanors motion well or ill,
All but the pieties of lovers' hands.[10]

I cannot pretend to understand fully what this long, beautiful, convoluted sentence means, but several critics in the last fifty years—from Samuel Hazo to Herbert Leibowitz to R.W.B. Lewis to Lee Edelman to Sherman Paul to Brian Reed—have done so in lengthy, creative, and appreciative accounts of this and other Cranian descriptions of the ocean and its analogues, perhaps in an effort to fend off further accusations of "obscurity" reminiscent of the kind Crane so often endured during his lifetime. He knew his poetry was considered by most to be "difficult," but Crane defensively told Winters in 1927: " 'The Voyages' (that is the series as a whole) I think are more articulate than you judge them."[11] "[A]rticulate" may mean something different to Crane than to Winters and other critics, but what certainly shines through in the poem, however much one feels it does or does not articulate, is an ambition to describe the sea with a metaphorical specificity and loftiness of diction not often attempted since the sixteenth century. (It should come as no surprise that two of Crane's poetic heroes are Marlowe and Donne.) A. Alvarez humbly offers the best explication of the first of these two stanzas by working through its associative qualities:

> Without a verb the action of the verse is difficult to plot; indeed, at first sight it seems to be made up only of a number of questionably connected phrases describing the sea. But seen from closer up it becomes clearer how the connections were made: how "wink" brought "rimless," which moved with a jump, into "unfettered"; how there is a connection between the curve of the sea's eye and the curve of her "belly"; how "sheeted," "belly" and "love" interact, and how the "great wink" turns into "laughing."[12]

The electricity Alvarez tracks between these words and their connotations is hard to dismiss. But what he generously ignores in line 4 is to me worth pausing over in any case: the word "wrapt," spelled with a "w" rather than an "r"—as in "Laughing the wrapt inflections of our love"—since there is no such correct spelling of that word in our language anymore. (I say "anymore" only because there is an instance of Milton's spelling it this way in *Comus* in 1637 and another in the first folio edition of Shakespeare's *Macbeth*).[13] Crane in fact misspells this word twice—again a few years later in the "Atlantis" section of his long poem *The Bridge*:

> O Thou
> Whose canticle fresh chemistry assigns
> To wrapt inception and beatitude,—[14]

Both of these errors—the "wrapt" inflection in "Voyages" and the "wrapt" inception in "Atlantis"—seem to me good candidates for his friends' embarrassment insofar as they are technically incorrect, "defects of the surface," so to speak, however much they are informed by Crane's extensive reading (in the manner of Robert Browning's mistake in my second chapter).[15] "Wrapped," with its double "p," may reasonably be said to have an archaic version spelled with a "t," but to claim Crane mainly has this meaning in mind when he uses the word, and not "rapt" (as in "rapture") is probably wishful thinking—particularly given the subject matter.

And yet this mistake in "Voyages II"—which appears in Crane's earliest drafts of the poem—comes with an ever-increasing history of justifications by critics that makes it an especially rich case for distinguishing between the poet's "flaws" and his very substantial powers of invention, for it seems that Crane's loyal readers are as determined to read and interpret this mistake as the poet was to write it in the first place. Sherman Paul, for instance, approaches this line with the dubious provocation that "[i]ts descriptive accuracy is not in question" (such unequivocal assertions are almost always suspect):

> "Laughing" gives a jewellike, tinkling sound as well as a sense of the visual play of moonlight on water. The sea, according to the syntax, is not laughing at the lovers but *laughing them*, or *laving* them (see

"Voyages III"), supporting and washing and cradling them in the waves whose very movement depicts their ardor. "Wrapt inflections" evokes the image of waves breaking and flowing back on themselves—waves as innocent-seeming as those in "Voyages I"—and "wrapt" contains the several meanings of *wrapped* (as in embraced), *rapt* (the complete involvement of being "wrapped," the rapture in which time and death are forgotten), and the protection love grants (a notion advanced in the next stanza by "All but the pieties of lovers' hands"). The "inflections" are the movement, of both the waves and "our love," that causes the laughing. Laughter is the language, the "inflection," of love.[16]

I love the poetical nature of this effort—especially the leap from laugh to "lave," which is a very beautiful connection, if almost entirely unsubstantiated as far as I can tell (even etymologically these words are distinct—"Laugh" coming from the Old English *hlæhhan* and "lave" deriving from the Latin *lavare*). In an early draft of the stanza, "laughing" was actually a noun rather than a verb and situated in the previous line:

> [In?] laughter bends thy undinal vast belly
> moonward the wrapt inflection our love[17]

Paul's subsequent trifold reading of "wrapt"—that the inflections are simultaneously hugging one another, in rapture, and protected by their union—gives the word a talismanic effect on the line as a whole, as though it could mean almost anything.

But then, what does it mean exactly? Herbert Leibowitz reads the same lines and produces a much soberer riff:

> When the sea mockingly laughs at the "wrapt inflections of our love,"
> it is laughing at the self-enclosed isolation of the lovers, but also at
> the lovers so rapt by their emotions that they do not see its impending
> dissolution of the sea's exemption from such restraints. Crane is obviously punning on the words, he is not merely being an amusingly bad
> speller as Philip Horton has said.[18]

Indeed, Philip Horton, Crane's earliest biographer, glancingly records the poet's error near the end of his biography by suggesting that his "lack of education" caused him to "commit such amusing mistakes as confusing 'cask' and 'casque,' 'wrapt' and 'rapt,' and apostrophizing Whitman as 'Panis Angelicus' under the impression he was hailing him as Holy Pan."[19] But according to Leibowitz, Crane amalgamates the meanings of "self-enclosed," or "wrapped up," and "rapt" by purposefully spelling the word wrongly. Again, it seems to me that his insistence on this effect—"Crane is *obviously* punning"—like Paul's ("its descriptive accuracy is *not in question*"), injects some doubt in the matter despite his best efforts to justify it. Critics are often on shakiest ground when most insistent (e.g., elsewhere in his study Leibowitz writes, "[t]hat Crane learned from [Joyce's bravura with language] *is hard to doubt*").[20] These are actually some of the least intuitive assumptions regarding Crane's poetry, as any thorough reading of the body of criticism dedicated to his work will attest. The extent to which Crane was careless versus insistently precise with his language is not obvious, and his ability to assimilate Joycean techniques into his own writing is actually fairly easy to doubt (even if it is the case). Similarly, the idea that Crane's prosody is "perfectly" suited to his subject is hardly an "*ineradicable* sign of his poetic skill," as Leibowitz later notes, given how subjective an assertion that perfection is in the first place.[21] These kinds of hyperbolic defenses do less for Crane than some of the more tentative accusations by his detractors; one immediately bristles at the critic who claims the obvious, the indubitable, the ineradicable anything.

Still, another early reader, R.W.B. Lewis, also accepts the misspelled "wrapt" but is less sure of its intentionality:

> The sea's laughter, unimpeded by the customary preposition "at," fairly pours down upon the wrapt nature of the lover's rapture (an arguable pun) and almost drowns it.[22]

Whether "obvious" or merely "arguable," this "pun" clearly piques the interest of all of these readers despite Horton's good-natured objection. And as if this cascade of associative connotations for "wrapt" did not take it far enough, Thomas Yingling suggests yet another:

Because the sea is allegorically cognate with the lovers' own experiences of transformation, it may now be said to laugh "the wrapt inflections of [their] love"—the secret ("wrapt") raptures and inflected (transformed) signs through which they recognize one another and their home in the world.[23]

Yingling reads "wrapt" as "under wraps" while simultaneously suggesting its implied rapture. Are these secret raptures really in the poem too? Well, possibly—Crane's poem, as we know from his letters, is in part about Emil Opffer, a sailor with whom Crane had a short but passionate relationship (he once wrote that he could not imagine "anything more profound and lovely than this love").[24] And yet to limit his misspelling to this kind of literal secret—which was indeed no secret to the poet's friends—feels disingenuous. Brian Reed, one of Crane's best recent critics, attempts to bridge all of these possibilities for the word by making possibility the point:

> "Wrapt inflections"? "Wrapt" as in "wrapped"—if so, by what? "Wrapt" as in "rapt attention"? Or as in "rapture"? . . . "Voyages" II somehow manages to be rhetorically effective, sweeping a reader, giddy, onto glorious terrain, even though (or perhaps because) its semantic meaning remains indeterminate.[25]

For Reed, what is giddy-making and glorious about Crane's poem may also be linked to its error. But he is careful not to specify whether or not "wrapt" is an intentional pun or a neologism or just a careless misspelling, even as he questions the plausibility of "wrapped" (with its double "p") as a logical descriptor for "inflections" in the first place. His solution, to point to and celebrate the indeterminacy of Crane's language, falls on neither side of the debate. Marjorie Perloff, in her study of what she calls "the poetics of indeterminacy" in the work of several modernist writers—Stein, Williams, Pound, and others—groups Crane not with these poets but rather among the more "symbolist" writers of the period, including Yeats, Eliot, and Auden.[26] The implication is that she still believes there to be something more "articulate" about his language, despite its difficulty.[27]

In the end, it may be Crane himself who presciently offers the best so-called defense of these kinds of critical interventions and justifications when he imagines in his essay "General Aims and Theories" what a poem ought to do:

> It is as though a poem gave the reader as he left it a single, new *word*, never before spoken and impossible to actually enunciate, but self-evident as an active principle in the reader's consciousness henceforward.[28]

"Voyages" literally gives the reader several "new word[s]"; but the problem with applying this theory to the misspelling of "wrapt" is that it leaves the poet's own intentions for the word in the dust (unless the poet's intention is simply to engage the minds of his readers). Such a mode of reading, which relies heavily on active principles in readerly consciousness, may have been attractive to Crane, but it does not account for the fact that readers do not always wish to be—and are not always able to be—poetical. Even for those who are comfortable enough engaging with Crane on his level, the problem of error still persists—for how does the critic who would not misspell such a word, who would not pun, or who does not believe in the arbitrary nature of punning "close read" such a word without recommitting the mistake himself? Indeed, several of the critics I have just quoted leave themselves no choice but to delight in using the mistakenly spelled "wrapt" in their own interpretations of the line. It may be worth noting that most of them also eventually mention "rapt" or "rapture"—as if acknowledging tacitly that this single meaning, this particular spelling, haunts their own associations, whatever Crane's intentions were.

This kind of critical reinscription of error may be interesting for the potential readings it produces, but it also has the odious, unnecessary effect of undoing the wrongdoing. How can we distinguish Crane's flaws from his flourishes if we are hell-bent on seeing them as one and the same? As we saw in the case of Emily Dickinson, from whom Crane learned a great deal in terms of technique, there can be finely calibrated distinctions between a poet's cultivated freedom with language and his or her haphazard use of it. He even speaks to such distinctions in the verses he dedicates to Dickinson when he writes that, in her singing, "Eternity possessed / And plundered momently in every breast."[29] His adverb "momently" is especially Dickinsonian—very close to "momentarily," but rarer, and crucially different from it, too, suggestively carrying the paradoxical meanings of both "every moment," or continually, as well as the opposite, "for a single moment."[30] Crane inherited and internalized not only Dickinson's decadence with words but also her predilection for carelessness; he could be studiously archaic in one line and carelessly mistaken in the next. Tate—in a sense Crane's first major critic—warns us of this trap when he points out optimistically that the poetry's "peculiar value cannot be separated from its limitations."[31] William Logan more recently makes the same argument, but with exasperation, when he concedes that "Criticism, however put, can never harm Crane in the eyes of the devoted, because what such a critic despises is exactly what those readers adore."[32] My suggestion in this still-raging debate is that we be willing to call a mistake a mistake in Crane when we see one, regardless of how interesting, even ingenious, its connotations are. This is not to call into question Crane's suitability for writing poetry but rather to prevent readers' own creativities, however well-meaning, from getting in the way of seeing exactly what Crane does so well.

His critics' reluctance to concede mistake may partly come from Crane's errors being particularly hard to identify among all the ornate language and grammatical constructions that crowd them. Delineating mistake from invention can be difficult in poetry so openly devoted to changing the nature and uses of words. In the lines of "Voyages" I quote, for example, "wrapt" is not the only word that gives pause. "[L]eewardings" also stands out as a tenuous noun—obviously related in some way to the more usual adjectival form, "leeward." But as Joseph Warren Beach has convincingly shown, Crane actually lifts this nominalization from *Moby-Dick*—"Such lovely leewardings," Ahab says in chapter 135—along with other phrases from Melville's novel.[33] Similarly, the word "processioned," which Crane appears to use as a past participle, defies any obvious sense; there is no such verb as "procession"—only "process." And yet Crane probably does mean something more closely related to the noun "procession" than to the verb "process" (one can readily see why he would not choose the much less magisterial "proc*ess*ed," or even worse "*pro*cessed"—especially on the heels of the rhetorically high "Samite sheeted"). His writing is full of suggestively creative language, much of which is intentional rather than misjudged or accidental. "[D]iapason knells" followed by "sceptred terror" and "sessions rends" obviously ask a lot of the reader too—and it takes more than a few tries to untangle the parts of speech in this stanza (to be honest, I'm still not entirely sure of all of them). But these phrases and clauses are classically Cranian—and less likely to be accidental than "wrapt," which has more to do with spelling than with sense. Likewise, his changing of the word "motion" in the ninth line into an act performed by the noun "demeanors" suggests a particular kind of antiauthoritarian stance toward grammatical law. But such a position, misguided or not, is different from a mistake. One *takes* a stance or a position, after all. And most of the time, Crane was deliberate: "What I want to get," he tells Sherwood Anderson, "is just what is so beautifully done in [John Donne's 'The Expiration'], an 'interior' form, a form that is so thorough and intense as to dye the words themselves with a peculiarity of meaning, slightly different maybe from the ordinary definition of them separate from the poem."[34] Crane wants to turn language into something bespoke—to use words in a way that renders them impossible to extricate from the verses to which they belong.

His success in this regard often put him at odds with the very editors he most wished to impress. When he submitted his short lyric "At Melville's Tomb" to Harriet Monroe at *Poetry Magazine* in 1926, she could not make heads or tails of it and told him so. Crane's reply to her query has all the makings of a modern manifesto:

> as a poet I may very possibly be more interested in the so-called illogical impingements of the connotations of words on the consciousness (and their combinations and interplay in metaphor on this basis) than I am interested in the preservation of their logically rigid significations. . . . The nuances of feeling and observation in a poem may well call for certain liberties which you claim the poet has no right to take. I am simply making the claim that the poet does have that authority.[35]

This "forthright" appeal to poetic license may well have seemed to Monroe like the poet's asking for a get-out-of-jail-free card,[36] but she did eventually publish Crane's poem, along with her letter and his reply (perhaps as a safety measure). Crane's argument, now known as "the logic of metaphor," gives the poem, and the poet, freedom from institutionalized meaning in service of "illogical" and often very personal associations that rely on the reader's own impulses to work them out (in the manner of Alvarez, above). "It implies (this inflection of language)," Crane tells Monroe, "a previous or prepared receptivity to its stimulus on the part of the reader. The reader's sensibility simply responds by identifying this inflection of experience with some event in his own history or perceptions—or rejects it altogether."[37] Whether or not these "inflections" of language and experience encompass the "wrapt inflections of our love" is another matter; the word "inflections" is clearly an important one for Crane, who uses it flexibly to describe aspects of language, life, and love that are palpably dynamic and almost always good. He may have taken his cue here from Wallace Stevens, who pits "inflections" against "innuendoes" in "Thirteen Ways of Looking at a Blackbird":

I do not know which to prefer,
The beauty of inflections
Or the beauty of innuendoes,
The blackbird whistling
Or just after.[38]

Crane admired Stevens—"There is a man whose work makes most of the rest of us quail," he once said—and read him with enthusiasm long before *Harmonium* first appeared.[39] Stevens's "inflections," described by Helen Vendler as the "heard melodies" of the bird as opposed to the secondary sensations left to the listener once the song has ended, become in Crane's writing mere abstractions.[40] But as in Stevens, they are primary insofar as they (the "inflections") represent experience itself, rather than its knock-on effects. Readers thus encounter inflections in Crane's poetry as in life, and must subsequently *do* something with them (i.e., make innuendo). Luckily, according to Crane, readers' innate "receptivity" makes this possible. He evidently trusted his readers a great deal.

There is a fair amount of criticism devoted to the idea of poetry-as-experience in Crane. Paul Ramsey is praising the poet when he suggests that "Crane offers . . . a poetry primarily of experience rather than understanding."[41] And Leibowitz, who calls "Voyages" Crane's "highest achievement and fascinating to read for its verbal experiments and effects," understands the experience to be the style, with all its "verbal crisscrossings and extraordinary plays with connotations and sounds that make the texture of the poem so rich and clotted."[42] In the same year he was composing "Voyages," Crane tells Jean Toomer, "I try to make my poems experiences, I rather don't try, when they are good *they are*."[43] What this means in practice is that much of the "poetry" in Crane's poetry consists in its potentiality for the reader. His rich and difficult style, which owes much to the Elizabethan poets he read and loved, becomes, according to John Irwin, "an implicit compliment to the reader whose feeling for verbal nuances is trusted to supply the link between tenor and vehicle."[44] Perhaps unsurprisingly, Irwin has a particularly well-honed "feeling" for verbal nuances and is among Crane's best close readers.

But all "verbal nuances" are not created equal and should not be treated as such. For instance, Crane loved taking liberties with language, both in terms of changing words' usage and allowing them to metamorphose into other words altogether. Many of these liberties have important uses in their specific contexts: phrases like "diapason knells," which hangs in suspension grammatically, and "unfettered leewardings," which is charmingly onomatopoeic if somewhat nonsensical (its nod to Melville notwithstanding), add layers of argument and innuendo to a primarily descriptive moment in the poem. And a surprise coinage like "transmemberment"—a word Crane invents at the end of the third section of "Voyages," which probably means something like transformation, remembering, and dismemberment all in one—requires the poet and the reader to be positively in cahoots. These sorts of pairings and neologisms arguably enhance the texture of the poetry and are particularly angled to a transhistorical style toward which Crane strained as he tried to differentiate himself from other modern writers who were, in his eyes, overly eager to disassociate themselves from their predecessors. Speaking of his modernist contemporaries, Crane writes,

> The deliberate program, then, of a "break" with the past or tradition seems to me to be a sentimental fallacy. . . . The poet has a right to draw on whatever practical resources he finds in books or otherwise about him. . . . I put no particular value on the simple objective of

"modernity." The element of the temporal location of an artist's creation is of very secondary importance. . . . His picture of the "period" . . . will simply be a by-product of his curiosity and the relation of his experience to a postulated "eternity."[45]

One of the ways Crane's poetry performs this critique of the "sentimental fallacy" in modern writing is through efforts at sounding antique. Langdon Hammer notes of this diction: "Crane's intention . . . is to deny the obsolescence of the high style as if the prohibition against it (conventional in high modernist verse, and particularly Eliot's) were not yet in effect; as if, in fact, it were *not yet an old style*."[46] For instance, Crane uses "thy" and "unto" in his poems without so much as a blink; and most of his Elizabethan tendencies—unlike Eliot's—proceed without irony.

But it is most likely that "wrapt" is neither an archaism nor a new word so much as a misspelled homonym masquerading as a pun. It basically means the same thing as the word it sounds like: "rapt," or "wrapped," or both. Neologisms ask for consideration; mistakes ask forgiveness. When Crane's critics treat the range of his "verbal nuances" as though they are one and the same, as some of Dickinson's critics also misguidedly do, they miss an opportunity to distinguish between inflections of language that call for innuendo and ones that are mere mishaps. Differentiating between the two might even quell some of the controversy among scholars, since presumably it would be as empowering for Crane's detractors to name his errors (without risk of assassination) as it would be for his admirers to mention them in passing without having to perform interpretive acrobatics to make them seem plausible. Calling out genuine mistakes throws other "effects" into relief. After all, neologisms are more than simply persuasive errors (though certain errors may transform into neologisms over time). No one shouted "erroneous!" when Lewis Carroll invented the "chortle";[47] no one accused Shakespeare of carelessness when he had Prince Henry mention "luggage."[48]

Part of the difference between mistakes and neologisms lies, of course, in intention; but part of the difference is also bound up in the effect. For example, "transmemberment" is an invention whose connotation combines several unlikely bedfellows: memory or remembrance, transformation, and body parts (of any which kind). When Crane uses this word in "Voyages

III," the ideas, taken together, amount to a kind of redemption for the lovers:

> and where death, if shed,
> Presumes no carnage, but this single change,—
> Upon the steep floor flung from dawn to dawn
> The silken skilled transmemberment of song;
>
> Permit me voyage, love, into your hands.[49]

One doesn't have to *like* "transmemberment," or Crane's decision to use it, to hear it working over and through these ideas. The occasional moments of sense in these lines hint at Crane's confidence in trying out the word: only a "silken skilled" poet would attempt it—and one vulnerable enough to ask to be "[p]ermit[ted]." And the context suggests its own connotations by offering basic counterparts to at least some of the possibilities bound up in the word. "[T]rans" remembers "change" above it, and points to "voyage"; "member" becomes "hands"; and "death" lends a sinister aspect to "-memberment." Other critics take the reading further than I have just done, linking both the word and the trope to Crane's admiration of Melville. Hammer writes that "[a]s a figure for historical relation, the neologism 'transmemberment' eschews the lesser reconcilements of memory to affirm the transfiguration of the past in the present. As a rhetorical strategy, the term indicates the mode of transumptive allusion . . . in Crane's work. For Crane, the goal of such a strategy is to admit no distance—or rather: no distance that cannot be spanned—between his own song and, in this instance, Melville's."[50] Thinking more literally, Paul notes that "[i]n its immediate visual sense . . . 'transmemberment' evokes the intertwined limbs (members) of lovers (as in the case of Queequeg and Ishmael in *Moby-Dick*), the union that the poem, this 'song,' accomplishes."[51] Leibowitz hears in transmemberment "a brilliant new word that expresses the tension in the poem between creative and destructive process, between love and death. The word, like the love, is made up of transubstantiation and dismemberment, the one impossible without the other."[52] Because of its context, then, "transmemberment" changes and enhances the meaning of

"Voyages"; it is an invention with multiple effects both on and below the surface.

I am aware that these readings of "transmemberment"—mine and those of other critics—sound similar to the creative readings of "wrapt," despite the fact that "wrapt," as a figure, is not nearly as far-reaching. Such creativity on the part of a critic is a dangerous enterprise in any case. Crane asks his critics to read with their imaginations, but can a reader take too much liberty? One never wants to cross that threshold. Lewis teeters on the brink when he quotes the following lines from the end of "Voyages IV" and then tries to fix them:

In this expectant, still exclaim receive
The secret oar and petals of all love.

Something is obviously wrong with either the grammar or the punctuation of the first of those lines (the worksheets do not help). One can move the words around experimentally; but they are curiously inert and heavy counters. I suppose "still" to be the noun intended, and the comma to be misplaced, and read it: "In this expectant still, exclaim [and] receive," etc. In any event, it is plainly a moment of final celebration, and the gift of the symbols of universal love.[53]

I appreciate Lewis's nod to error here, even as I question his willingness to smooth it over. As critics, we are not exactly permitted to rearrange the words and sentences of poems to our liking or understanding, are we? We must work with what is there—or else risk turning the interpretive act into the poetical one at the expense of the author and his choices. R. P. Blackmur—on the whole a Crane skeptic—suggests that "in reading Hart Crane we must make allowances for him . . . whereby we agree to forgive or guess blindly at those parts of the poems which are unintelligible."[54] But I worry about making allowances for poets. Don't—shouldn't—poets make allowances for their readers, and not the other way around? Can we not look for and expect greatness in poems, if not all the time, some of the time—and be willing to say when we do not find it? I doubt Crane wished for allowances so much as admiration.

In describing the origin of Crane's neologisms, Leibowitz appeals to the influence of Joyce—a connection he is probably right to make given Crane's early appreciation of the novelist. (Crane was among the first American readers of *Ulysses*, having asked a friend to bring him a copy before it was readily available.)[55] Leibowitz connects Crane's "transmemberment" to words like Joyce's "blandiloquent," for instance, and hears in the poetry some of the richness and intricacy bound up in Joyce's "bravura gifts."[56] But there are important differences too. A poet like Crane requires a creative reader like Leibowitz in a way that Joyce—and, Nabokov, to mention another "magical manipulator of words"—did not.[57] Joyce's plays and puns rarely need to be solved or defended. In comparing what these writers ask of their readers, I find myself wondering not only about poets and their sense of creative license but also about the creative license *critics* take in reading difficult passages—some of which occasionally contain mistakes. One of the pleasures of reading Crane's poetry lies in the fact that it raises these sorts of questions. You can hear Crane's own awareness of these issues bubbling up to the surface in his letter to Monroe when he claims:

> If one can't count on some such bases in the reader now and then, I don't see how the poet has any chance to ever get beyond the simplest conceptions of emotion and thought, of sensation and lyrical sequence. . . . [A]s long as poetry is written, an audience, however small, is implied, and there remains the question of an active or an inactive imagination as its characteristic.[58]

I am not advocating that critics be unimaginative or inactive. But I do question the lengths to which we sometimes go in such activities. When a sensitive reader's imagination makes manifest the beauty of a pent-up word or line, he puts his critical faculties to good use. But when he turns a simple spelling mistake into a disquisition, when he is found to be squeezing juice from a pit, he had better look for riper fruit.

The value in Crane's work is not always intrinsically tied to his mistakes and does not require those mistakes to be anything other than mistaken. Good poets are not always good spellers, nor are they right all of the time. Crane's poetry in particular seeks out an especially honest reader. Blackmur has suggested that Crane "puts an impossible burden on the reader, the burden of reading two poems at once, the one that appears and the 'real' poem which does not appear except by an act of faith."[59] Faith is a tricky enterprise. Sometimes it involves genuine feeling; sometimes it involves deceiving oneself in order to make the implausible plausible. Reed, in his take on Crane's "Elizabethan crazy quilt," says that the poetry "delights in its half-intelligibility and its inconsistences."[60] But is it possible that what *we* love about Crane is the feeling of half-intelligibility and inconsistency? Are these the qualities Crane himself loved about his work? He was, after all, a careful and talented reviser, as the manuscript versions of his poems show—even if he did write his first drafts rather haphazardly in the middle of the night while drunk and listening to the Victrola.[61] He was a poet who believed in form, prosody, and polish. He once told his mother, "My work is becoming known for its formal perfection and hard glowing polish, but most of those qualities, I'm afraid, are due to a great deal of labor and patience on my part."[62] If celebrating Crane's "half-intelligibility" and "inconsistency" involves overlooking the specificity of his own aims for poetry, then we are being remiss in our work as readers. As ever, it is not my wish to mar Crane's reputation in pointing out that his poems contain errors—only to demonstrate the implications of our ways of reading them. When we smooth over Crane's rough edges, we do so at the expense of his own sense of polish.

At the time of Crane's death in his early thirties, on an actual sea voyage from Mexico to New York in the spring of 1932, his self-esteem bore little resemblance to the self-conscious swagger of the young poet writing letters to friends and family at the beginning of his career. Critiques of his poetry's obscurity, along with financial difficulties and alcoholism, got in the way of his progression as a poet. Whether Crane died by deliberate suicide or accidental drowning remains an open question—he had purportedly propositioned a sailor on the ship and was beaten for it; he was drunk and unhappy. But intention and outcome do not live in perfect accordance, nor do they have neat boundaries. Crane may have wished to jump overboard, or simply fallen, or indeed both. Likewise, his poems, whose accidental-seeming qualities often reveal (under scrutiny) signs of careful deliberation but occasionally betray failures in the pursuit, overstep poetry's usual bounds in interesting, purposeful ways while also performing mishaps from time to time. Crane believed in the associative qualities of language, in inflection and innuendo—but it does not follow that all of his words are inflected equally well. Nor is it possible for us, as readers, always to square our admiration for the prodigious talent in his work with the mistakes we sometimes unwillingly encounter cohabiting there.

CHAPTER 6

Fact-Checking Elizabeth Bishop

Journalists stick to the facts, but must the principle hold for poets? In workshops, poet-teachers tend to put it less dogmatically: "write what you know." But then, what do we know—even about ourselves? Elizabeth Bishop was a poet who adored facts but in other ways claimed to know very little about anything. She was both autobiographical in her writing yet also extremely reticent about her private life. Her tone in poems often feels personal and impersonal at once; to many readers, her way of describing things, always down to the tiniest detail, gives the verse an encyclopedic, prosy feeling—something like, or toward, reportage. In "The Bight," for instance:

> The frowsy sponge boats keep coming in
> with the obliging air of retrievers,
> bristling with jackstraw gaffs and hooks
> and decorated with bobbles of sponges.
> There is a fence of chicken wire along the dock
> where, glinting like little plowshares,
> the blue-gray shark tails are hung up to dry
> for the Chinese-restaurant trade.
> Some of the little white boats are still piled up
> against each other, or lie on their sides, stove in,
> and not yet salvaged, if they ever will be, from the last bad storm,
> like torn-open, unanswered letters.[1]

This is obviously full of detail, and yet not quite journalistic or wholly objective; the subjectivity behind the minutiae comes through in metaphors like "air of retrievers" and similes like "unanswered letters," which complicate the otherwise scientific matter-of-factness of the boats and their habitat. Bishop herself has seen—or is at the moment of seeing—the bight, and although one of her principal concerns in describing it seems to be factual accuracy, the poem, which appears in her second book, *A Cold Spring* (1955), ultimately offers a personal, idiosyncratic description of the place. It also bears a crucial epigraph: "[*On my birthday*]."[2] The date is important not only for the air of specificity it gives the poem but also because it confirms what we already suspect about the poem's descriptions: that the inner life of the poet is at play, and on display, here, too. Who goes to such a bight on her birthday? Why are the letters unanswered? Facts tell all sorts of stories, on and below the surface. They can be fictive, too, if not fictitious.

Many of Bishop's later poems reveal more of her inner life and do so less subtly than "The Bight." The late poem "In the Waiting Room" is, on the face of it, very obvious in its autobiographical inflections. It relates the experience of an almost-seven-year-old child named "Elizabeth" sitting in the waiting room of a dentist's office while her aunt receives some kind of treatment. The poem explicitly draws on real facts from Bishop's own childhood; we know this not only from her interviews and letters about the poem but also from an episode that she records and publishes in her short memoir "The Country Mouse," about her move at the age of six away from her maternal grandparents in rural Nova Scotia to live with the wealthier, paternal side of her family in Massachusetts. The last paragraph of that memoir very closely resembles the narrative of "In the Waiting Room" but is written in prose:

> After New Year's, Aunt Jenny had to go to the dentist, and asked me to go with her. She left me in the waiting room, and gave me a copy of the *National Geographic* to look at. It was still getting dark early, and the room had grown very dark. There was a big yellow lamp in one corner, a table with magazines, and an overhead chandelier of sorts. There were others waiting, two men and a plump middle-aged lady, all bundled up. I looked at the magazine cover—I could read

most of the words—shiny, glazed, yellow and white. The black letters said: FEBRUARY 1918. A feeling of absolute and utter desolation came over me. I felt . . . *myself*. In a few days it would be my seventh birthday. I felt, *I, I, I*, and looked at the three strangers in panic. I was *one* of them too, inside my scabby body and wheezing lungs. "You're in for it now," something said. How had I got tricked into such a false position? I would be like that woman opposite who smiled at me so falsely every once in a while. The awful sensation passed, then it came back again. "You are you," something said. "How strange you are, inside looking out. You are not Beppo, or the chestnut tree, or Emma, you are *you* and you are going to be *you* forever." It was like coasting downhill, this thought, only much worse, and it quickly smashed into a tree. *Why* was I a human being?[3]

The question with which Bishop ends her piece can be answered simply—because she was born human, on February 8, 1911. The arbitrariness of this fact frustrates the girl; birthdays mark us each as individual, but they also remind us of our common humanity. It would be *her* particular birthday soon—but then everyone has birthdays, grows up, grows old. Bishop begins to understand that she is at once a master of her own experience (she "could read," after all) and also a subject of that experience ("inside" her "scabby body"). The lesson leaves a deep impression. Bishop would formalize this memoir's tale of dawning subjectivity into poetry six years later, keeping many of its details and adding more:

IN THE WAITING ROOM

In Worcester, Massachusetts,
I went with Aunt Consuelo
to keep her dentist's appointment
and sat and waited for her
in the dentist's waiting room.
It was winter. It got dark
early. The waiting room
was full of grown-up people,
arctics and overcoats,
lamps and magazines.

My aunt was inside
what seemed like a long time
and while I waited I read
the *National Geographic*
(I could read) and carefully
studied the photographs:
the inside of a volcano,
black, and full of ashes;
then it was spilling over
in rivulets of fire.
Osa and Martin Johnson
dressed in riding breeches,
laced boots, and pith helmets.
A dead man slung on a pole
—"Long Pig," the caption said.
Babies with pointed heads
wound round and round with string;
black, naked women with necks
wound round and round with wire
like the necks of light bulbs.
Their breasts were horrifying.
I read it right straight through.
I was too shy to stop.
And then I looked at the cover:
the yellow margins, the date.
Suddenly, from inside,
came an *oh!* of pain
—Aunt Consuelo's voice—
not very loud or long.
I wasn't at all surprised;
even then I knew she was
a foolish, timid woman.
I might have been embarrassed,
but wasn't. What took me
completely by surprise
was that it was *me*:

my voice, in my mouth.
Without thinking at all
I was my foolish aunt,
I—we—were falling, falling,
our eyes glued to the cover
of the *National Geographic*,
February, 1918.

I said to myself: three days
and you'll be seven years old.
I was saying it to stop
the sensation of falling off
the round, turning world
into cold, blue-black space.
But I felt: you are an *I*,
you are an *Elizabeth*,
you are one of *them*.
Why should you be one, too?
I scarcely dared to look
to see what it was I was.
I gave a sidelong glance
—I couldn't look any higher—
at shadowy gray knees,
trousers and skirts and boots
and different pairs of hands
lying under the lamps.
I knew that nothing stranger
had ever happened, that nothing
stranger could ever happen.
Why should I be my aunt,
or me, or anyone?

What similarities—
boots, hands, the family voice
I felt in my throat, or even
the *National Geographic*

and those awful hanging breasts—
held us all together
or made us all just one?
How—I didn't know any
word for it—how "unlikely" . . .
How had I come to be here,
like them, and overhear
a cry of pain that could have
got loud and worse but hadn't?

The waiting room was bright
and too hot. It was sliding
beneath a big black wave,
another, and another.

Then I was back in it.
The War was on. Outside,
in Worcester, Massachusetts,
were night and slush and cold,
and it was still the fifth
of February, 1918.[4]

Bishop dramatizes the child's crisis here much more than in her memoir. She also offers richness from the stories in the magazine, their characters colliding with those in her own life in cold, slushy Worcester. This poem is somewhat extraordinary for Bishop in that she rarely strikes such overtly personal notes: here we have not only autobiographical details—a dentist's office in the city where Bishop lived, a magazine that was of particular interest to her, and a first-person narrator who is identified as "an Elizabeth" and who shares her birthday—but also an unusual intimacy of tone, elevating the anecdotal to a high but naturalistic rhetoric. Bishop's qualities of accuracy and descriptive detail also apply themselves a little differently, first to a magazine that is itself descriptive, and then to the inner life of the speaker, who is herself a reader ("I could read") prefiguring *us* as readers both of this poem and ultimately of her. Bishop bookends her experience by naming the magazine twice: "I read / the *National Geographic*" she begins; and then, "I—we—were falling, falling, / our eyes glued to the cover / of the *National Geographic*, / February, 1918." David Kalstone has suggested that the magazine's literalness, "with its date and familiar yellow and black" acts as an "anchor" for the poet.[5] Jamie McKendrick comments similarly that "[t]he statement of the external place and time have a talismanic importance as though the gulf into which the girl that she was falls could only be re-approached through the actuality of its setting."[6] The factual specificity of the date is certainly important (as we know from the memoir too); Bishop repeats it at the end of the poem—"it was still the fifth / of February, 1918"—and it allows her to connect the personal (it was three days before her seventh birthday) with the universal ("It was winter" and "the War was on"). The poem itself becomes a figure for the connection between inner and outer life.

But the magazine's date, February 1918, which grounds the imaginative and subjective reading experience of the child in the cold, hard facts of the world, also presents the reader with an interpretive crux: for although there really was a war on, and the real Elizabeth Bishop did live in Worcester and turn seven and visit the dentist, the actual *National Geographic* magazine published in February 1918 contains no such narrative of the adventurers Osa and Martin Johnson, no dead man roasting on a pole, no African women and children "wound round" with wire and string. What's more, these details *are* based in fact—right down to the caption "Long Pig"—but they mostly come from a different issue of the magazine, published more than a year later. Only the initial material about the volcano can be found in the February 1918 issue, in a story about Alaska called "The Valley of Ten Thousand Smokes." "My memory," Bishop explains later in an interview, "had combined two . . . issues of the *Geographic*."[7]

How—or whether—Bishop's factual slip alters the effect of her poem depends on the way one reads the facts in it more broadly. The magazine's details tell multiple stories. They certainly alert the child in the poem to her own selfhood and the strangeness of it; but in doing so, they also connect her to a wider world made up of actual people and historical events of real significance (the Johnsons, for example, and World War I). Critics of this poem have attended to Bishop's inaccuracy from very early on and are almost unanimously generous in their response: Anne Stevenson comments that "Of course the poem suffers not at all from this minor lapse in otherwise perfect recall. Its masterly execution . . . depends not on whether the facts are exact but on how convincingly they are deployed."[8] Kalstone points out that Bishop, who often insists on the literal accuracy of her poems in her letters, uses truth not just to represent what happened but also as a way of keeping "pain within bounds"—of transforming subjective, autobiographical experience into something "literal" (i.e., made of letters).[9] So in this poem, the mere impression of fact, Kalstone suggests, is enough to counteract the child's feeling of falling off of the world. The mistake, he claims, does not "matter in our reading of the poem. The point is the presence of the magazine at all and the vital role it plays in the child's awakening and distress."[10] Lee Edelman uses similarly nuanced logic to explain away the error:

> The truth that interests Bishop . . . is not the truth of history or fact *per se*, but the more "delicate" matter of representation. . . . Bishop's is a poetry conscious of the difficulty and the necessity of reading, conscious of the inevitable mediations of selfhood, the intrusions of the "I," that make direct contact with any literality—with any "truth"—an impossibility.[11]

Edelman's is a beautiful account of the poem and its layers of meaning, but his treatment of this particular inaccuracy makes awfully complex what was initially, for Bishop, an accidental snafu. He suggests that part of the work of Bishop's poem is to "revise[ ] simplistic conceptions of 'fact' or literality."[12] Perhaps that is the case for some of the poem's readers—and perhaps for others (like Kalstone and Stevenson), the mistake really makes no difference at all.

But these kinds of arguments did not relieve Bishop herself from the worry she felt, both during and after the writing of this poem, over getting its details right. In fact, the first thing she did when she finished a draft of "In the Waiting Room" was go straight to the New York Public Library to check its accuracy. It was the summer of 1967, and she had written the poem while visiting her friend Jane Dewey's farm in Maryland. "The poem I wrote there," she explains to her friend Robert Lowell, "requires an afternoon's work in the Public Library, alas—then I'll send it—."[13] The verse came to her, she tells him, while she was sleeping: "It is one of those I dream—woke up one morning at Jane's with almost the whole thing done."[14] It isn't hard to imagine how Bishop might have blurred the details between two magazines during the more than fifty years that intervened between the actual episode in the waiting room and her composition of the poem—especially if the writing happened in a dream. She was actually surprised, at the library, to discover just how accurate her dreaming was: "It was funny—queer—I actually went to the Library & got out that no. of the *NG*—and that title, 'The Valley of 10,000 Smokes'—was *right*, and has been haunting me all my life, apparently," she subsequently tells him.[15] She doesn't mention, in this letter, the problem of the African material, but we know from her later drafts of the poem that she spent a good deal of time trying to change that section so that all of the details came from the February issue she mentions at the beginning and the end.[16]

But February's article about the volcanoes, and another about Canadian pork production, did not furnish Bishop with the right notes. She writes in a letter to her friend Frank Bidart,

> I did go to the library in N.Y. and look up that issue of the *National Geographic*. . . . I had remembered it perfectly, and it was all about Alaska, called "The Valley of Ten Thousand Smokes." I tried using that a bit but my mind kept going back to another issue of the *National Geographic* that had made what seemed like a more relevant impression on me, so used it instead.[17]

Bishop's choice to carry on with the poem as it was initially written is convincing: the relevance of the African material to the other autobiographical aspects of the poem is strong. Those babies and mothers, their heads and necks "wound" with string and wire, and those "horrifying" breasts, are perhaps the most noteworthy elements of the story—and suggestive, too, of the poet's attitudes toward identity, sexuality, and gender. That is to say, they are thematically accurate, if not literally so. It is hard to imagine "In the Waiting Room" without those breasts in particular: the little girl's shyness over them, and our own subsequent shyness as readers, gives way to Bishop's beautiful meditation on womanhood and collective identity—and the threat each poses to the child's sense of self:

What similarities—
boots, hands, the family voice
I felt in my throat, or even
the *National Geographic*
and those awful hanging breasts—
held us all together
or made us all just one?[18]

Comparing the women in the waiting room to those naked women (who must have seemed, to a young girl in 1911, of a different world altogether) and eventually to herself is half of the revelation. The word "awful" carries off its double meaning especially well here; shame and awe coexist as the most palpable results of "Elizabeth's" newfound subjectivity. Bishop has used "awful" to similar effect before—at the end of "The Bight":

The bight is littered with old correspondences.
Click. Click. Goes the dredge,
and brings up a dripping jawful of marl.
All the untidy activity continues,
awful but cheerful.[19]

What is full of ugliness in the bight is also full of interest—dredge, litter, marl. The winking rhyme of "jawful" two lines above paves the way for the wit of that poem's closing line: birthdays can indeed be awful and cheerful at the same time. For the almost-birthday girl in "In the Waiting Room," the sexually charged nature of those "awful" breasts and their connection to motherhood makes them particularly complex as an image. Bishop's own mother was institutionalized for mental illness and taken from her—one of many circumstances that led to her being in that waiting room with an aunt in the first place.

Such revelations notwithstanding, Bishop never became fully comfortable with the mistake. When submitting her poem to editors at the *New Yorker*, where it was eventually published, she confesses that "[i]t cheats a bit, so you may not want it for your super-honest weekly."[20] (Bishop was well aware of that magazine's famously meticulous fact-checkers.) "If you do want it, however—" she goes on to say, "I doubt very much that anyone else would look it up except a junior English major or something like that—."[21] She was wrong, of course, but the *New Yorker* editors at the time were not deterred:

> Your poem arrived before Howard left for the summer, but he left before it had gone through, and so it falls to me to tell you how much we all liked it, and that we want it for the magazine. We can't see that the fictitious "National Geographic" magazine matters at all. And we don't feel bound to publish in a February issue.[22]

Her editors' lenience was perhaps emboldening for a poet who otherwise showed extreme care about the facts in her poems. The poem appeared on July 17, 1971, and she was proud of it despite returning to its inaccuracy in several later interviews.

But Bishop's confessions in these interviews reveal more than mere defensiveness about her "error." They are a window into her process of composition—its thirst for, and its occasional desire to subvert, fact as it relates to memory:

> You know, I am inaccurate, though. And I get caught. The poem about being almost seven, in the dentist's office, reading *National Geographic*? . . .Something's wrong about that poem and I thought perhaps that no one would ever know. But of course they find out everything. My memory had confused two 1918 issues of the *Geographic*. . . . When I sent the poem to *The New Yorker* I wrote Howard Moss and said I must confess that this is a little wrong. The magazine was nice about it and said it would be alright. But, since then, two people have discovered that it isn't right. They went and looked it up! I should have had a footnote.[23]

It can be hard to read the tone of such an admission. Bishop may, after all, be hedging—making more of the error than her true feelings reflect, both to be funny and in her characteristically devious way of downplaying what she knows to be an extraordinary quality in her work. (Interestingly, she makes a further error here, for the African material was not published in 1918 at all.) Elsewhere she confesses to other slight transgressions:

I *always* tell the truth in my poems. With *The Fish*, that's *exactly* how it happened. It was in Key West, and I *did* catch it, just as the poem says. That was in 1938. Oh, but I did change *one* thing: the poem says he had five hooks hanging from his mouth, but actually he only had three.[24]

And in another interview, about her poem "The Moose":

It was all true. The bus trip took place before I went to Brazil. I went up to visit my aunt. Actually, I was on the wrong bus. I went to the right place but it wasn't the express I was supposed to get. It went roundabout and it was all exactly the way I described it, except that I say "seven relatives." Well, they weren't really relatives, they were various stepsons and so on, but that's the only thing that isn't quite true.[25]

Here her little anecdote about wrong buses and right destinations serves as a kind of preamble to the "error" itself: Does it matter which route you take if you get where you meant to go? In the case of "In the Waiting Room," we might understand her predicament with the magazine in this way: sometimes you don't know where you mean to go until you mistakenly end up there.

But Bishop is wry. By bringing up the errors of her own accord, and by talking of truth only to undermine its importance moments later ("that's the only thing that isn't *quite* true"), she is able to straddle the fence on the matter of fact. Poems routinely alter certain elements of reality, she suggests, as necessity requires. In "The Fish," perhaps her poet's ear was bent on having the sound of "five big hooks" rather than "three," or her eye was set on the image of a "five-haired beard of wisdom / trailing from his aching jaw," or her imagination wanted to connect the wounds of the fish to the five wounds of Christ during the Crucifixion.[26] One interesting aspect of these confessed inaccuracies is that Bishop appears, on some level, to *want* her readers to know when she isn't "*quite*" right. No one but those passengers on the boat with her could possibly attest to there being three hooks instead of five, yet she brings it up as though it is a necessary admission. Here the positive aspect of her defensiveness—the pleasure she takes in the naysaying (i.e., my poem is *not* true—"I did change *one* thing")—makes up for the guilt of inaccuracy.

At the same time, Bishop's confessions appeal to a purity that she aspired to in poetry—a purity she reluctantly compromised in "In the Waiting Room" because of competing needs in the poem. "We must admire her perfect aim," she writes of the huntress in her poem "The Colder the Air."[27] As readers we often catch sight of Bishop in the act of self-correction, as though she is compelled to make sure of her own accuracy even as she attempts to show her reader just how hard it is to get things exactly right. For instance, in the opening descriptions of "Brazil, January 1, 1502" (another poem insistent about its date), she writes, "and flowers, too, like giant water lilies / up in the air—up, rather, in the leaves—";[28] in "The Armadillo," she explains of the fire balloons,

Once up against the sky it's hard
to tell them from the stars—
planets, that is—the tinted ones:
Venus going down, or Mars,

or the pale green one.[29]

In "Sandpiper," the bird runs "straight through" the water, "watching his toes. / —Watching, rather, the spaces of sand between them."[30] At the end of "Loves Lies Sleeping," she describes a person whose "open eyes" are "inverted and distorted. No. I mean / distorted and revealed."[31] Of "The Monument," she explains that it is "built somewhat like a box. No. Built / like several boxes in descending sizes."[32] These small intrapoetic revisions give the poems immediacy—as though the eye of the writer is perceiving at the very moment the poet is recording what it sees—but they also say a lot about Bishop's dedication to accuracy. They simultaneously reveal her to be extra careful as well as constantly susceptible to, and accepting of, mistake. She is in this respect like "The Gentleman of Shalott," who, she writes in that poem, "loves / that sense of constant readjustment."[33] Her choice to keep the whole process live—to leave the error and the correction—hints that both sides of this coin may be worth putting on display. Why deny mistakes when you can claim them? Bishop mentions in one interview that her friend Marianne Moore's "greatest influence" on her "was a thirst for accuracy. She would go to incredible pains to get things right."[34] Bishop's own finical "rathers" and "ors" feel like a meticulous but fallible poet's due diligence: they suggest modesty and self-righteousness in equal measure. (Colm Tóibín has suggested that they might also be "a trick, a way of making the reader believe and trust a voice, or a way of quietly asking the reader to follow the poem's casual and then deliberate efforts to be faithful to what it saw, or what it knew.")[35] But they also celebrate the mistakenness that proves inevitable even for the most careful of poets. Mistakes may not be welcome, at least consciously, but they are inescapably part of the process.

Truth, or "rightness," thus presents itself as always precariously situated next to exaggeration or falsehood. In her dramatic monologue "Crusoe in England," Bishop's character laments various inaccuracies relating to his famous story: "None of the books has ever got it right," he says of the name of his island, and about his friend Friday's arrival, "[a]ccounts of that have everything wrong."[36] And yet elsewhere in the poem, Bishop winks at her reader through Crusoe's own errors—as when the stranded man cannot remember the final words of Wordsworth's famous lines, forgetfully reciting, " 'They flash upon that inward eye, / which is the bliss . . .' The bliss of what?"[37] Crusoe's mistake on "solitude" obviously gets to the heart of the poem's wider meanings and represents an instance where forgetting is simply a different form of remembering. And when he dreams of "slitting a baby's throat, mistaking it / for a baby goat," Bishop means for her reader to hear the unconscious symbolism behind such an error, for dreams are where unintended mistakes can become intentional.[38] Moore strikes a similarly psychoanalytic note when she includes an epigraph to her *Complete Poems* saying that "Omissions are not accidents."[39] And yet—the intentionality behind Moore's editorial decisions in that collection notwithstanding—sometimes they are. Freud's theories about mistake were not unknown to Bishop (or Moore); in fact, she openly celebrates the productivity behind certain accidental slips in her early poem "The Man-Moth," whose title and subject—a creature, half-man, half-moth, who "always seats himself facing the wrong way"—she invents after reading a newspaper article that mistakenly spells the word "mammoth" that way.[40] Commenting on that poem later, Bishop remarks, "the misprint seemed meant for me."[41] She knows that inaccuracy sometimes ends well.

The letters Bishop writes to Lowell about his poems in the years following her publication of "In the Waiting Room" reveal fittingly complicated
and strong feelings about the "truths" literature should and should not
tell. In one, she practically begs Lowell not to alter the facts of his relationship with Elizabeth Hardwick when he records them in his collection *The
Dolphin*:

> I can't bear to have you publish something that I regret and that you
> might live to regret, too . . . Here is a quotation from dear little Hardy
> that I copied out years ago—long before DOLPHIN, or even the *Note-
> books*, were thought of. It's from a letter written in 1911. . . . "What
> should certainly be protested against . . . is the mixing of fact and
> fiction in unknown proportions. Infinite mischief would lie in that.
> If any statements in the dress of fiction are covertly hinted to be fact,
> all must be fact, and nothing else but fact, for obvious reasons."[42]

The repercussions of Lowell's fabrications about his dissolving marriage are
of course very different from those resulting from Bishop's appropriations
of the African material. Yet she suggests that altering historical fact in any
way places the poet on a slippery slope—and perhaps especially in a poem
like "In the Waiting Room," where, to use Hardy's phrase, "fact and fiction"
do exist "in unknown proportions." The poem makes no *absolute* claim to
autobiography, but its speaker is overtly "an Elizabeth"—one whose age
corresponds with the poet's age in 1918 and whose world borrows directly
from the places and scenarios recognizable to Bishop's own life. And although Bishop had no aunt named "Consuelo," other aspects of the poem's
narrative come straight from her memoir. In this case, the difference between autobiographical fact (as represented, say, by her aunt's name) and
historical fact (as represented by stories and dates in an actual magazine)
becomes important. Bishop seems to show less compunction in changing
the former than in changing in the latter.

This distinction between historical and autobiographical fact is especially
contentious as it relates to "In the Waiting Room" because it highlights a
topic that the poem itself brings to the surface: the relation between inner
and outer life. Much to her own dismay, the child's experience as herself—
her selfhood, so to speak—is inextricably linked to the world around her

(including her aunt, the other people in the dentist's office, and of course those women with their horrifying breasts). What begins as internal to the speaker becomes externalized in her surroundings as well as in the magazine. Very quickly the private, or personal, experience of the child loses its edge over the universal; what begins as autobiographical indeed becomes historical in the end: "Outside / . . . were night and slush and cold" and "the War was on." And so the subjectivity or inner life that "Elizabeth" discovers is both crucial and disconcertingly limited. Separating facts as they are experienced individually (especially in memory) from facts as they are "known" historically is less easy than both the child and the poet would choose. Bishop grapples with this dilemma at the end of her poem "At the Fishhouses"—another coming-of-age tale:

> It is like what we imagine knowledge to be:
> dark, salt, clear, moving, utterly free,
> drawn from the cold hard mouth
> of the world, derived from the rocky breasts
> forever, flowing and drawn, and since
> our knowledge is historical, flowing, and flown.[43]

Knowledge here is both "free" and yet also "drawn from the cold hard mouth of the world" and "derived from its rocky breasts." These breasts are metaphorical rather than literal; their universality and perpetuity ("forever") counter the presupposition that understanding comes from within rather than without. The individual experience that defines knowledge is always subject to history because it necessarily derives from it: knowledge is both "drawn" and "flown" (Bishop uses the past participle to emphasize its passivity). Inner experience may feel like fact—but it cannot subsume fact. Bishop knows this as she writes and revises her later poem, and she likewise knows it when she confesses to transgressing fact in other poems that make certain claims toward truth that cannot be reconciled with what actually happened.

It may be the case that "In the Waiting Room" is no worse for its factual slip (indeed one could easily make the argument that it is better because of it). But to say that such a slip does not *matter* is to resist a crucial aspect of the making of this and so many of Bishop's poems. She is attentive to questions of fact, and what it means to her to "get things right" (as she says about Moore) changes over time. For instance, Bishop continues to pester Lowell about *The Dolphin* right up until its publication, but in doing so, she seems to contradict herself about his handling of autobiographical detail:

> I feel I've annoyed you more than enough, no doubt, as it is, on that subject, but I can't resist this from Kierkegaard: "The law of delicacy according to which an author has a right to use what he himself has experienced, is that he is never to utter verity but is to keep verity for himself & only let it be refracted in various ways."[44]

The extent to which young Elizabeth Bishop's experience is refracted in her poem "In the Waiting Room," as opposed to reflected within it, may never be known, but it is certainly the case that some fact lies therein. Whether or not the presence of any fact then necessitates that "all must be fact" is less clear-cut than either Hardy or Bishop would have us believe. The misplaced facts embedded in the poem are rich not only because they reveal a wish, on the poet's part, to relate her own life to the lives of African women and children and feminist explorers, but also because they make very clear how important the poet considers her unconscious imagination to be even when she is at the stage of correcting her drafts. For Bishop, not even the worry over her inaccuracy can trump the "relevance" of the African material. It must be slipped in—the way Crusoe's dream allows for certain mistakes he cannot contemplate while awake. Her continued guilt over including the material suggests it to be founded in "error," and her insistence upon its place in the poem proves that inaccuracy can be inexorably tied to craft—which may have its own parameters for truth. ("The Man-Moth" is only her most explicit example.) Our considering her poem to contain a factual mistake does not preclude our admiring it: the inaccurate date becomes, like Crusoe's imagined baby, a point of interest—a site that contains the tension between the value of what the poet dreams up, perhaps unconsciously, and what she means to put down on the page.

It seems doubtful that such a mistake—with respect to printed material especially—could be carried off today. The stringent fact-checkers at the *New Yorker* would likely find it harder to permit this sort of factual inaccuracy in an era when magazine archives are, for the most part, digitized, and when historical information of the kind Bishop mentions in her poem might only be an Internet click away. Paul Muldoon, who served as the *New Yorker's* poetry editor from 2007 to 2017, interviewed the poet Tracy K. Smith for one of the magazine's podcasts, asking her how she felt about dealing with the magazine's "famous" fact-checkers (who had followed up on a song recording she had quoted in a poem). Her answer is noncommittal and telling:

> I like that there is obviously a little bit of room, wiggle room, as it were, in a poem. But poems do sometimes deal in the material of the real world, and, you know, as much as poetic license is important, sometimes it's nice to know what that real material is rooted in, even if we're going to move away from it.[45]

For Smith, as for Bishop, facts are where the poem starts—its "roots"—even if they are not always reflected in its ends. (The words Smith quotes in her poem are in fact accurate.) But how much room is wiggle room? Muldoon is equally unsure in his reply:

> I think that's right, and there are a couple of famous instances in the history of poetry where it would have been much better if the poem had benefited from a little fact-checking—a few things that have gone badly wrong.[46]

It is doubtful that Muldoon is thinking of Bishop's poem here, though he may well have Keats's Cortez/Balboa blunder, and other mistakes mentioned in this book, in mind. Ironically, Muldoon appeals to Bishop earlier in this podcast episode—as an example of a poet who strives for perfect accuracy and precision in everything she writes. The same meticulous eye and ear that keeps her poetry so alive to facts is what makes her inaccuracy in "In the Waiting Room" so valuable. What she brings to the poem from her own imaginative, if "confused" memory is itself rooted in what Smith calls "the material of the real world." Its being so is surely part of why her readers continue to insist that the poem's mistake is also its gain. But whether we like the material she adds to the February 1918 issue, and whether we find it suited to the purpose of the poem (at least as Bishop saw or experienced it), are separate issues from our knowing the material to be mistaken.

About a decade before composing "In the Waiting Room," Bishop began an essay about writing poetry that she never finished. In it she names the three qualities she admires most in her favorite poems: "*Accuracy, Spontaneity, Mystery.*"[47] It is not easy to imagine how these qualities cohabitate, if they do. Accuracy and spontaneity are often at odds, the steady needs of the former warding off the dynamism prerequisite for the latter. And mystery surely finds its enemy in the knowledge accuracy requires. But Bishop offers a solution to the paradox toward the end of her draft—not surprisingly through a metaphor that is complicatedly personal and objectively scientific:

> My maternal grandmother had a glass eye. It fascinated me as a child, and the idea of it has fascinated me all my life. . . . Quite often the glass eye looked heavenward, or off at an angle, while the real eye looked at you. . . .
>
> Off and on I have written out a poem called "Grandmother's Glass Eye" which should be about the problem of writing poetry. The situation of my grandmother strikes me as rather like the situation of the poet: the difficulty of combining the real with the decidedly un-real; the natural with the unnatural; the curious effect a poem produces of being as normal as *sight* and yet as synthetic, as artificial, as a *glass eye*.[48]

For Bishop, differences between the real and the unreal, fact and fiction, are differences that poetry can hold in the balance—not unproblematically but nevertheless necessarily. Her inaccuracy in "In the Waiting Room" may be one version of her grandmother's looking "off at an angle" while simultaneously looking straight at you. What is not factual may still give a *sense* of accuracy—one that courts the spontaneous and mysterious elements of poetry that "cold, hard" facts occasionally preclude. Enjoying the accuracy of her mistakes is part of the fun.

CHAPTER 7

Misremembering Seamus Heaney

On a summer's evening in 2010, Seamus Heaney read his poems to a large and admiring crowd at St. Oswald's Church in the center of Grasmere Village in the eastern part of the Lake District. The church stood not far from the cottage where, a little more than two hundred years before, William Wordsworth lived and wrote with the company and encouragement of his sister Dorothy. Their graves lie in the churchyard there. The reading was arranged in conjunction with the annual Wordsworth Summer Conference, and afterward, at a dinner in Heaney's honor, I shyly asked the poet if he would sign my copy of his latest collection, *District and Circle*. His generous inscription reads:

> for Erica—
>   in the windermere (mistake)
>   district—
>
> fondest wishes—
> Seamus Heaney
>
> Grasmere July 2010

Heaney, the ever-humane wordsmith, was presumably trying to personalize his note by associating the physical "lake district" within which we found ourselves with the title of his book. But his chance mistake—"windermere" for "lake"—put an end to the pun, highlighting instead the fallibility to which all people, even famous poets, are subject. Heaney modestly acknowledges his small "(mistake)" and then takes a second stab at place. "Grasmere July 2010" reads as a declaration of regained footing.

But twenty-four pages into *District and Circle*, there is further trouble. In his short poem "Wordsworth's Skates," which commemorates *The Prelude*'s ice-skating episode and was initially published in the *New Yorker*, Heaney again bungles the locale:

> Star in the window.
>   Slate scrape.
>   Bird or branch?
> Or the whet and scud of steel on placid ice?
>
> Not the bootless runners lying toppled
> In dust in a display case,
> Their bindings perished,
>
> But the reel of them on frozen Windermere
> As he flashed from the clutch of earth along its curve
> And left it scored.[1]

Heaney spins an extraordinary image of the young Wordsworth in his final three lines from ordinary elements: star, slate, skates. Neil Corcoran has described this compositional tactic elsewhere in Heaney's work as a process of "revelation" whereby "the close act of attention, which is always firstly the manifestation of descriptive capacity, is extended beyond itself into an excess or superabundance in which the initial object or image becomes vision."[2] The visionary capacity in the final stanza is made possible by the mundane observations that precede it. But a geographical error in line 8 puts the poet himself on thin ice. As readers of *The Prelude* may remember, it was almost certainly Esthwaite Water, near Hawkshead, where he went to school, on which Wordsworth skated as a child, not the much larger Windermere, which is farther afield and rarely freezes.[3] Wordsworth mentions Esthwaite multiple times in *The Prelude* in connection with his childhood; it was on the shores of this lake when he was "not nine years old" that the young poet discovered a "heap of garments" belonging to a drowned man.[4] And less than a hundred lines after his skating passage in book 1, Wordsworth recalls playing games indoors when "From Esthwaite's neighboring Lake the splitting ice" sounded "distant yellings" that he memorably compares to the "noise of wolves / . . . on the Bothnic Main."[5] Esthwaite—a small and relatively shallow lake—was frequently covered with ice, often for several weeks during winter. As was the case with Bishop's "In the Waiting Room," the fact-checkers at the *New Yorker* either did not pick up on the error or did not care.

One wants to agree with them and say immediately of Heaney's mistake, if I may presume to call it that, "of course it does not matter." But doesn't it matter a little? After all, Heaney was a poet who cared deeply about places and their names. Poems like "Anahorish," "Broagh," and "Toome" demonstrate his attentiveness to the specific locations connected with his own childhood and the words and sounds that describe them. He also knew how important such details were to Wordsworth, who wrote, among many other poems about place, "Poems on the Naming of Places," and was a "local" poet in more ways than one. In fact, Wordsworth's influence on Heaney stems in part from Heaney's sense of their shared regionalism and affection for rural communities; it was a literary inheritance he readily acknowledged throughout his life.[6] In an interview with Dennis O'Driscoll, he remarks, "in May 1974 I went to Grasmere to spend three or four days getting to know Wordsworth's Dove Cottage and the surrounding district for a TV programme; it was immediately afterwards that the first [Glanmore] sonnet was written—the one beginning 'This evening the cuckoo and the corncrake' "[7] That sonnet and the sequence to which it belongs would make much of the association between place and poetry. It also made Heaney's debt to Wordsworth explicit. The sestet even invokes him by name:

> I had said earlier, "I won't relapse
> From this strange loneliness I've brought us to.
> Dorothy and William—" She interrupts:
> "You're not going to compare us two . . . ?"
> Outside a rustling and twig-combing breeze
> Refreshes and relents. Is cadences.[8]

These lines self-consciously initiate a comparison between Heaney and his wife, lately arrived to a small house on the Glanmore estate, and Wordsworth and his sister living at Dove Cottage. The woman here, presumably Marie Heaney, balks at the association, perhaps, as Barbara Hardy has suggested, because "the Wordsworths are too illustrious or homely or brotherly-and-sisterly for this comparison."[9] But whatever Marie's reluctance, Heaney is certainly thinking about Wordsworth in relation to his own sense of place and belonging. The home that the Wordsworths adopted in the Lake District as adults represents for him a successful precedent as he enters a new phase of his writing life, and the homophonic rhymes in these lines—"us to" and "us two"—invite this transhistorical link even as the sense of the sonnet calls it into question. "Us too" is perhaps what Heaney will not put into words, but the poem sounds it out anyway.

In this way Wordsworth acts as a tutelary spirit across several of Heaney's books and much of his prose; Heaney returns to him again and again, along with Frost, Hopkins, Kavanagh, and Eliot. Notwithstanding the two erroneous instances of "Windermere" in my copy of *District and Circle*, Heaney demonstrates substantial expertise about Wordsworth's life and work throughout his career, publishing several critical essays about his poetry and even editing a selection of his work for Faber and Faber. That is to say, whatever the cause of his misremembering the lake, he was much more than a casual reader of Wordsworth, as his essay "The Makings of a Music," which addresses *The Prelude*'s ice-skating passage specifically, shows:

> The exhilaration of the skating, the vitality of the verbs, "gleaming," "sweeping," "spinning," "wheeling," the narrative push, the *cheerfulness*, to use one of the poet's favourite positive words—all these things have their part to play in the overall effect of this writing. But what distinguishes it as Wordsworthian is the gradual allaying of the sensation which is not, however, a diminution of awareness. It is as if a lens of apprehension opens wide and holds open. It is achieved by pacing, a slow, gathering but not climactic movement, repetitive but not monotonous, a walking movement. We might say, in fact, that Wordsworth at his best, no less at his worst, is a pedestrian poet. As his poetic feet repeat his footfalls, the earth seems to be a treadmill that

he turns; the big diurnal roll is sensed through the poetic beat and the
world moves like a waterwheel under the fall of his voice.[10]

The attentiveness of this reading dismisses any charge of carelessness on
Heaney's part with regard to Wordsworth's long poem. And yet one thing
Heaney does make clear is that he is primarily interested in the *manner* of
Wordsworth's writing—his way of apprehending and expressing—more
than what he is saying specifically; the story of the child skating on the ice
transforms for him into a figure for the footfalls of the poet's own lines
(figure skating at its best). The facts of the scene—whatever the name of
the lake—operate as a platform on which Wordsworth can make his own
poetical "movements," a musical term that Heaney deliberately connects
with the physical one. Poetry, its sounds and its sensations, matters here
more than the event that sparks it. In fact, the give and take between poetry's sounds and history's facts may have something to do with his
mistake.

Heaney's reading of these "movements" in *The Prelude* prefigures his
underlying gesture in "Wordsworth's Skates." The last stanza of that poem,
with its pun on musical "score," suggests a comparison between the lines
the young Wordsworth drew on the ice and the verses his memory later
makes of them. The whole poem is likewise interested in transposing aspects of the physical world into inscribed, poetical terms. The first line's
"star in the window" reduces the depth of the universe into a two-
dimensional frame: Heaney is likely thinking here of Wordsworth's similar
move in the lines, "To cut across the image of a star / That gleam'd upon
the ice," which rewrite the heavens by literally drawing on their reflection.[11]
"Slate scrape" in line 2 may refer to a sound, but it also recalls the primitive
act of inscription. The "bindings" on the original skates, which lay bare the
steel implements of writing, quietly gesture to the poet's books. Even as
Heaney develops the concept of ice-writing—Wordsworth's lasting earthly
imprint, or "score"—he also puns on what is "real": "Not the bootless runners . . . but the *reel* of them on frozen Windermere." These movements of
the poet-child, his "reel"—a word that recalls the dance form but perhaps
also *The Prelude*'s cinematic qualities—long outlast the reality.

Heaney's poem thus counterintuitively uses objects and aspects of life
to remember poetry rather than the other way around.[12] His backward-

facing approach allows him to concede that he loves poems as much as he loves the life from which they spring—and is consistent with nearly all of the statements Heaney makes about poetry's life-giving properties in his interviews, speeches, and prose.[13] The display case in question really exists and isn't far from St. Oswald's; anyone who visits the Dove Cottage Museum can see Wordsworth's skates there, gathering motes of dust. (These steel runners are not likely the ones he used as a child—Wordsworth was an avid skater even into his sixties, as a letter written by his sister at that time confirms: "He is still the crack skater on Rydal Lake.")[14] But because Heaney cares less for relics themselves than the visions they conjure, he closes his poem not with the professed subject of its title but with an actively imagined scene illustrating what memory, when played upon, can produce. This memory is actually a memory of somebody else's memory—a remembering of Wordsworth's remembrance rather than his life. Heaney is interested in Wordsworth's remembering (i.e., his poem) because he has read *The Prelude* and understands that within it, "each man is a memory to himself."[15]

The many layers of this poem complicate Heaney's misremembering within it. How might a mistaken memory like "Windermere" work in a poem that so self-consciously generates a remove between remembrance and real life, with its attendant facts? Heaney is not a poet beholden to rightness or fact per se, though he is, like Wordsworth, a poet of remembered places and events. "[M]emory," Heaney says, "was the faculty that supplied me with the first quickening of my own poetry."[16] *Death of a Naturalist*, his first collection, is a book of childhood memories perhaps more appropriate to the reflection that comes with middle age, despite its author being in his twenties. This is a quality he may have learned from Wordsworth, who wrote many of the childhood-related passages in *The Prelude* before he was thirty. For both poets, memory is less of a device for nostalgia than a strategy for quickening the here and now as it becomes manifest in words. Remarking on Wordsworth's "originality" in mining childhood memory for poetry, Heaney marvels how, "by intuition and introspection he recognized that such moments were not only the foundation of his sensibility, but the clue to his fulfilled identity."[17] David Bromwich has described this phenomenon in Wordsworth's poetry of the 1790s:

> [F]or Wordsworth the moments of a life may have as much distance
> separating them as the moments of different lives. . . . [M]emory is a
> kind of experience. . . . The connecting of memories drawn from the
> past can lend to memory itself a depth, and yield for the mind a long
> perspective all its own.[18]

Wordsworth lives memory presently; blending multiple remembrances
from effectively "separate selves" gives the remembering mind its own distinct "experience."[19] Such experience often involves, Bromwich goes on to
say, a connection to place: "The strangeness of the 'other being' who is also
oneself can be remedied only by the thought that such a being has internal
relations to itself, in the form of memories that link it to a chosen landscape."[20] If Heaney has gleaned this art from Wordsworth, then the link to
landscape seems especially critical to his mode of recollection.

In the poem "Fosterling," Heaney both acknowledges and challenges this
innate connection between the actual places of his childhood and his writing self:

> At school I loved one picture's heavy greenness—
> Horizons rigged with windmills' arms and sails.
> The millhouses' still outlines. Their in-placeness
> Still more in place when mirrored in canals.
> I can't remember not ever having known
> The immanent hydraulics of a land
> Of *glar* and *glit* and floods at *dailigone*.
> My silting hope. My lowlands of the mind.
>
> Heaviness of being. And poetry
> Sluggish in the doldrums of what happens.
> Me waiting until I was nearly fifty
> To credit marvels. Like the tree-clock of tin cans
> The tinkers made. So long for air to brighten,
> Time to be dazzled and the heart to lighten.[21]

The sonnet's octave is cheerful about the hold and sway of "place" in the
mind; Heaney uses local words—*glar* (mud), *glit* (slime), and *dailigone*

(dusk, or "daylight is gone")—to characterize the connection between a landscape so familiar to him that he "can't remember not ever having known" it and the poetry it produces. But the sestet begins to wonder what happens when "in-placeness" stops feeling original, causes boredom (i.e., "the doldrums" of poetry). Heaney is testing out "marvels" here—considering what might come of trading his *actual* experience of landscape for the differently credible, partly imagined experience of memory—one that is not purely indebted to "place," "being," or "what happens." Such a trade-in produces that wished-for "lightening" at the end of this poem; it also serves as an opening out into the sequence of poems called "Squarings," which begins with a section called "Lightenings" and immediately follows "Fosterling" in the collection *Seeing Things*. Heaney's Wordsworthian reliance on place now involves a similarly Wordsworthian skepticism about memory's pastness. In "Fosterling," remembrance may not necessarily be a recollection of "what happen[ed]," with its requisite "in-placeness," so much as a belief that memory can be something that happens presently and need not always be tied to the actual. "Fosterling"—which predates "Wordsworth's Skates" by more than twenty years—articulates the same impulse to replace the remembered "real" with the "reel" of memory itself.

Memory's tenuous connection to "what happens" may also lie behind Heaney's mistake in "Wordsworth's Skates." The connection between remembered things and real life is complicated and always personal. For Heaney, especially as his career progresses, the question of poetry's roots in the actual becomes a charged one: the troubled political situation in Northern Ireland, his native place, imposes a specific kind of pressure on his poetry—not unlike, as he once acknowledged in a 1984 lecture given at the Wordsworth Summer School in Grasmere, the pressure Wordsworth felt at his own revolutionary leanings despite being an "Englishman" during the French Revolution.[22] For Heaney, poems—particularly their formal qualities—act as both a solution to, and an absolution from, the poet's predicament of being Northern Irish:

> The only reliable release for the poet was the appeasement of the achieved poem. In that liberated moment, when the lyric discovers its buoyant completion, when the timeless formal pleasure comes to its fullness and exhaustion, in those moments of self-justification and

self-obliteration the poet makes contact with the plane of consciousness where he is at once intensified in his being and detached from
his predicaments. It is this deeper psychological compulsion which
lies behind the typical concern of Northern Irish poets with style,
with formal finish, with linguistic relish and play.[23]

When Heaney writes here of "being" and "predicaments" he refers to the
poet's responsibility to write from and about lived experience. But for him,
one of the challenges of writing involves finding ways of circumventing
actual atrocities while remaining true to "what happens." What happens in
the *poem*—self-justification and self-obliteration at the same time—develops into a strategy of resistance that simultaneously constitutes political
action and self-appeasement. Elmer Andrews suggests along these lines that
Heaney's poetry, "by virtue of its organic form, resolves the conflicts of
mind and history";[24] resolutions of this kind are not limited to what is
"true" in narrow terms:

> His primary obligation is not to the "facts." His own poetic experi-
> ment with the "facts" in Part 2 of *North* demonstrated the resultant
> entrapment and thwarting of his creative powers. He seeks to com-
> pose, not a pseudo-reality, but those facets of reality that bring what
> we do not know—or do not want to know—about ourselves to
> light.[25]

Memory's ability to derange fact but remain true to imagined experience
holds a special provenance in Heaney's poetry for this reason. Andrew
Murphy describes this derangement in terms of "alchemy": "[Heaney's
poems] posit a transformative, alchemical power for poetry: the power to
take the ready material of the everyday and to fashion it into something
astounding."[26] When Heaney fashions recollected material, he tries very
hard to keep the real and the imagined in balance. For some of his critics,
this balance teeters on the edge of rebellion: " 'Insouciance,' " Robert Welch
writes, "is one of Heaney's favoured words: it counters another one that
haunts him—'obedience.' "[27] While I do not consider Heaney's poems, even
at their most imaginatively conceived, to be particularly "insoucian[t]," I
do think that his mistake on "windermere," especially the published one,

speaks indirectly to the possibility that obedience to memory might involve expanding one's sense of what experience entails.

But when and where is memory allowed to be wrong? Writing about experience without feeling limited by experience—or being hemmed in by facts or particular subjects—has always been an explicit theme in Heaney's poetry. It sometimes takes the form of a debate between the virtues of the "given" and the "made." In the early poem "The Given Note," Heaney describes a violinist whose music seems to come "from nowhere" and is neither remembered nor learned:

> So whether he calls it spirit music
> Or not, I don't care. He took it
> Out of wind off mid-Atlantic.
>
> Still he maintains, from nowhere.
> It comes off the bow gravely,
> Rephrases itself into the air.[28]

The proxy-poet in this poem seemingly does very little; like Coleridge in "The Eolian Harp," Heaney celebrates the kind of music that "[r]ephrases itself" and cannot be shaped by the thinking or arranging mind. The given here is pure and earthly—"wind off mid-Atlantic" (even a qualifying article like "the" would disturb its authenticity). Its distinguishing feature is that it has no human source—possibly no source at all. "Whitby-sur-Moyola," another poem about a naturally "gifted" artist, makes a related claim:

> And all that time he'd been poeting with the harp
> His real gift was the big ignorant roar
> He could still let out of him, just bogging in
> As if the sacred subjects were a herd
> That had broken out and needed rounding up.[29]

In these lines, Caedmon—the farmer-poet celebrated in Bede's *Ecclesiastical History*, whose vocation to sing did not stop him from mucking in—retains an "ignorant roar" Heaney admires over the cultivated one. Here "poeting," as distinguished from the inner poetry that needs to be "let out," loses its luster in the battle with pure instinct.

But other poems challenge the given in favor of poetry's imaginative meddling and tendency toward make-believe. In "The Settle Bed," Heaney negatively reframes the givens of Irish politics and historical memory as a piece of old, heavy furniture, "an inheritance" that is

> willable forward
>
> Again and again and again, cargoed with
> Its own dumb, tongue-and-groove worthiness
> And un-get-roundable weight. But to conquer that weight,
>
> Imagine a dower of settle beds tumbled from heaven
> Like some nonsensical vengeance come on the people,
> Then learn from that harmless barrage that whatever is given
>
> Can always be reimagined, however four-square,
> Plank-thick, hull-stupid and out of its time
> It happens to be.[30]

In these lines, the "given note" he admired in the violinist's music, which simply came off his bow, has transformed into an "un-get-roundable weight" that has "come on" the poet. The only thing to do with such "[p]lank-thick" inheritances, Heaney suggests, is to reimagine them. He is not just thinking of political and personal history as it comes on the poet through givens but also poetic inheritances and forms, which are always available for reimagining. "The Settle Bed" appears in the same volume as "Fosterling," with its near-injunction "Time to be dazzled," and a few pages before the poem "Wheels within Wheels," which similarly exclaims, "Who ever saw / the limit in the given anyhow?"[31] When Heaney collects all of these poems in *Seeing Things*, he is registering his belief in the poet's capacity for turning the actual—"what happens"—into something else.[32] The last poem in the book's long sequence, "Squarings," turns this transformation on its head, going so far as to claim that what is imagined—"things in the offing"—may indeed *become* historical, or "foreknown":

Strange how things in the offing, once they're sensed,
Convert to things foreknown;
And how what's come upon is manifest

Only in light of what has been gone through.[33]

For Heaney, the process of "credit[ing] marvels" involves believing in a future that is able to shape the past. His memory here, far from obedient to what has happened, is retroactive: it "foreknows" things only after they have occurred. Events in the offing can be as historical as events gone by.

Heaney understands he is on conceptually shaky ground: the whole of *Seeing Things* admits to its own deceptions. It is as though the poet is asking after the fact whether or not it could be possible to imagine experience into being: the title phrase simultaneously means itself and its opposite—perceiving what is real (*seeing* things) and also making things up (am I *seeing* things?).[34] Heaney wants his poetry to constitute an experience with its own set of parameters for truth. (Under these conditions, poetry might even be capable of making its own memories.) His readers have generally been willing to accept these terms for the book, partly because he is so forthcoming about his ambitions. Corcoran cheerfully notes, "*Seeing Things* is a volume that sees things with the pellucid clarity which turns them into something other than themselves; and a large number of its poems define this process of translation itself."[35] Catharine Molloy similarly comments that within the poems,

> [m]emory functions to augment discourses that attempt not so much to perfect a recollection as to see it for its evocation of something true and lasting. The remembered event may be seen with multiple facets: as it originally happened and as time has changed and broadened the speaker's perception of it. Memory, therefore, does not serve so much to embellish a recollected event as to unleash its possibilities for meaning.
>
> The discursive emanations from these memories help to reshape the speaker's past as he reflects upon their relevance for the present.[36]

Her assessment of Heaney's use of memory focuses on the truth memory "evokes": "what happens," according to Molloy, becomes not so much embellished as reshaped according to the meanings latent in the speaker's own "re-seeing." It is a psychoanalytically inflected approach to the past that may indeed hold some sway with Heaney himself, who once referred to his religion as "Jungian."[37] Michael Cavanagh likewise points out that "moments from [Heaney's] rural past are bathed in the enchanting spotlight of memory"—and Cavanagh's word "enchanting" affords a good deal of freedom to the act of remembrance, making it almost akin to magic.[38] For him, Heaney's "[m]emory generates vision out of past experience, recognizing in retrospect the timeless in the midst of what seemed to be the flow of time."[39] He goes on to suggest that the visionary memory in *Seeing Things* is inherently connected to the poetry of Wordsworth—

> a connection that is only encouraged by Heaney's 1998 essay on Wordsworth, in which he speaks of Wordsworth's effort "to retrieve for the chastened adult consciousness the spontaneous, trustful energies unconsciously available in the world of childhood." According to Heaney, Wordsworth's poetry in the years after 1795 was about a midlife journey of retrieval.[40]

But what is being retrieved? Not memory or historical fact per se; rather, "energy," "spontaneity," "trust"—what Bromwich calls memory's "experience" or the mind's own "long perspective."[41] If Heaney is taking his cue from Wordsworth, he is digging less for what happened than for his own youthful sense of it. Perhaps for this reason, one critic has referred to the tone of the poems in the "Squarings" sequence as "oracular";[42] another detects a "rapid surrender to the impulses of writing as the poet struggles through one memory after another";[43] another notes how "the visionary and the real are symbiotic rather than exclusive."[44]

But does Heaney's Wordsworthian "visionary gleam" actually absolve him from mistake, or does it simply shine a light onto its processes?[45] Heaney himself may be less sanguine about memory's lapses than his readers are. A pair of related poems in "Squarings," which deal explicitly with memory's mistaking, seem less certain about the poet's license to get things wrong. I detect in them the same impulse as the one that caused him to acknowledge the "(mistake)" in his inscription to my book—an impulse to confess memory's mishaps rather than sweep them under the rug. The first, a poem of childhood recollection, figures a poet-in-the-making discovering his own relation to the real world around him:

VI

Once, as a child, out in a field of sheep,
Thomas Hardy pretended to be dead
And lay down flat among their dainty shins.

In that sniffed-at, bleated-into, grassy space
He experimented with infinity.
His small cool brow was like an anvil waiting

For sky to make it sing the perfect pitch
Of his dumb being, and that stir he caused
In the fleece-hustle was the original

Of a ripple that would travel eighty years
Outward from there, to be the same ripple
Inside him at its last circumference.[46]

This poem admits changing perspectives and far-flung hopes. Young Hardy plays with his own negative capability as much as he plays dead—and what Heaney seems to enjoy especially about this remembered scene (lifted from Hardy's biography—officially written and published by his wife Florence, though likely ghostwritten by Hardy himself) is the connection between the central act, Hardy lying in the grass, and its final effect. The future here is "foreknown," mapped out among predictably concentric ripples, but not fully realized until many years afterward when Hardy's playing dead ultimately transforms into the dead Hardy playing poetry. It is an important anecdote for Heaney, whose sequence sets out to consider the multitude of vantages, gestures, and postures that contribute to his experience of what happens. These "Squarings," as Heaney calls them, importing a metaphor from the game of marbles, are

Test-outs and pull-backs, re-envisagings,
All the ways your arms kept hoping towards

Blind certainties that were going to prevail
Beyond the one-off moment of the pitch.[47]

Heaney's many "Squarings," like Hardy's infinite possibilities for reception, come together to prove that re-envisagings and blind certainties about the future sometimes do prevail. And so, early in the sequence, Heaney's recollection of Hardy's Wordsworthian game of "wise passiveness" provides him with a lovely figure for his own credulity.[48] Except for one little problem: it isn't true.

In the very next poem in the sequence, Heaney corrects his own mistake:

VII

(I misremembered. He went down on all fours,
Florence Emily says, crossing a ewe-leaze.
Hardy sought the creatures face to face,

Their witless eyes and liability
To panic made him feel less alone,
Made proleptic sorrow stand a moment

Over him, perfectly known and sure.
And then the flock's dismay went swimming on
Into the blinks and murmurs and deflections
He'd know at parties in renowned old age
When sometimes he imagined himself a ghost
And circulated with that new perspective.)[49]

Heaney apparently likes to put his corrections in parentheses—for example, "(mistake)" in my copy of *District and Circle*. If he had managed to build hopes for memory's experiential power in the first Hardy poem, they are dashed in the opening sentence of this one. His unexpected, parenthetical shift—another kind of "pull-back" or "re-envisaging"—after consulting the biography may, on the one hand, affirm the underlying concern in "Squarings" with changing and evolving perspectives. But on the other hand, what had been an aptly coincidental, even inevitable, tale of a poet whose verse exemplifies the very qualities of timelessness and transport Heaney wants to celebrate, now seems somewhat fanciful and made-up, rather than serendipitously fit for its occasion or "foreknown." The charm of Heaney's readiness to confess his misremembering makes up for this small disappointment, but the more sober truth in Hardy's actual childhood memory continues to worry the hopefulness of Heaney's first version. In the corrected story, young Hardy is anything but passively receptive; his actively going down "on all fours" seems at odds with that earlier experiment with infinity. The child here engages with the ewes rather than playing dead; and instead of waiting for the sky to bestow him with perfect pitch, he mitigates his own loneliness with their panic. Hardy's real experience in the field is still "original"—it prefigures the poet's future social experience—but the outer ripples of Hardy's life in this second scenario have less to do with poetic pitch than they do with personal sorrow. Heaney reimagines the "flock's dismay" as the "witless" reception an aged poet must endure at parties. And in the final stanza, a child's fanciful game of pretend transposes into an unsettling allegory about a living poet imagining himself already as a ghost, "circulating" among people the way only his books now do.

Both of these poems, the mistake and the correction, treat lived and remembered experience as part of a continuum in which prior events "know" future ones "proleptically." (In the first of his sonnets in "Glanmore Revisited"—a self-consciously Wordsworthian title—Heaney recalls a moment of the past that "felt remembered even then, an old / Rightness half-imagined or foretold.")[50] Memory for him is capable of taking on an anticipatory quality: we might even ask whether it is possible for poems to remember things their poets do not. Heaney has written about the poet's "disposition to be affected by all positions, negatively rather than positively capable," and this Keatsian view of what the poet does when he writes from multiple perspectives turns the Hardy poems, taken together, into a kind of *ars poetica*.[51] There may, in effect, be more than one poet—and so more than one set of memories or facts to which the poem must adhere. These are the challenges Heaney's misremembering presents beyond the more literal, local discrepancies in the Hardy story. The relation between poetic narration and fact is necessarily a murky one, but in these two Hardy poems, Heaney emphasizes the truth of his narration (by insisting that he correct his mistake at the beginning of the second poem) while also calling into question the narration's status as fact (by allowing the more compelling, false remembrance to remain in the sequence even after it is revealed to be untrue). This posturing helps to remind the reader that both of these anecdotes are merely representational. Of course all poems, with their tropes and symbols, make themselves susceptible to such a charge, but Heaney's "Squarings" sequence especially brings this quality to the fore. As Helen Vendler writes: "The powerful effort of re-imagining everything—not representing it mimetically as it happened; not representing it embalmed by memory; but representing it on an abstract and symbolic plane that presents itself as such—this is the strenuousness that underlies the hieroglyphs of *Seeing Things*."[52] If these poems tell the story of a future they foreknow as much as of a past they recount, then Heaney's error in remembering nearly absolves itself.

Nearly. Heaney is both a dreamer and a historian—on the one hand suggesting that language is capable of imagining its own stories while on the other suggesting that the poet retains some agency over what he writes. In a kind of parallel logic, Heaney's straddling the fence between fact and fiction allows Hardy to encompass both personae—the poet of perfect pitch and the sorrowful aged one—at once. It may well be that the poem has brought into being, by accidental misremembrance, Heaney's own ambivalence about who Hardy was as a poet. Heaney writes in an essay about Philip Larkin of Hardy's two characters, saying that later in his career, "Larkin turned to Hardy, the poet of human sadness, rather than to Hardy, the witness of irrational hope."[53] Giving both Hardys credence is just another way for Heaney to explore the question of whether the imagined and the real, the accidental and the planned, reside in the same house. "Squarings," Heaney writes in *The Redress of Poetry*, "is a parable about the way consciousness can be alive to two different and contradictory dimensions of reality and still find a way of negotiating between them."[54] It may well be the case that what Heaney misremembers is simply another dimension of what he calls "reality"—a willed rehearsal of the mind's own sense of truth, admitted through the back door. But the truth of what happens will out—as Heaney is also compelled to acknowledge through his parenthetical confession of getting it wrong.

Heaney treats these categories—the recollected and the imagined—as fluid; in fact, even his corrected version of the Hardy poem rewrites part of the story. The Hardy biography actually says:

> He recalled how, crossing the ewe-leaze when a child, he went on hands and knees and pretended to eat grass in order to see what the sheep would do. Presently he looked up and found them gathered around in a close ring, gazing at him with astonished faces.[55]

It is not hard to note the discrepancies. For one, Florence Hardy explains clearly that the child goes down on all fours "in order to see what the sheep would do"—not, as Heaney suggests, to mitigate his feelings of loneliness. And while in Heaney's version the flock looks on with a dismay linked proleptically to sorrow, the biography's account merely describes the sheep's "astonishment"—hardly a synonym for "dismay." So Heaney's second squaring, like his first, puts projected feeling before fact. This does not make it correct, but it does mean his mistake is a productive one.

Most readers, including myself, can appreciate (if not excuse) these changes, but they also bring to mind the passage I quoted in chapter 6 from Elizabeth Bishop's letters to her friend Robert Lowell about the "mischief" inherent in "mixing fact and fiction." It was wisdom she had learned from none other than Thomas Hardy:

> I can't bear to have you publish something that I regret and that you might live to regret, too. . . . Here is a quotation from dear little Hardy that I copied out years ago—long before DOLPHIN, or even the *Notebooks*, were thought of. It's from a letter written in 1911 . . . "What should certainly be protested against . . . is the mixing of fact and fiction in unknown proportions. Infinite mischief would lie in that. If any statements in the dress of fiction are covertly hinted to be fact, all must be fact, and nothing else but fact, for obvious reasons."[56]

Though Heaney's creative retelling of Hardy's memory is not equivalent to what Bishop cautioned Lowell against (i.e., publishing rewritten versions of private letters between himself and his wife), it may be worth bearing in mind that Hardy himself took a nuanced view toward memory's relation to printed recollection. Not all of Heaney's critics have been cheerful about these two anecdotal poems, despite his gesture of confession. Barbara Hardy quips that Heaney's "revision" is "wittily parenthesized" and ultimately suggests that his errors turn the poet Hardy into a caricature:

> Heaney's correction is complexly inaccurate, because in fact the first sonnet wasn't entirely inaccurate but a misremembering and also a confusion of two stories. The boy Hardy did once lie flat on his back on the ground, looking at the sun through the gaps in a straw hat on his face, and though he didn't start off by miming death, he rose feeling that he didn't want to grow up. It has been suggested to me by Michael Baron that Heaney's first version of Hardy's prone reflections may have been suggested by what Coleridge called a hooked atom, the account in Dorothy Wordsworth's journal of how she and William lay close together in a sheep-field, and William imagined death: "sweet thus to lie so in the grave, to hear the peaceful sounds of the earth and just to know that our dear friends were near." Perhaps not two but three striking stories about the imagination, linked by proneness, stillness and sheep, were rewritten. A poem isn't a thesis, and the errors in fact aren't errors of poetry, but the source-muddled allusion reduces Hardy and promotes a stereotype.[57]

This assessment of Heaney's retelling of the older poet's "experiment in empathy"—that it removes some of the original episode's crucial oddity—may overlook the fact that Heaney seems to be performing his own such experiment on Hardy himself, empathizing with the young boy's curious recalibration (his physical and emotional stance) as his poem puts pressure on the idea of perspective.[58] Her suggestion that Heaney confuses several stories or amalgamates them into one—with Wordsworth's own prone encounter in a sheep field at the center—is very convincing. And yet her conclusion, that these elisions promote a stereotype, appears to fall on the wrong side of mistake. That is, she claims that while Heaney's misremembering mars the poem, it is not an "error[ ] of poetry." But poetry does not have to be a thesis to contain or accommodate mistake. I would suggest the opposite: Heaney's misremembering is exactly an error of poetry—but it doesn't mar the poem.

One reason why Heaney gets away with his mistakes, beyond his openly recognizing them, is his sophistication in turning mistake into something poetically useful. Corcoran has accounted for this deft handling in his discussion of how Heaney makes memory "act restoratively within language and form":

> "Squarings" is a series of hymns to portent and concentration. . . . The geometry of the sequence is, then, the plotting of a graph of the trajectory in which portent and concentration become self-aware enough to articulate themselves; a process in which, as poem xi has it, "accident got tricked into accuracy," in which desire exceeds restraint, achievement catches up with intimation, reach coincides with grasp in poems lucidly mobile with their own meanings. In this sense, these poems are interestingly read in the light of Gaston Bachelard's observation that "it is not until late in life that we really revere an image, when we discover that its roots plunge well beyond the history that is fixed in our memories."[59]

To plunge, as Bachelard describes, beyond the history memory offers up could mean introducing mistakes or simply imagining a separate world out of fixed recollections. Heaney allows for both possibilities, but the "accuracy" accident becomes is crucially not the accuracy of a historian. Language, for Heaney, has an inherent power that may give access to histories "beyond" those "fixed in our memories": words can be sites where things or ideas are born, not merely represented or seconded. This is an idea he explicitly associates with Hardy in a different poem, "The Birthplace," published long before "Squarings" was conceived. Its third and final section concludes:

> Still, was it thirty years ago.
> I read until first light
>
> for the first time, to finish
> *The Return of the Native?*
> The corncrake in the aftergrass

> verified himself, and I heard
> roosters and dogs, the very same
> as if he had written them.[60]

Again Heaney turns to the corncrake, a small bird that commonly builds its nest in hayfields, to help link his own rural experience with that of another writer (his Glanmore sonnet about William and Dorothy Wordsworth begins with "the cuckoo and the corncrake"). Here the bird's self-verification aids the poet in his own process of realizing other "givens" like roosters and dogs, which come less from the reality to which they belong than from the otherworld of language from which that reality suddenly seems drawn. The poem begins with a visit to Hardy's literal birthplace in Dorset but ends in the figurative; by giving elements of life the stamp of veracity through their "sameness" to the images and sounds Hardy creates in his novel, Heaney locates the birthplace of memory in language itself. Bernard O'Donoghue has called these lines "an extraordinary declaration of the priority of writing and verbal form over event," pointing out that "not only spoken language but the reality it refers to loses its signifying priority over the written."[61] If it is a declaration about verbal form, it is likewise a self-fulfilling prophecy with regard to his own work. When he later arrives at "Squarings," he has already established the way words can mean more than facts: it is Hardy who teaches him this lesson and Hardy's life that furnishes him, in the later poems, with the recorded history on which to test it out.

Hardy appears again in *Electric Light* (2001) in a poem called "The Loose Box," which, as its title suggests, begins in a literal open stable (a "loose box" is an enclosed space where horses do not need to be tied and can move around freely) but soon moves to the metaphorical possibilities of such a place. The second section of the poem suggests that talking about a loose box (or indeed any aspect of land) offers the poet

> a purchase come by
> By pacing it in words that make you feel
> You've found your feet in what "surefooted" means
> And in the ground of your own understanding—[62]

The feet of the horse and the feet of the poem work in tandem here; real stables and mental stability connect by multiple puns in the words of a poet who wants to signal that poems themselves, with their stanza-rooms, can be their own versions of a loose box. Across his books, Heaney makes much of the connection between his family's farming background and his vocation as a poet, but here the corroboration between physical space and human "understanding" is brought to bear on Irish politics through wordplay and associative misdirection—or what Heaney calls the "must and drift of talk about the loose box."[63] The fourth, penultimate section of the poem begins with the pun on stable and uses Hardy once again to emphasize how memory of the printed word can be linked to actual experience—indeed replaces such experience in the mind of a child for whom words can be as powerful as events:

> Stable child, grown stabler when I read
> In adolescence Thomas *dolens* Hardy—
> Not, oddly enough, his Christmas Eve night-piece
> About the oxen in their bedded stall,
> But the threshing scene in *Tess of the D'Urbervilles*—
> That magnified my soul.[64]

What Hardy's language offers the child here is a screen on which to place his own memories—words that cause his own experience to come "flowing back" in a different form.[65] Barbara Hardy again takes issue, complaining he "appropriates rather than appreciates" Hardy:

> Heaney's memory takes over the threshing, in more ways than one. The poet inserts his italicized Latin between the novelist's given and family names, but his version, which may or may not elide his reading with his actual farming experience, ignores the way in which the book and the passage are dolorous.[66]

But the critic Hardy's concern over Heaney's "eliding" the memory of his own childhood with the language of the novel does not take into account Heaney's underlying ambivalence in this and other poems about how to turn actual experience into language that *means* in a universal sense. To ask for fact (appreciation without appropriation) in a poem that takes as its subject "the must and drift of talk" is to miss the context of the poem-as-*loose*-box. Heaney is aware of what gets lost in such translations—indeed, he is scrupulous elsewhere in admitting his own mistakes and misremem-berings—but he is also honest about his susceptibility to being drawn to-ward them. The linguistic play and associative drift that characterizes this poem in particular is Heaney's way of conveying the foreknowledge of language over history in certain circumstances. Reading—whether Hardy's *Tess* or the biography of the Irish revolutionary Michael Collins (the "text" Heaney sets against childhood memory in the final section of the poem)—counterintuitively carries the poet away from fact and opens up a world of recollected experience that sees language itself, more than event, as its source. Whether Heaney means for Hardy to preside over this process across multiple poems is difficult to know, but his presence in them helps contextualize his self-confessed mistake in "Squarings."

Because Heaney is comfortable with the foreknowledge of language di-recting his poetic line, he is also willing to concede that memory—despite being a record of the past—cannot be composed without a longed-for fu-ture associated with it. The opposite is also true, as the last poem in "Squar-ings" attests: "what's come upon is manifest / Only in light of what has been gone through."[67] With past and future so inexorably linked, memory becomes less a recorded history than a lens through which to process expe-rience on all levels. Misremembering also becomes a lens, not of experience per se, but of the feeling of *un*knowing it, which for Heaney is not neces-sarily a bad thing. Two poems in the middle of the sequence try to articu-late experience's "shifting tenses"[68]—a term that enlists the rhetoric of lan-guage to describe the feeling of time—by portraying felt time as constantly in flux:

> I was four but I turned four hundred maybe
> Encountering the ancient dampish feel
> Of a clay floor. Maybe four thousand even.[69]

These lines, which remember from childhood the feeling of entering an old building, elide the experience of a four-year-old with the place's first occupants. It is less a poem about an actual event than a poem about an inheritance that *doesn't* change over time:

> Out of that earth house I inherited
> A stack of singular, cold memory-weights
> To load me, hand and foot, in the scale of things.[70]

Whatever the weight of memory, it operates in balance here with what the present and future have to offer. Heaney is not explicit about whether or not the scale is tipped in one direction, but he makes it clear that past and future are always understood in relation to each other. The poem that follows it similarly puts poetry at the intersection of recollection and anticipation:

> Sand-bed, they said. And gravel-bed. Before
> I knew river shallows or river pleasures
> I knew the ore of longing in those words.
>
> The places I go back to have not failed
> But will not last. Waist-deep in cow-parsley
> I re-enter the swim, riding or quelling
>
> The very currents memory is composed of,
> Everything accumulated ever[71]

The longing Heaney describes in these opening lines is not a particular longing but rather an innate sense that what is remembered is preparatory in some way—always keeping an eye toward the future. The "ore" of longing, with its pun, simultaneously wishes for what was and will be. Heaney complicates this feeling by acknowledging that places themselves do not last—perhaps because places in this context are always "composed" and therefore subject to the changeable conditions of recollection and its contingent human experience. Heaney also puns on memory's "currents," which flow in various directions but always rely on the present to come into being. Partly for this reason, many of the words in this poem are compound words—accumulations of a language that knows things that the speaker of it may realize only after the fact. Memory can be discovered in the future as well as in the past.

And so one thing "Squarings" offers beyond the specifics of particular memories and narratives is an account of how seen or known things turn themselves into unseen but longed-for things. In this sense, the whole series lends itself to misreading and misremembering historical events in order to construe them into the facts we wish for, or could use: it is language that wants to play itself into reality. Heaney is toying with his own memories, treating them like playthings out of which poems rise. The poem beginning "I misremembered" could be less of a confession than a statement of prior (if not consciously known) intent. Misremembering is something poets do because it is something everybody does; but because part of what poets also do is conjure alternate realities into being, their mismemories necessarily compose the future even as they compromise the past. Robert Pinsky, an American poet and near contemporary of Heaney's, has said that misremembering lines from beloved poems for him amounts to receiving a "creative writing lesson" from the original poet, simply because what a reader mistakenly attributes to a poem underscores desires and designs on the part of the original poet that can never be fully anticipated by the reader, who brings to the poem his own needs and desires.[72] Christopher Ricks similarly hypothesizes in an essay on "Matthew Arnold, Walter Pater and misquotation" that the line between criticism and creation can be difficult to distinguish—that there is often something disturbingly creative, or creatively disturbing, about a critic's misremembering what another writer has said or written.[73] Both Pinsky and Ricks notice how the impulse of longing—for what one lacks, or requires—feeds into creative production; this impulse is for Heaney a seemingly arbitrary one (I write "seemingly" because impulse, like intention, may have origins in unconscious desire). Heaney writes of the structure of "Squarings":

> The 12-line form felt arbitrary but it seemed to get me places swiftly. So I went with it, a sort of music of the arbitrary that's unpredictable, and can still up and catch a glimpse of a subject out of the blue. There's a phrase I use, "make impulse one with wilfulness": the wilfulness is in the 12 lines, the impulse in the freedom and shimmer and on-the-wingness.[74]

Heaney describes a willingness to be led by unaccounted-for impulse—to follow one's nose. If the form of the poem represents its given, then its subject matter constitutes what the mind will make of such arbitrary gifts. Willfulness in this equation is less about deliberate choice than surrender to gut feeling, associative drift, and creative mismemory. Heaney fundamentally understands that surrendering has its perks. Ricks has also written of Heaney's work in particular that, "like the acrobat half-feigning a faltering Heaney's poems often tremble with the possibilities of misconstruing and misconstruction which they openly provide but which only a predator would pounce upon."[75] His point is not that misconstruction isn't to be found in these poems, but rather that Heaney on some level courts such falterings—partly because he knows they are productive, and partly because he believes them to be as authentic and unavoidable as all impulses are.

It follows that for Heaney, the poet's task necessarily involves trusting the reader not to misconstrue misconstruction. Misrememberings do not have to be fatal to the poem, but they should at least be genuinely born of impulse or accident. In his essay "Feeling into Words," Heaney comments that

> [a] poem always has elements of accident about it, which can be made the subject of inquest afterwards, but there is always a risk in conducting your own inquest: you might begin to believe the coroner in yourself rather than put your trust in the man in you who is capable of the accident.[76]

According to Heaney's formulation, readers interested in poets' mistakes act out the role of the coroner. But Heaney does not object to the profession so much as he objects to the possibility of a poet's performing the duty on himself (which is perfectly reasonable, given the metaphor). As coroners, we must content ourselves with knowing that the poet may never have consciously intended what we encounter as we read. Likewise, we can never be sure if what we suspect to be accidental in the poem is premeditated or whether it has simply hardened into what Corcoran calls "accuracy" after the fact. This burden of unknowing importantly belongs to us, not the poet, and constitutes one of the most salient aspects of what it feels like to read poetry.

Heaney mostly absolves himself from the problem of misremembering by believing in the power it has to transform language into its own type of experience. But where he runs into trouble, if we can call mistake "trouble," is in the misrepresentation of fact as it pertains, not to his own memory, but to the memories or experiences of others. In these instances—as in his "(mistake)" on "windermere district" or his misremembering Hardy's biography—his conscience overrides his willingness to follow poetry's inherent "on-the-wingness." Accident turning into accuracy is what Heaney wishes for even as he battles his own sense of right and wrong as determined by fact alone. He describes the beginnings of "Squarings" in these terms during an interview with Dennis O'Driscoll:

> The title of the first section, "Lightenings," arrived by accident, when I found a dictionary entry that gives it to mean "a flaring of the spirit at the moment before death." And there were also the attendant meanings of being unburdened and being illuminated, all of which fitted what was going on as the first poems got written. The one about the boat in the air above Clonmacnoise, for example. Or the ones about Thomas Hardy as a child, on his back among a flock of sheep, gazing up at the heavens.[77]

It is clear from these comments that Heaney especially values the role accident plays in determining both the language for and direction of these poems. "Lightenings" strikes him suddenly as the appropriate term for poems that were already coming into being, and his passing remark about the Hardy poems confirms that, despite his admission, the first poem, with its misremembering of Hardy's position in relation to the sheep, remains for him the lasting record of the event.

Heaney's long-standing interest in how accident propels itself into poetry may seem to weaken the case for mistake within his work (accident and mistake are distinct, after all)—but he carefully maintains a distinction between both the imaginative play that occasionally finds itself at odds with fact and the more serious instances of misremembering that require some form of redress. He quotes with admiration Wallace Stevens's line "the imagination presses back against the pressure of reality" to characterize how he conceives of his own processes of composition, particularly with reference to his task of writing poems in the face of violence in Ireland.[78] But he simultaneously valorizes poetry's morality, which for him is never wholly disconnected from truth, or "what happens"; answering the question "What has poetry taught you?" in an interview, his reply straddles both sides of the fence:

> That there's such a thing as truth and it can be told—slant; that subjectivity is not to be theorized away and is worth defending; that poetry itself has virtue, in the first sense of possessing a quality of moral excellence and in the sense also of possessing inherent strength by reason of its sheer made-upness, its *integritas, consonantia,* and *claritas.*[79]

This Dickinsonian approach to truth—as we have already seen in the case of Dickinson herself—is an ambivalent one; it must encompass "moral excellence" even as it makes itself up within the poem. Heaney is importantly not defending mistake here, only subjectivity, which offers him an escape route from the "pressures" reality places on poems that would or might go elsewhere.

Heaney's subjectivity is also what keeps him separate from Wordsworth and Hardy. It should be no surprise that Heaney feels compelled to confess his misremembering when it reconstitutes Hardy's experience rather than his own. Perhaps he feels more license to misremember his own history into vision than that of another writer. Significantly, in both of the published mistakes discussed in this chapter, the events Heaney misremembers are themselves memories from childhood—that is, he does not simply bungle Wordsworth and Hardy's life events, he bungles their memories of those events—whose relation to fact may be unquantifiable. Riffing on the memories of others is naturally a more dubious business than turning one's own mismemories into something poetically "accurate."

There may be other factors beyond a faithfulness to subjective experience at play in Heaney's willingness to err and also his contrition when doing so infringes upon other people's stories. Mistake as a persona-making, character-building device is critical to several of Heaney's poems: it sometimes helps him strike the right note between pretension and condescension. (This is related to, but slightly different from, the "feign[ed] faltering"

Ricks notices in the poems of *Field Work*.)[80] O'Donoghue has written persuasively about this function of mistake in the elegies of Heaney's "Clearances" sequence, which explicitly make use of grammatical errors to absolve him of seeming highfalutin in the eyes of his own mother:

> I'd *naw* and *aye*
> And decently relapse into the wrong
> Grammar which kept us allied and at bay.[81]

The right grammar for the poet to use here is also the wrong one. As O'Donoghue points out, getting his words wrong in his mother's presence amounts to keeping allied with her even in the face of his increasingly distancing professional vocation.[82] "Fear of affectation made her affect / Inadequacy," Heaney says at the beginning of this sonnet. In these poems, he mostly employs the trick himself—not just to pay his respects and remain close to her but also to avoid the affectation that mourning, as a poetical mode, can take. Mistake here is one of the strategies Heaney uses to keep both the reader and his own grief "at bay." In an earlier sonnet in the sequence, he imitates his mother's voice directly, incorporating her grammar into the sonnet's higher register:

> Sandwich and tea scone
> Were present and correct. In case it run,
> The butter must be kept out of the sun.
> And don't be dropping crumbs. Don't tilt your chair.
> Don't reach. Don't point. Don't make noise when you stir.[83]

Almost as if to explain in advance the subjunctive grammar of the verb "run," Heaney describes the table in terms of its own propriety: "present and correct."

Heaney's toeing the line between wrong and right in "Clearances" may also have something to do with how he thinks about his own Irishness with regard to social class and English-Irish relations. In these elegies, he is careful to present grammatical mistake within the context of a cultural inheritance of which he is proud, and he refers to such an inheritance in various ways throughout his writing life. For example, during a keynote address at a conference in Cork, he recounted an anecdote about two Irish schoolboys suspected of plagiarism. According to the story, the schoolmaster concocted a plan to find out which boy was cheating: after assigning both boys an essay titled "The Swallow," he allowed them to sit next to each other for a few minutes before separating them for the duration of the assignment. The studious boy produced a long essay on the characteristics of swallows, beginning by pointing out that "the swallow is a migratory bird" and then continuing in this vein for several pages. By contrast, the plagiarist's essay contained just two sentences: "The swallow is a migratory bird. He have a roundy head." Heaney uses this story (according to the journalist who recorded it) to describe the "clash between the formal correctness of textbook English and the faulty grammar of [what he called] 'the resurrected afterlife of the Irish,'" suggesting that the charmingly rogue plagiarist had in fact written a succinct "two-sentence history of Anglo-Irish literature."[84] What makes the second sentence of the boy's essay mistaken is also what makes it fundamentally Irish—and, as such, a fitting protest of the limitations imposed by English grammar on children with a richer literary heritage than the textbooks might suggest. For Heaney, the wildly different registers of the boy's two adjacent sentences testify to complex differences between England and Ireland, urban and rural life, and central and peripheral literary traditions. They also remind him and his audience that "wrong" and "right" can coexist.

Their coexistence in "Squarings" is perhaps that sequence's most lasting impression. Its eighth poem—the one that immediately follows his Hardy confession—is well placed to comment upon its lesson about historical facts and misremembering:

VIII

The annals say: when the monks of Clonmacnoise
Were all at prayers inside the oratory
A ship appeared above them in the air.

The anchor dragged along behind so deep
It hooked itself into the altar rails
And then, as the big hull rocked to a standstill,

A crewman shinned and grappled down the rope
And struggled to release it. But in vain.
"This man can't bear our life here and will drown,"

The abbot said, "unless we help him." So
They did, the freed ship sailed, and the man climbed back
Out of the marvellous as he had known it.[85]

Like the Hardy poems, this story of a marvel centers on the issue of perspective. The "marvellous" here is also the ordinary. To the praying monks,
a floating ship and descending man represent a heavenly vision; but to the
descending man, it is the monks who are "marvellous." So, too, in the two
Hardy poems, perspective comes from different directions, and Heaney is
reluctant to prioritize one over the other. There is Hardy himself, gazing at
the sheep eye to eye; there are the sheep, gazing back; and there is Heaney,
also gazing—but looking forward, imagining Hardy less as he was than as
he would become, and what that future might mean in terms of his own
way of "seeing things." As O'Donoghue puts it, "the marvellous is what is
seen to be marvellous."[86]

This point could equally apply to facts and mistakes. What happens, at
least in poems, depends on how we experience (or remember) what happens. Heaney celebrates the power of subjectivity, but he also understands
the nuance involved in making subjective experience the primary arbiter
of narrated event. At the same time that he affirms the capability of the
individual imagination, he also calls into question the perilously creative
depths of mismemory, noting slyly in an interview about the Clonmacnoise
poem that

[t]he story was unforgettable: it's there in Kenneth Hurlstone Jackson's *A Celtic Miscellany*, but the version I have is a bit different because I misremembered some of the details. In the original, the boat's
anchor "came right down on to the floor of the church," whereas I
have it hooking on to the altar rails—somehow it enters miraculously
through the roof and the crewman shins down a rope into the sanctu-
ary. That wasn't a deliberate alteration, although I'm sure the image

in the first "Lightenings" poem of an unroofed wallstead and an unroofed world must have prompted it.[87]

Heaney takes this opportunity to set the record straight even as he declares
his poem to be a legitimate version of the story. The phrase "I misremembered" circles back here to involve not only Hardy's history but also other
written sources. The pun in this half-confession, half-affirmation—Heaney's
insistence that his inserting an "altar" into the story "wasn't a deliberate
*alter*ation"—retains the playful spirit of accident and reminds us how powerful the unconscious intentions of the poet can be. "I wanted to affirm,"
Heaney says about this poem in his essay "The Frontiers of Writing," "that
within our individual selves we can reconcile two orders of knowledge
which we might call the practical and the poetic; to affirm also that each
form of knowledge redresses the other and that the frontier between them
is there for the crossing."[88] In light of Heaney's tending to the distinction
between practical and poetic knowledge, we might note that this poem
begins with reference to a written history—"The annals say"—when in fact
the annals *don't* say exactly this. Perhaps the annals never do say, or never
can say, with absolute certainty.

That the poet and the poem are mistaken could be a truth more comforting than it initially seems. Mistakes happen and rarely ruin whole poems.
Heaney's modest affirmations of them—including his misremembering and
subsequent confessions—are reminders that poetry occurs in and around
truth. Denying Heaney's mistakes about Wordsworth and Hardy would
also deny him the truths these mistakes evoke. In this book's first chapter,
I described an inadvertent grammatical mistake in Wordsworth's lines
about a deceased "boy of Winander," whose shock of mild surprise "has
carried far into his heart" nature's sublimity despite such a carrying being
temporally impossible. In this chapter, I explore the ways that Heaney, always under Wordsworth's spell, understands such mistaking as a fundamen-
tal principle of poetic composition. Quoting lines by Zbigniew Herbert in
The Government of the Tongue, Heaney says,

The poem makes us feel that we should prefer moral utterance to
palliative imagery, but it does exactly that, makes us *feel*, and by

means of feeling carries truth alive into the heart—exactly as the Romantics said it should.[89]

Moral utterance, which involves truth in some capacity, and the "palliative imagery" of poetry, which often prefers vision to "what happens," are two sides of the same poem. In saying so, Heaney also happens to be remembering and reappropriating a line from the "Preface to *Lyrical Ballads*," where Wordsworth writes of "truth . . . carried alive into the heart," a phrase that may well reflect Wordsworth's own remembrance—or misremembrance— of the very line in "There was a boy" with which I began this study.[90] Heaney is more interested in what poetry carries forward than what it leaves behind. Mistake is one vehicle for such carrying forward. As I have tried to emphasize throughout this book, it is usually worth noting the means by which we have arrived.

Mistaking on Purpose

This book has moved from a grammatical mistake in Wordsworth's lines about a boy of Winander to Heaney's mistaking Windermere, the modern name for Winander, for a different lake in the life of the boy Wordsworth. In each chapter, I have considered the circumstances surrounding a mistake or set of mistakes committed by a poet whose writing I admire. I have been led in this process by my belief that it is both more natural and more enriching to do so than not. One of my suggestions throughout has been that readers can get closer to poets and poems by knowing when they are wrong rather than by insisting that they are right. I have argued that poets usually wish to be treated as craftspeople as much as mystics (the former being vulnerable to mistake, the latter magically immune from it); we can tell so from the ways they scrutinize their own compositional practices within a broader culture that continues to understand mistaking as a phenomenon to avoid. Relating artists and literary critics, David Bromwich has written:

> There are so many ways of being bad. To recognize the skill with which the artist averts them all is to realize as Coleridge once said that in depth of judgment every true artist is already a critic. The miracle of great art is to look as if the right way through the labyrinth of error was inevitable.[1]

True artists are their own best critics. But for readers still willing to have a go, the miracle of great criticism may involve recognizing that the labyrinth of error is itself sometimes inevitable, that in many great poems there is no right way through, and that, in any case, error need not preclude greatness. Critics must be willing to concede that greatness does not always avert badness. Discovering a poet's journey through the "labyrinth of error"—regardless of whether he or she makes it out the other side—is one of the pleasures of reading.

Even so, it would be wrong to deny that poets, including several considered in this book, frequently suggest in their poems as well as in their prose that mistakes can make poems better. Hardy, in spite of his insistence on fact, writes in his notebooks about the advisability of producing "dissonances" and "irregularities" within otherwise metrically even verse because they "give more charm than strict conformities": "Ars est celare artem," he points out—to conceal art is art.[2] For Hardy, the mistake would be too much evenness rather than the other way around. His "irregularities" may be purposeful, but even unintended mistakes can prove beneficial, as W. H. Auden discovered when Faber misprinted one of the lines of his poem "Journey to Iceland":

And the traveller hopes: "Let me be far from any
Physician"; And the ports have names for the sea;[3]

Writing to his friend Christopher Isherwood, Auden clarifies:

Thank you for your letter. No, you were wrong. I did not write: "the *ports* have names for the sea" but "the *poets* have names for the sea." However, as so often before, the mistake seems better than the original idea, so I'll leave it.[4]

Letters from Iceland accordingly preserves both the misprint as well as Auden's explanatory note to Isherwood, giving his readers a sense not only that unintended mistakes can be better than initial conceptions but also that they are worth acknowledging; for Auden, a description of how the mistake came about merits an appearance in the book alongside the mistake itself. (In later editions of his poetry, Auden silently emends the line to "every port has its name for the sea.")[5] John Fuller has proposed that "port" is better than "poet" "[b]ecause to ascribe human agency to a thing and not to a person requires greater imagination in the reader."[6] His assessment of Auden's decision rings a Hart-Cranian note and suggests that readerly imagination is always at play in meaning. But Auden may have had other reasons: perhaps reappropriating the printer's mistake, consciously making use of it, was one way to regain control of a compositional process that felt out of his hands. In other words, Auden possibly preferred "ports" *because* it was wrong.

A mistake like "ports," when acknowledged and subsequently accepted, ceases to be one. It was never really Auden's mistake anyway, only his publisher's. (Another beautiful and famous line probably created by a lucky printer's error has forever lifted the reputation of the Renaissance playwright and poet Thomas Nashe: "Brightnesse falls from the ayre," the lovely figure Joyce plays upon in *Portrait of the Artist as a Young Man*, was likely a misprint for the more literal "Brightnesse falls from the hayre"—arguably less profound, if easier to picture.)[7] By bringing his poem's typographical error to the fore, Auden—like other poets who turn error into a subject in its own right—deliberately casts a shadow of doubt over his readers' belief in poetry's inalienable rightness. The poetry that comes out of mistake is surely a testament to error's abiding presence, not its lack. In these closing pages I rest my case on a few examples where mistake becomes an explicit feature, if not the point, of the verse. Mistakes can be full of treasure—especially when they bring material to the poem that would otherwise be inaccessible (as was the case with the African material Bishop drew from the "wrong" magazine). And mistakes certainly have much to offer interpretation, as the readings throughout this book show. Critics are not only drawn to errors in the texts about which they write but also, as Alexander Freer has noted, to mistakes and omissions in the criticism surrounding them.[8] Wrongness breeds scholarship. Frank Kermode, a meticulous and unerring critic himself, remarks in an essay that "[t]he history of interpretation . . . is to an incalculable extent a history of error."[9] In saying so he aligns critics and writers, giving the example of the seventeenth-century metaphysical poet Henry Vaughan, whom he accuses of misinterpreting the Bible in his poem "The Night." "It is easy to see," writes Kermode, "that Vaughan distorts the original, yet few would deny that this is a great poem."[10] Kermode titles his essay "The Uses of Error" and subsequently gives that title to the collection of essays to which it belongs—implying that errors of interpretation on the part of readers can healthily coincide with "ambiguit[ies]" and "antithetical senses" within the literature they read and love. "We have always been pretty sure that literal sense is not enough, and when we try to go beyond it we may err, but sometimes splendidly," he writes.[11] Poets have always known this and often err splendidly. That many are willing to say so in poems should come as no surprise. Their willingness to concede error and to use it productively should suggest to critics how crucial mistakes are to the process of making—and also the loss we incur when we needlessly gloss over them or justify them away.

If mistaking has a history as long as poetry itself, many of the occasions on which poets purposefully write about their own mistakes are contemporary. Perhaps this is because our epoch has been nourished by psychoanalytic principles that persuasively unbottle the relation between mistake and need; today's poets may be more comfortable recording and incorporating their own errors because they understand them to be connected to unfulfilled or repressed desires. Or perhaps our poets simply write for a public they trust will understand. Whatever the reason, the private, prone-to-mistake self behind the poem feels more accessible today than ever before, highlighted especially in the confessional posture of poems that admit to their own accidents, inefficacies, and unconscious motives. For instance, in a poem that comments on the smears and smudges of "action painting," Robert Hass notes, "The typo would be 'paining.'"[12] By ushering the specter of Freudian parapraxis into his line, Hass turns a small, easy slip of the keyboard into a psychological exploration. The meaning of his imagined typo reverberates: we are to deduce from it that making something, whether with paint or with words, can be as painful as it is rewarding. His line does not constitute an actual mistake—Hass's slip is both purposeful and only conditional ("The typo *would be* paining")—but it reminds his reader how mistake and creativity might occasionally cooperate for the good of the poem rather than to its detriment. Dan Chiasson makes a similar move:

> I did it, though my lungs hurt,
> though my lungs felt sandpapered after.
> I almost wrote "sadpapered" there; isn't it weird
> the way the mind works, . . .[13]

What accident, or presumed accident, unexpectedly brings into this poem (spoken by a circus elephant) becomes more important to it than the actual words it records. As Brunella Antomarini points out in her book *Thinking through Error*, "a chance error can have *positive* results. Sometimes what we call an 'error' is not an error, neither before we make it (because we think it is the correct choice) nor after (because it turns into its contrary)."[14] Like Hass's "paining," Chiasson's suppressed but leaked mistake "sadpapered" describes the feeling of the poem more accurately than the intended word. These poets are acknowledging and exploiting the creative potential of unforced error; neither makes any real mistake, but by using error productively, both suggest its plausibility in their work.

Other poems use and transform the mistakes of others, as in James Merrill's "Days of 1964," whose narrative about the poet's inheriting his grandmother's old apartment in New York turns on somebody else's mistake:

Today's memo from the Tenants' Committee deplores
Even the ongoing deterioration
Of the *widows* in our building.[15]

The committee's inadvertent typo allows Merrill a pun that later brings his poem to its point: "My grandmother—an easy-to-see-through / Widow by the time she died—made it my own. / Bless her good sense."[16] The poet understands here the psychoanalytic possibilities for meaning bound up in errors of language. In the manner of a mind voicing unconscious desires through parapraxes, Merrill's poem uses error to propel itself forward without seeming overly sentimental.[17] Robert Lowell likewise takes advantage of error's ironic plausibility and psychological relevance at the end of "Sailing Home from Rapallo" when, traveling back to America from Italy with his mother's corpse, he notices that

In the grandiloquent lettering on Mother's coffin,
Lowell had been misspelled *LOVEL*.[18]

This mistake imparts upon language an autonomy that momentarily relieves the poet of his duty to compose (and stay composed); for Lowell, the comedy of error becomes a way of getting at inexpressible love.

Highlighting the capacity mistake has for improving poems, as these and other poets do, may seem to run counter to the argument of this book. Ending among such examples certainly puts my contention that mistakes should be considered *mistaken* on shaky ground. I have taken care to point out the extent to which poets have erred according to their own parameters for truth or accuracy, hypothesizing in each case about the regret they likely would have felt had they learned of their own transgressions. In the two cases I include where poets were made aware of their mistakes, Browning innocently denies any knowledge of the word he wrongly used, and Bishop glumly remarks that her misdated magazine should have included a footnote. If mistake were something only to be celebrated, such regret would surely seem either disingenuous or out of place. And yet my sense is that, in using their own errors to improve or deepen their work, poets also concede that mistaking exists within poetry's broader remit regardless of whether or not they mean to do it. Such an idea is central to my purpose too. Mistakes can be wrong and also valid or apropos. In fact, there is an appealing paradox underlying many poets' faith in mistake as being somehow integral to their process, as Anne Carson suggests in her poem titled "Essay on What I Think About Most":

> what we are engaged in when we do poetry is error,
> the willful creation of error,
> the deliberate break and complication of mistakes
> out of which may arise
> unexpectedness.[19]

Here what is broken is also the fix. One of Carson's aims—"unexpectedness"—justifies her "creation of error." Her method is similar to that of many contemporary poets, who often consciously write against the grain of traditional lyric in order to frustrate expectations about what poetry looks like and how it works. Nerys Williams, in her book about several writers of the L=A=N=G=U=A=G=E school (including Charles Bernstein, Michael Palmer, and Lyn Hejinian), points out that these poets "share a mistrust of poetry as a mastery of form, and the linguistic indeterminacy of their poetry could be read as a strategy safeguarding against the dangers of an authoritarian rhetoric."[20] She suggests that a poet's "erring" and a reader's "errancy," which she defines as wandering through the text in a way that makes productive use of error, defends against the notion that poetry must be accurate or represent any one thing.[21] But purposeful errancy, or wandering, in this sense—which angles toward a kind of compositional freedom—is far from the literal definition of mistake as a "misconception of the meaning of something." Williams proposes that error "offers us a possibility of countering literary history's tendency to define the contemporary lyric as a static model of personal expression."[22] She and the contemporary poets she admires read and write erringly, but they do so intentionally—not by mistake. Unintended mistakes in poetry, as manifest in most of the examples I have described in this book, necessarily work against conscious forms of expression. This does not make them uninteresting to readers, but it does make them fundamentally different from more purposeful forms of errancy, including Carson's in the poem I have quoted above. Carson's position—that errors are what give rise to poetry's necessary unexpectedness—does not try to obviate the problem of will. Even as she celebrates error's creation, she concedes its twin aspect of intentionality, suggesting that the particular sort of error she imagines in and *as* her poem remains distinct from what I have been identifying, throughout these chapters, as unintended mistake. To break something willfully is not to err, exactly—though the effect it produces could perhaps be called error. In this formulation, erring and mistaking may well be opposed.

From the above examples alone, it should be clear that many poets would at least prefer to think about mistakes in positive terms. Given the prevalence of mistaking even in excellent poetry, it is easy to understand why. But poets' acknowledgment of the virtues of mistake should not be taken as permission by critics to read poetry's wrongs as rights. Rather, when poets openly appreciate mistake, they articulate the value of an element of form they see as inevitable and therefore intrinsic to the making of their art. And so celebrating mistakes is not the same thing as disqualifying mistakenness as a category. In fact the opposite is true: when poets highlight their capacity for—and interest in—mistake, they also cement mistake as a firm possibility and a facet worthy of their readers' acknowledgment. As we attend to their mistakes, we might remember that inevitability is not the same thing as intentionality. Mistakes may be a forgone conclusion, but they still constitute flaws regardless of whether or not poets or readers find them appealing. A mole can be appreciated as a mark of beauty and still be a mole.

There are certain errant, or digressive, styles of poetry, especially from the last hundred years, that may still seem to resist the category of mistaking I have been laying out in these pages. Identifying unintentional mistakes in poems that advertise their own unintentionality—poems that bring their own accidents and contingencies to the fore—may appear an impossible task, or at any rate a too risky one. John Ashbery's work offers a prime example: his first book includes a poem titled "Errors" that makes no explicit mention of any, implying that errors may well pervade the whole:

> Jealousy. Whispered weather reports.
> In the street we found boxes
> Littered with snow, to burn at home.
> What flower tolling on the waters
> You stupefied me.[23]

Ashbery's fine-tuned sense of colloquial speech here—his characteristic way of keeping meaning at bay without sacrificing tenor or tone—makes these lines hard to paraphrase. One can readily see how they might subscribe to the broad category of "error"—jealousy is usually a mistake, weather reports are nearly always wrong, and so on—but it might also be an error to limit their ways of signifying based on that title alone. The word "Errors" merely qualifies what comes after it in some way—as all titles qualify the poems they presume to label in this way or that. Ashbery is interested in turning up the unexpected valences of words by enacting seemingly unwarranted collisions (e.g., "What flower tolling on the waters / You stupefied me."). It would be fruitless to fault the grammar here, not because it is correct (surely it isn't) but because grammar is precisely not the point. "Poetry," Ashbery once said, "is even freer than the visual arts to make up its own universe and then make up the laws that govern it."[24] The effect for him has priority over the means, or in some cases *is* the means. Dan Chiasson writes in the *New Yorker* that Ashbery's "poems conjure a massive mental errata slip made up of what they almost say and nearly mean" and that his style "prizes such mistakes and misapprehensions, as though looking for the word on the tip of the tongue."[25] Misapprehensions might well be the more accurate way of describing what some readers have felt to be sloppiness in Ashbery's language; for instance, Terence Killeen, in an otherwise admiring essay published in the *Irish Times* shortly after Ashbery's death, notes that the poet was

> quite capable of misusing words: in the poem And Socializing he refers to "cohorts" when he means companions (a very common error—this is the sub-editor in me coming out) and in the long poem And the Stars Were Shining he refers to something being "remonstrably a cause" when he clearly means "demonstrably" (there is no such word as "remonstrably"). One might put that down to a typo were it not that there are so many other examples of what can only be called malapropisms throughout the work.[26]

It may be the case that such "malapropisms" are part and parcel of the idiom of a poet who has pointed out in his critical writings that spoken language and written language are fundamentally "at odds": "the spoken language," Ashbery clarifies, "is the one I use when I write poetry."[27] Elsewhere he praises the "imperfection" of poets like John Clare, and in his poem "The Bungalows," he addresses a "you" who "avoided / The monotony of perfection by leaving in certain flaws."[28] The possibility of there being purposeful flaws and errors in every poem is an appealing act of resistance against mistake (as a category) that also manages to celebrate it. For Ashbery, being boring is much worse than being wrong.

But let us not close the case of Ashbery (and other recalcitrant poets like him) too soon. Does leaving in certain flaws *on purpose* necessarily preclude the existence of others that are less purposeful? Do the "laws that govern" the universe *never* apply to such poets? Ashbery's is a tricky and therefore ideal example—and where better to test it than in the opening line of his best-loved and most-anthologized poem, "Self-Portrait in a Convex Mirror"? His long, ekphrastic meditation on a sixteenth-century painting by Francesco Parmigianino of the same title begins with the following words:

> As Parmigianino did it, the right hand
> Bigger than the head . . .[29]

But anyone who has looked at Parmigianino's well-known painting could see that this isn't quite right. The hand depicted there is in fact not Parmigianino's right hand but his left one—reversed in the portrait by the properties of the convex mirror at which he stares in order to paint it. What Ashbery sees when he looks at the picture is Parmigianino's reflection, "of which the portrait," he notes a few lines down, "is the reflection once removed."[30] What looks right is actually left. His mistake is minor, but it has major implications, since the poem bills itself as attentive to the distortions produced by artists like Parmigianino (a proxy for Ashbery himself), whose "Realism," the poem tells us, "[n]o longer produces an objective truth, but a *bizarria*."[31] The bizarreness of mirrors and self-reflexivity is certainly at play throughout. In the first line, the wrong "right hand" cannot objectively be true—but by the end of the poem, a reader could reasonably ask: How important is truth in a poet's critique of realism?

Regardless of intent, Ashbery's mistake is certainly understandable: mirrored reflections are notoriously difficult to conceptualize, even when one "gets" how they work. The poet actually demonstrates he knows the physics when he writes later in the poem that the forms "are / Finally reversed in the accumulating mirror."[32] And there is even a very early poem of his about hands and mirrors—written when he was still in high school at Deerfield Academy—in which there appears to be no confusion:

> Always the left hand flickers, falls to right;
> The eyes groping at mirrors
> Strike the sought self, opaque and firm,
> Safe in its frame.[33]

These opening lines could mean a number of things; but if the left hand in line 1 corresponds to the eyes in the line below it, then perhaps the hand that "flickers" does so between reality and reflection—the actual self and the "sought self" that lives safely in the mirror's frame. What is left in real life indeed "falls to right" in the mirror. This prompts the question: Does Ashbery's recognition of mirror games in a piece of juvenilia written thirty years before "Self-Portrait," along with the otherwise careful explication of the painting's properties in that poem, exonerate him from the glaring mistake in its first line? In other words, was the mistake on purpose?

As usual, Ashbery's critics have stepped in to save him from any embarrassment. Some simply treat the mistake as if it isn't one, insisting on the hand's rightness in both senses, as David Lehman does when he proposes that "The picture suggests that Parmigianino is left-handed, as Ashbery is."[34] His connection here may be factually incorrect (Parmigianino was clearly right-handed—the actual right hand, *not* pictured, was occupied in painting the portrait), but it raises the point that Ashbery may well have desired the painter to be left-handed like him—as part of the identification going on between the poet and artist throughout the poem. And that desire may well have something to do with the error's coming into being. James Heffernan's book on ekphrasis similarly gets it wrong when it refers to "the absence of the left hand (which was no doubt occupied in painting the picture)"; both of these critics either willfully assume Ashbery's own position as mistaken viewer or are just as confused by the mirror image as the poet apparently was.[35] Other readers take the bait and run with it, insisting that the mistake simply isn't one. Ben Hickman launches his defense by appealing to the following formulation in the work of French philosopher Paul Ricœur: "[t]he tension between sameness and difference characterises the logical structure of likeness." Hickman writes that "[s]uch a structure is suggested by Ashbery in the very first line of the poem, which has "the right hand" thrust at the viewer when it is actually the painter's left hand that we see."[36] Hickman's point about likeness—the poem, after all, begins on the word "As"—rings true for the poem as a whole, but its logic with regard to the first line's hands depends on a degree of subtlety that Ashbery may not yet have earned within the poem (being only a few words in). William Elford Rogers is more literal in his justification of the "switch," pointing out logically that

[i]t is possible to imagine that the right hand is extended only if (1) the viewer in imagination assumes the spatial position of the figure depicted "inside" the mirror; or (2) the viewer imagines that the image is real—for example, that a real though distorted other is extending his right hand. Under the assumption that Ashbery was not just confused by mirror games, this switching of left and right is perhaps an overly ingenious way of talking about how the portrait works—namely, by causing an identification with the artist (as in

lines 237ff.) while preserving a strong sense of "otherness, this / 'Not-being-us.'"[37]

Ashbery certainly is identifying with the artist here—but his "way of talking about how the portrait works" in the rest of the poem is not so "overly ingenious" as to confuse the reader between right and wrong, truth and its mirrored imaginary. Rather Ashbery methodically points out, sometimes even quoting historians and art critics, exactly how such distortions and identifications operate.

Among the justifiers, John Shoptaw comes closest to conceding actual mistake, but then immediately appears to walk it back: "'Self-Portrait,' he writes, "begins with an obvious (though hitherto unnoticed) mistake, or error, or open-secret."[38] An error and a secret are certainly not the same thing—but his equivocation points to a quality of Ashbery's writing that makes it especially resistant to the kind of reading of mistake I have been proposing. A poetry of secrets (and secret errors) is not an easy poetry to probe for intention or its limits. After his hedging elision of categories, Shoptaw commences his own act of interpretation:

> What (if anything) lies behind this misrepresentation of Parmigianino's portrait, this reversal of left and right? Since Ashbery makes a point of reminding us that everything is "reversed in the accumulating mirror" (SP ["Self-Portrait"] 73), this sleight of hands should be related to the many reversals within the poem. Parmigianino's single, enlarged, phallic hand "thrust at the viewer" is sexually disorienting; it may be left or right. To see Parmigianino's left hand as his right is to imagine that the painter has taken the place of his portrayed mirror image within the globe.[39]

These all would have been perfectly good reasons for switching right and left hands had Ashbery been thinking consciously about whether or not such a mistake would be fruitful for readings of his poem. They offer his reader convenient ways of using the mistake productively in making sense of other aspects of the work. But they also have the same ring as many of the justifications of error I have cited throughout this book, which prioritize the creativity of the reader's interpretation over its plausibility with respect to the poet's own intentions. In the case of Ashbery, such readings might feel marginally more plausible because we know him to be a poet at pains to blur the distinction between reality and imagination—and also because he is a poet who does not shy away from error as a muse or source. But poets who resist taking too much care and are intrigued by imprecision—poets who, in their recalcitrance, call into question the very act of representation with which they find themselves preoccupied—are in fact no more immune to mistake than those who are scrupulously attentive to their craft. To absolve such poets from the possibility of mistaking would be to imply that all of their mistakes are on some level purposeful. But even a deliberately sloppy poet makes mistakes. While it is true that mistakes can be longed for, part of that longing involves the paradox of wishing for something that is necessarily unwanted.

Ashbery's mistake in "Self-Portrait" fits within the context of his own style and also chimes with several of the meanings behind his poem, but its being apropos does not diminish the likelihood of its being unintentional. In fact, its unintentional quality becomes all the more important. What happens when poets take their eye off the ball is worth understanding *for*, not *in spite of*, its own wrongness. Contemporary poets frequently celebrate the power of errancy; like Ashbery, they may even seek it. But just as there is no poem that can entirely escape its poet's will, there is also no poem wholly incapable of being mistaken (since where there is intention there is also the possibility that such intention will be unintentionally betrayed by one contingency or another). As Ashbery himself implies in his early poem "The Painter," the only "perfect" painting—or poem—is the one that either remains unwritten or is erased, "the canvas / perfectly white." Any mark of a painter or poet is a mark that is subject to mistake.

Though Ashbery's poem may not mistake willingly, what should we be looking for in poems that *do* wear their mistakes on their sleeves? Deciphering intended meanings cannot be our only aim, if it ever was, since other virtues openly announce themselves. (We could also ask ourselves whether it is right to think such poems demand anything different from us at all.) Paul Muldoon makes this dilemma the centerpiece of "Errata," a poem composed entirely of mistakes:

> For "Antrim" read "Armagh."
> For "mother" read "other."
> For "harm" read "farm."
> For "feather" read "father."
>
> For "Moncrieff" read "Monteith."
> For "*Beal Fierste*" read "*Beal Feirste*."
> For "brave" read "grave."
> For "revered" read "reversed."[40]

It goes on like this for thirty-two lines, suggesting the list could be—is—endless. Muldoon asks without asking: What can be read as itself in poetry anyway? Don't poems always say one thing and mean another? Where most poems produce surprise and ambiguity by means of metaphor and other similarly "poetical" figures, this one knocks seemingly unrelated words or conceptions against one another using mistake as the vehicle. Muldoon isn't upending metaphor as the dominant trope so much as he is suggesting metaphor and error may be related. Metaphor, as Walker Percy noted in his classic essay "Metaphor as Mistake," is always partially " 'wrong'—it asserts of one thing that it is something else—" and "its beauty often seems proportionate to its wrongness or outlandishness."[41] His principle certainly still holds true for these errata: the spelling difference in *Fierste* and *Feirste* is notable but rather mundane; on the other hand, putting "mother" beside "other," or, later in the poem, "anecdote" with "antidote," proves not only comic but lastingly suggestive. The worse the mistake in these instances, the better. (In the real errata list for Muldoon's *Poems, 1968–1998*, he mentions mistaking "aureoles" for "areolae"—a coupling so outlandish I suspect he prints the list for the sole purpose of including it.)[42] Mistake's serendipitous rightness in many of this particular poem's lines also brings the subjectivity of metaphor into focus—what Percy calls the "cognitive dimension" of analogy.[43] What one person sees as "married" another might see as "marred," literally and figuratively.[44] One of the playful implications of Muldoon's poem is that mistakes may not only be as common as other kinds of poetic tropes but also as difficult and provocative.

Yet still there is a further seriousness at the bottom of his exposé of error—a sense of mistrust directed at poets, or readers, or both. It is worth noting that "Errata" is a poem that records mistakes but does not actually make any (on the contrary, several of its subtle rhymes are almost virtuosic). Instead, it shines light both on the slipperiness of language and poets' proneness to slippage. For all his fun, we should not assume Muldoon is cheerful about being prone. Starting in line 16, for instance,

For "ludic" read "lucid."

For "religion" read "region."
For "ode" read "code."
For "Jane" read "Jean."
For "rod" read "road."[45]

What would happen if readers actually made the substitutions this poem dictates? For one thing, they would be forced to remember that games are often more illustrative than anyone might wish. What is ludic may also be seen through (including the poem). Similarly, religion and regions some-times go together, sometimes not. In Muldoon's native region of Northern Ireland, differences in religion cause major rifts: assuming one's religion from one's region can have violent consequences. Even the lighter mistakes here have a sharper edge; "Jean" is the name of the poet's wife, so he wouldn't really want to call her "Jane," would he? Muldoon hints at the darker side of this and other poems in an interview, noting that what seems playful has "a serious enough undertone":

> It is after all some version of the slippage that brings us to the shib-boleth and the shibboleth is after all still very much the mode in Northern Ireland. There are places in Northern Ireland, certainly where I was brought up, where mispronouncing a word, how one *spelled* a word, depending how one pronounced the letter H, whether or not you sounded it, you could be dead. It was indicative of whether you were Catholic or Protestant. So I mean that that kind of slip could be your last slip.[46]

The flippancy of his "Errata" only partially resists what may be an underly-ing suspicion on his part that mistakes hide and haunt—and that the poem is only ever a letter or two away from its own ruin. For Muldoon, as for Heaney (his onetime mentor and fellow Northern Irishman), mistakes in meaning, in pronunciation, in grammar might indicate all sorts of things, including social status and national allegiance. The sense of play throughout this poem involves its own series of warning signals.

If there is a cautious celebration of error's power in "Errata," several of Muldoon's other poems seem to betray his own compunction at not always getting things right. But they do so without covering up his mistakes. For example, at the beginning of "Yarrow," a long, segmented, and richly complex elegy for his mother, Muldoon admits to misremembering the Latin used by "young Ignatius of Loyola," who,

> raising the visor of his bucket,
> pledged himself either *Ad Major*
> or *Ad Majorem Dei Gloriam*, I can't quite remember which.[47]

A quick search would have afforded Muldoon the answer—it is *Majorem*—but the possibility of his own error ends up being an important theme across the poem and so is worth mentioning at the outset. Later in the elegy he refers to a god who has "lost his bit of Latin."[48] The most emotionally available lines in the elegy are roughly four-fifths of the way through, when the poet finally comes out and says what all the grief is for:

> The bridge. The barn. Again and again I stand aghast
> as I contemplate what never
> again will be mine:
>
> "Look on her. Look, her lips.
> Listen to her *râle*
> where ovarian cancer takes her in its strangle-hold."[49]

Muldoon's admission of the disease, and his helplessness to save his mother from it, is blunt compared to the allusive and seemingly unrelated subjects that make up the rest of the poem. But he returns to this kind of evasiveness almost as soon as he utters the word "cancer": the next two sections take an

unexpected turn and compare Muldoon's mother's battle with cancer to the
battles fought by the Muslim leader Salah-ed-din during the Crusades:

> Sharp was her end as the scimitar of Salah-ed-din
> with which he cut through . . . what?
> A cushion? A pillow? That was the year Richard the Lionheart
>
> floated barrage-
> balloons all along the coast between Jaffa and Tyre;
> the year Lionheart smote an iron
>
> bar with such force as so far,
> so good, while Salah-ed-din, ever the more delicate,
> sliced through the right Fallopian.
>
> ———
>
> And there lay the mare—after they sliced her open—
> there lay the mare with her nostril all wide
> while Badhbh, daughter of Cailidin,
>
> cried out on her behalf, "Whosoever
> looketh upon a woman with carnal desire
> as after the water brooks panteth the hart . . ."
>
> "Ovarian," did I write? Uterine.
> Salah-ed-din would slice through in his De Havilland Mosquito.
> "American," did I write? British.[50]

The way in which Muldoon's mother's tale converges with Salah-ed-din's—
the sword likened to the scalpel—surprises a reader who at this point in the
poem expects a more personal note. Just when Muldoon finally seems to
be broaching the subject, he rather whimsically elides her surgeon with a
medieval sultan and then confesses he has misdiagnosed her cancer: " 'Ovarian' did I write? Uterine." Is this mistake, an embarrassing one for a son
who has recently lost his mother, worth keeping in the poem instead of

discarding? As readers, should we disregard or believe it? It would have been easy enough for Muldoon to correct during the drafting process. Or is the mistake a plant?

We can conjecture, but no explanation feels definitive. Maybe he keeps "ovarian" so that he can write the line about "slic[ing] through the right Fallopian." But "uterine" doesn't absolutely preclude "Fallopian." Maybe he prefers the sound of "ovarian" and wants to reserve the rhyme between Salah-ed-din and uterine for the end. Maybe he keeps the mistake for ideological reasons—his belief in the "serendipity" of language[51]—since earlier in the poem he has a "post-Sausserian" person remark that "the word is a suspect device."[52] Or maybe the mistake stays in the poem simply because it has been made, error being somehow the intention of the poem rather than the poet. In fact, the whole poem is full of slips and misre-memberings, as his guilty "American" versus "British" slip confirms two lines later.[53] Even Muldoon's "ma" mistakes the name of Arthur Griffith, the Irish writer and founder of the political party Sinn Féin, for "Arthur Griffin" at one point in the verse.[54] It is a poem of deep regret that incorporates error in the texture of its language. (This is the same poem that once had "aureoles" for "areolae.") The poet's feelings of loss become his poetics, and mistake plays a crucial role in that displacement.[55] "Yarrow" in this way foregrounds its own errors and deflections. Getting it wrong temporarily acts as a proxy for grief. The truth about the poet's mother is subjugated to the truth about the poet's way of feeling—the same hierarchy that is at work in Heaney's mistake in "Squarings," where historical fact is ultimately too limiting for a poet wanting to explore the experiential possibilities of memory.

Muldoon's own elegy for Heaney, "Cuthbert and the Otters," similarly appears to obviate mistake by calling attention to it: "Did I say 'calamine'? / I meant 'chamomile,' " he writes in a welcome moment of bathos amid otherwise raw lines that humanize the poet at the same time as they idolize his subject.[56] His inclusion of both the mistake and the correction calls attention to his own fallibility while also inviting the reader to interrogate the psychological meanings behind seemingly accidental slips—as if mistakes, and the poems in which they figure, might have an intentionality all their own. But if Muldoon partly atones for error by overtly capitulating to it, his spirit of confessing also contains in it a note of uneasiness about a poet's natural tendency toward getting things wrong. (Indeed there *are* mistakes that he does not account for—like when he refers, in his poem "The More a Man Has the More a Man Wants," to "the hedge-sparrow's / *Littlebitofbreadandnocheese*," despite that sound's famously describing the song of a yellowhammer, not a sparrow.)[57] Mistake in Muldoon may seem to be wished for, but it is never fully absolved. "Aware of the human cost of mistakes," John Kerrigan has noted, "Muldoon does not muddle words without a sense of potential damage."[58] No matter how explicit his poems are about their own errancy, the feeling of being wrong for him may still more closely resemble shame than desire. For instance, in forcing his corrections to be accompanied by the mistakes that occasioned them, Muldoon enacts the poetical version of what psychoanalysis terms reaction-formation, or "the tendency of a repressed wish or feeling to be expressed at a conscious level in a contrasting form."[59] The wish to get it right in Muldoon may appear as a perverse delight in being mistaken: "'Ovarian,' did I write? Uterine." The sense of control he displays here in the exaggerated acceptance of his own errors is a mastery developed in response to the initial disturbance. Few poets—not least ones as technically skillful as Muldoon—actually enjoy getting it wrong.

For certain poets plagued by the guilt of perpetual mistake, poetry itself becomes the purest medium of atonement. Such are the biblical inflections and proportions Geoffrey Hill invokes in his essay "Poetry as 'Menace' and 'Atonement'" when he concedes that despite living and working "in a world of actual terror," the poet can—and must—feel "remorse over a *faux pas*."[60] Hill is not a writer overly determined to correct his own poems, but his readers do have to contend with a meaningful revision to his early poem "In Memory of Jane Fraser," an elegy for someone who never existed, whose death in winter ("When snow like sheep lay in the fold")[61] nevertheless ushers in a spring that cannot quite console:[62]

> Her body froze
> As if to freeze us all, and chain
> Creation to a stunned repose.
>
> She died before the world could stir.
> In March the ice unloosed the brook

And water ruffled the sun's hair.
Dead cones upon the alder shook.[63]

So read the revised final stanzas of this poem as it appears in *King Log* (1968) and all subsequent selected and collected editions of Hill's verse. But the short lyric, as he originally published it in his first book, *For the Unfallen*, ends on a slightly different note:

And water ruffled the sun's hair,
And a few sprinkled leaves unshook.[64]

When Hill changes the ending and reprints this poem, he gives it the subtitle "AN ATTEMPTED REPARATION" and includes an explanation:[65]

"In Memory of Jane Fraser" was included in my first book, *For the Unfallen*, which is now out of print. I dislike the poem very much and the publication of this amended version may be regarded as a necessary penitential exercise.[66]

But what is Hill repenting, exactly? An elegy as a "penitential exercise" might suggest the poet feels the need to set something right about the memorialized subject of his verse. What wrong has he perpetrated against Jane Fraser in the first poem? The changes Hill makes, apart from one or two small revisions in punctuation, seem merely to involve transforming a somewhat inane ending into a significantly darker and more resonant final line. That is, Hill's "reparation" appears not to be for Jane at all but for himself and his book—a rigorous poet's "necessary" penitence for having written a less than perfect line of poetry.

There is no doubt something to atone for in that solecism "unshook," which appears to be the simple past tense of the verb from which we derive the past participle "unshaken" but here remains awkwardly intransitive. Does Hill mean that leaves fell from a tree—"shook off," as it were—or was he thinking of leaves that had already fallen and were "sprinkled" on the frozen brook, which, in melting, releases them? Or perhaps these were leaves of new foliage breaking through, as one might expect at the end of an elegy? No matter which, his pathetic fallacy grates, especially coming immediately after "the sun's hair" (itself not an unrisky personification); the revised poem's "shook," by contrast, allows for the wind to be doing the shaking—and in any case does not call its own grammatical correctness into question. "Sprinkled" is likewise better left unsaid; it is too precious a word for this poem and also hard to see: one could imagine the brook's being sprinkled *with* leaves, but "sprinkled leaves," before they have unshaken themselves, if that is what they are doing, suggests for a moment that they themselves are sprinkled with water or snow. Rhythmically it is hard not to prefer the newer version: "Dead cones upon the alder shook" resumes with deadly vigor the iambic march upon which the poem has relied from the beginning, a march that poignantly slackens a little in Hill's falsely redemptive penultimate line. "And a few sprinkled leaves unshook" is metrical but weak by comparison. Perhaps most important, the dead cones in the repaired line cling to the alder despite the season's renewal, bringing the final image in line not only with a meaning suggested by the original collection's title (*For the Unfallen*) but also with the point Hill makes more generally in the poem: the dead remain—we cannot shake them.

For all of these reasons, Hill's new version serves as an adequate reparation for the original. But we might also read his second publication—of a poem Hill claims *still* to dislike—as a form of quasi-religious self-flagellation. The "penitential exercise" of revising includes manifest improvements to the text itself, but it also involves a re-airing of the larger mistake (i.e., the disliked poem itself) by reproducing the whole of its lines within the broader context of reparation. To atone for poetry one dislikes through the act of republishing it is not as daft as it seems. Hill writes in his essay that the poet "may learn to live in his affliction, not with the cynical indifference of the reprobate but with the renewed sense of a vocation: that of necessarily bearing his peculiar unnecessary shame in a world growing ever more shameless."[67] The poet's shame is importantly "unnecessary" because it does not stem from man's original fallenness—the common and universalizing shame of humanity—but from something much worse: what Hill calls "empirical guilt," or his specific personal "anxiety about *faux pas*, the perpetration of 'howlers', grammatical solecisms, misstatements of fact, misquotations, improper attributions."[68] In other words, even for a spiritual poet like Hill, the poet's peculiar brand of shame often derives from the sort of lowly mistakes to which I have been calling attention throughout this book.[69] Because the poet must "hope to be taken seriously," his mistakes are painful; for Hill, they represent nothing short of "irredeemable error in the very substance and texture of one's craft and pride."[70] However, they do not keep him from going on: "one may continue to write and to publish in a vain and self-defeating effort to appease one's own sense of empirical guilt."[71] Seen in the most positive light, then, we might consider mistake for Hill a sustaining force; but we could not deny its menace.

For what mistakes should the *critic* be ashamed? Poetry presents those who would study and write about it with a peculiar kind of temptation to treat flaws as flourishes, to which many good readers succumb. We resist acknowledging its mistakes precisely because poems are, in and of themselves, forms of resistance—their forms resisting the grammatical, historical, and semiotic precision that so often characterizes other kinds of literary texts. Erring in novels and plays, to say nothing of prose nonfiction, usually announces itself more readily than in poems. Accordingly there has been more critical work done to expose the nature of errors in them.[72] But there is still work to be done in those genres too. Michael Anesko's preface to his book about mistakes in Henry James comments that the existence of the revised New York edition of James's novels and tales—which James himself scrupulously helped produce—means that "an unusually rich textual record survives from which we can learn much about the author's desire to correct 'mistakes' that he later perceived in the books as first printed."[73] Anesko's need to put the word "mistake" in quotation marks speaks volumes to the reluctant attitude readers still have toward error in literature they love. What could those quotation marks do but qualify or mitigate the wrongness implied by such a word? Most of the fascinating mistakes in *The Portrait of a Lady* that Anesko catalogs are as patently wrong as anything I have described in this book—more so, even. (He gives a lucid account of James describing a character as both sitting and standing at the same moment, among many others.)[74] But the urge to theorize mistake as something hard to pin down, to believe that an author simply could not have erred, or that a finished text is incapable of being wrong despite all evidence to the contrary, persists despite the fact that in many novels, historical inaccuracies, geographical errors, and inconsistencies in plot and character are easy to recognize (especially once they have been pointed out by careful textual scholars like Anesko). If "mistake" must still appear in scare quotes in relation to James, who has his most famous character announce at one point that "I can't publish my mistake. I don't think that's decent. I'd much rather die," then poetry, the much more capacious art in terms of license, seems forever doomed to have its bloopers codified as blessings despite poets themselves usually suggesting otherwise.[75] The pleasure of believing in authors' infallibility continues to be irresistible even when we are trying our hardest.

There may be something ungenerous, or unpoetical, in my literal approach to mistake. But I remember what Empson once wrote with regard to his treatment of ambiguity:

> literary critics have been so unwilling to appear niggling and lacking in soul that upon these small technical points the obvious, even the accepted, has been said culpably seldom.[76]

If I have niggled, it has been with an aim to redirect attention toward aspects of poetry that poets themselves consider most important. If my analysis of particular poems lacks soul or nuance in its dogged descrying of error, I hope it nevertheless displays rigor and honesty regarding details of compositional technique and—yes—intention, which often receive short shrift. I have insisted that readers of poems stop excusing mistake, but it does not follow that I would wish poets to put an end to their own mistaking. How could they? One of the premises of this book is that the ideal of a poem's unerring accordance with its poet's conscious intentions would be both impossible and impoverishing. Nor do I claim that mistakes necessarily cause poems to be bad; to suggest so would be to make an unsubstantiated and overly broad value judgment running contrary to the opinions of many poets who, from the examples I have provided in this conclusion, frequently consider their mistakes to be a boon. But mistakes do exist—and they exist *because* they are not meant to. Part of our task as readers involves noticing and identifying them as such. Denying a poem's mistakenness erases from the record an important quality bound up in its existence as a work of art. If doing so temporarily assuages our own guilt about potential misreadings, it much more perniciously promotes a false belief in poetry's invincibility that gets in the way of our ability to form genuine pictures of the art and artist. Few poets ever reached the heights of Parnassus without the slow, laborious pursuit of craft—a process that has always been distinguished by their waging a constant battle with and against mistakes. We need not fret about exposing them; mistakes have something perhaps even more pleasurable to offer than rightness, for they reveal to readers what poems and poets actually achieve as opposed to what they should, or mean to. Read and accepted in this light, the poet's mistake can deliver us momentary relief from our own nagging desire for perfection in the welcome insistence of things as they are.

Notes

Introduction. The Poet's Mistake

1. Sigmund Freud, *The Psychopathology of Everyday Life*, trans. Anthea Bell (London: Penguin, 2002), 216.
2. *Henry IV, Part One*, in *The Norton Shakespeare*, ed. Stephen Greenblatt et al. (New York: W. W. Norton, 1997), 1.1.35; subsequent references are to act, scene, and line from this edition unless otherwise noted.
3. *Julius Caesar*, 2.1.193. This particular anachronism has often been excused for its necessity in facilitating the plot of the play; it is certainly the case that Shakespeare is not a naturalistic dramatist.
4. *The Winter's Tale*, 3.3.1–3.
5. Sir Thomas Hanmer, ed., *The Winter's Tale*, in *The Works of Shakespear* (London: Printed for J. and P. Knapton, 1745), 2:513.
6. Edmund O. von Lippmann, "Shakespeare's Ignorance?," *New Review* 4 (1891): 250–54.
7. See, for example, Harold Bloom, *Dramatists and Dramas* (Philadelphia: Chelsea House, 2005), 121.
8. Wallace Stevens, "The Poems of Our Climate," line 21, in *Collected Poetry and Prose*, ed. Frank Kermode and Joan Richardson (New York: Library of America, 1997), 178. All subsequent citations refer to this edition.
9. Robert Frost, "The Figure a Poem Makes," in *Collected Poems, Prose, and Plays*, ed. Richard Poirier and Mark Richardson (New York: Library of America, 1995), 777.
10. T. S. Eliot, "Tradition and the Individual Talent," in *The Sacred Wood: Essays on Poetry and Criticism* (London: Faber and Faber, 1997), 49.

11. George Gordon [Lord] Byron, *Childe Harold's Pilgrimage*, 4.180.1617–20, in *The Complete Poetical Works*, ed. Jerome McGann (Oxford: Oxford University Press, 1981), 3:184. All subsequent citations to Byron are taken from this edition, with volume and page noted.

12. *OED Online*, s.v. "lay, *v*.1," "VII. Intransitive Uses corresponding with lie, *v*, 43a."

13. Gavin Hopps, "Byron and Grammatical Freedom," in *Liberty and Poetic License: New Essays on Byron*, ed. Bernard Beatty, Tony Howe, and Charles E. Robinson (Liverpool: Liverpool University Press, 2008), 166.

14. Matthew Arnold, *Poetry and Prose*, ed. John Bryson (London: Rupert Hart-Davis, 1954), 719.

15. See Tracy Miller, "What Remains: Matthew Arnold's Poetics of Place and the Victorian Elegy," *Victorian Poetry* 50, no. 2 (Summer 2012): 147.

16. Aristotle, *On the Art of Poetry*, chapter 25, trans. Ingram Bywater (Oxford: Clarendon Press, 1920), 86–87.

17. Stanley Corngold describes the difference between these two terms in his consideration of "Error in Paul de Man," *Critical Inquiry* 8, no. 3 (1982): 492: "Error is not *mistake*. The concept of the mistake is usable, perhaps, within the restricted teleology of pragmatic acts or within the quasi-rigorous language of scientific description. Mistakes (or what de Man sometimes calls 'mere error' [see, e.g., *BI*, p. 109]) are without true value: trivial, in principle corrigible according to a norm already known. But the skew of error implies a truth." The reference to *BI* here is referring to *Blindness and Insight* (New York, 1971).

18. *OED Online*, s.v. "mistake, *n*."

19. Edmund Spenser, *The Faerie Queene*, ed. A. C. Hamilton, 2nd ed. (New York: Routledge, 2013), 1.1.13.6, 1.1.20.6, and 1.1.22.7. References are to book, canto, stanza, and line(s).

20. Ibid., 1.1.13.6.

21. Seth Lerer, *Error and the Academic Self: The Scholarly Imagination, Medieval to Modern* (New York: Columbia University Press, 2002), 17.

22. Paul Muldoon, "Author's Note," in *Poems, 1968–1998* (London: Faber and Faber, 2001), xv.

23. Fernando Pessoa, *The Book of Disquiet*, trans. Richard Zenith (London: Penguin Classics, 2002), 83.

24. Adam Phillips, *Promises, Promises: Essays on Literature and Psychoanalysis* (London: Faber and Faber, 2000), 114.

25. Ludwig Wittgenstein, *Philosophical Investigations*, part 1, section 143 (New York: Macmillan, 1958), 57.

26. J. L. Austin, "A Plea for Excuses," *Philosophical Papers*, 3rd ed. (Oxford: Oxford University Press, 1979), 175–76.

27. Jonathan Bate, *Soul of the Age: The Life, Mind and World of William Shakespeare* (London: Penguin, 2008), 305.

28. Austin, "A Plea for Excuses," 176.

29. Ibid.

30. Freud, *The Psychopathology of Everyday Life*, 208.

31. Christopher Ricks, "Literature and the Matter of Fact," in *Essays in Appreciation* (Oxford: Oxford University Press, 1996), 286.

32. Ibid., 281.

33. John Ruskin, quoted in ibid., 310.

34. Byron, *Don Juan*, 7.42.331–34 and 7.42.349, in *The Complete Poetical Works*, ed. Jerome J. McGann (Oxford: Clarendon Press, 1986), 5:349.

35. Ibid., "Hints from Horace," lines 415–20, in *The Complete Poetical Works*, 1:304.

36. A. R. Ammons, "The Poem Is a Walk," in *Claims for Poetry*, ed. Donald Hall (Ann Arbor: University of Michigan Press, 1982), 4.

37. David Quint points out this mistake in *Inside "Paradise Lost": Reading the Designs of Milton's Epic* (Princeton, NJ: Princeton University Press, 2014), 197, 276n.

38. John Milton, "Lycidas," lines 70–76, in *Complete Shorter Poems*, ed. Stella P. Revard (Oxford: Wiley Blackwell, 2009), 76.

39. In the poem's first edition, the Aztec (Mexican) war god Vitzipultzi appears in line 13 despite the speaker seemingly identifying with the Incas (e.g., "Copac"). In later editions, "Vitzipultzi" is replaced with "Pachacamac," the Peruvian god of fire. See the original text in Robert Dodsley, ed., *A Collection of Poems* (London: Printed by J. Hughs, 1755), 4.209–10.

40. John Keats, "On First Looking into Chapman's Homer," in *The Major Works*, ed. Elizabeth Cook (Oxford: Oxford University Press, 2001), 32.

41. Alfred Tennyson, quoted in Francis Palgrave, *The Golden Treasury*, rev. and enlarged ed. (London: Macmillan, 1902), 367.

42. Ricks, "Literature and the Matter of Fact," 307.

43. Tennyson, "The Charge of the Light Brigade," lines 9–17, in *Tennyson: A Selected Edition*, ed. Christopher Ricks (Berkeley: University of California Press, 1989), 509.

44. Tennyson, "Locksley Hall," line 182, in *Tennyson*, 192. Ricks's notes to the poem include Tennyson's excuse.

45. John Kandl, "The Politics of Keats's Early Poetry," in *The Cambridge Companion to Keats*, ed. Susan Wolfson (Cambridge: Cambridge University Press, 2001), 3.

46. Charles Rzepka, " 'Cortez: Or Balboa, or Somebody like That': Form, Fact, and Forgetting in Keats's 'Chapman's Homer' Sonnet," *Keats-Shelley Journal* 51 (2002): 39.

47. The arguments of these critics are discussed in ibid., 35–75.

48. Ibid., 73–74.

49. William D. Robertson's *History of America* (1777) quoted in Daniel Watkins, *Keats's Poetry and the Politics of the Imagination* (London: Associated University Presses, 1989), 27.

50. Charles Cowden Clarke, "Recollections of Keats," in *Keats: The Critical Heritage*, ed. G. M. Matthews (London: Routledge and Kegan Paul Books, 1971), 391.

51. Jack Stillinger, *Romantic Complexity: Keats, Coleridge, and Wordsworth* (Chicago: University of Illinois Press, 2006), 80–84.

52. Richard Woodhouse, *The Keats Circle, Letters and Papers, 1816–1878*, ed. Hyder Edward Rollins (Cambridge, MA: Harvard University Press, 1948), 1.128–29. I have smoothed out the abbreviations and cancellations in this passage with as little alteration as possible in order to make it legible. I am grateful to Jack Stillinger's *Romantic Complexity* for bringing it to my attention.

53. Stillinger, *Romantic Complexity*, 86–87.

54. John Keats to J. H. Reynolds, 22 November 1817, in *John Keats: Selected Letters*, ed. Robert Gittings (Oxford: Oxford University Press, 2002), 39.

55. Willard Spiegelman, *Majestic Indolence: English Romantic Poetry and the Work of Art* (Oxford: Oxford University Press, 1995), 102.

56. W. K. Wimsatt and Monroe C. Beardsley, "The Intentional Fallacy," in *The Verbal Icon* (New York: Noonday Press, 1954), 18.

57. Ibid., 10.

58. Steven Knapp and Walter Benn Michaels, "Against Theory," *Critical Inquiry* 8, no. 4 (Summer 1982): 723–42.

59. Sean Burke, *The Death and Return of the Author: Criticism and Subjectivity in Barthes, Foucault and Derrida*, 3rd ed. (Edinburgh: Edinburgh University Press, 1998), 134.

60. E. D. Hirsch, *Validity in Interpretation* (New Haven, CT: Yale University Press, 1967), viii.

61. *OED Online*, s.v. "mistake, *n.*," sense 1a.

62. Rzepka, "Cortez: Or Balboa," 35.

63. Susan Wolfson, *The Questioning Presence: Wordsworth, Keats and the Interrogative Mode in Romantic Poetry* (Ithaca, NY: Cornell University Press, 1986), 221.

64. Robertson's *History of America*, quoted in Claude Finney, *The Evolution of Keats's Poetry* (Cambridge, MA: Harvard University Press, 1936), 1:126.

65. Finney, *The Evolution of Keats's Poetry*, 1:136.

66. Marjorie Levinson, *Keats's Life of Allegory: The Origins of a Style* (Oxford: Basil Blackwell, 1988), 15. This comment applies not only to what she refers to as the "Cortez/Balboa" moment but to all of the poem.

67. Jerome McGann, *The Poetics of Sensibility: A Revolution in Literary Style* (Oxford: Clarendon Press, 1996), 122–23.

68. I am indebted to Adam Phillips's discussion of *The Psychopathology of Everyday Life* for the succinctness of this description. Phillips, "Contingency for Beginners," in *One Way and Another: New and Selected Essays* (London: Penguin, 2013), 87–88.

69. Ibid., 89.

70. Ibid., 87.

71. Seamus Heaney, quoted in Andrew Bennett, *Ignorance: Literature and Agnoiology* (Manchester: Manchester University Press, 2009), 228.

72. Anne Ferry, *By Design: Intention in Poetry* (Stanford, CA: Stanford University Press, 2008), 1.

73. See, for example, Seamus Perry, "What the Poem 'Knows,'" *Times Literary Supplement*, no. 4962 (22 May 1998): 32.

74. Austin, "A Plea for Excuses," 201–2.

75. Edward Eigen's book *On Accident: Episodes in Architecture and Landscape* (Cambridge, MA: MIT Press, 2018) glosses the word "accident" more copiously: "the particular, the contingent, the incidental, and the seemingly singular" (xiii). But like Austin's, Eigen's account of accidental events still relies on the absence of will.

76. Hirsch, *Validity in Interpretation*, 22.

77. For complex versions of the latter, see in particular, Michael O'Neill, *Romanticism and the Self-Conscious Poem* (Oxford: Clarendon Press, 1997), xiv: O'Neill uses the phrase "self-conscious" specifically to describe "the recognition made by a poem that it is a poem."

78. Wordsworth, *The Prelude*, 6.596, in *The Fourteen-Book Prelude*, ed. W.J.B. Owen (Ithaca, NY: Cornell University Press, 1985), 129. All subsequent references to Wordsworth's poetry are to title of work, book number (if applicable), and line number(s), taken from the relevant volume of the Cornell edition, the title of which is abbreviated after the first citation.

79. Ibid., 5.389–413, in ibid., 103.

80. Hart Crane, "Voyages II," line 21, in *Complete Poems and Selected Letters* (New York: Library of America, 2006), 25.

81. Elizabeth Bishop, "In the Waiting Room," in *Poems, Prose and Letters*, ed. Robert Giroux and Lloyd Schwartz (New York: Library of America, 2008), 149–51.

82. Elaine Scarry, *On Beauty and Being Just* (Princeton, NJ: Princeton University Press, 2001), 12–13.

83. Keston Sutherland, "Wrong Poetry," *Textual Practice* 24, no. 4 (2010): 772–73.

84. On the contextual aspects of poetry and its meanings, see Virginia Jackson, *Dickinson's Misery* (Princeton, NJ: Princeton University Press, 2005); and Yopie Prins, "What Is Historical Poetics?," *Modern Language Quarterly* 77, no. 1 (March 2016): 13–40.

85. Horace, "Ars Poetica," line 359.

Chapter 1. Wordsworth's Imperfect Perfect

1. Transcribed from manuscript "JJ" contained within DCMS 19 (Dove Cottage); my italics.

2. Ibid.

3. Wordsworth, "Preface to the Edition of 1815," in *The Prose Works of William Wordsworth*, ed. W.J.B. Owen and Jane Worthington Smyser (Oxford: Clarendon Press, 1974), 3:35. All subsequent references to Wordsworth's prose are taken from this edition, hereafter referred to as *Prose Works*.

4. Wordsworth, *The Prelude*, 2.28–33, in *The Thirteen-Book Prelude*, ed. Mark L. Reed (Ithaca, NY: Cornell University Press, 1991), 1:125.

5. David Bromwich, *Disowned by Memory: Wordsworth's Poetry of the 1790s* (Chicago: University of Chicago Press, 1998), 149.

6. William Wordsworth, *The Fenwick Notes of William Wordsworth*, ed. Jared Curtis (London: Bristol Classical Press, 1993), 13. See also Curtis's editorial note to "There was a Boy," 107–8: "First appearing as a first-person narrative in an early manuscript of *The Prelude*, these lines were sent as a free-standing poem to STC [Samuel Taylor Coleridge] in late November or very early De-

cember 1798. Not part of the 1799 *Two-Part Prelude*, the account does appear in the longer versions (*Prelude* V, 389–422). Wordsworth discussed the poem in his *Preface* to *Poems*, 1815 (*Prose*, III, 35n.)."

7. See T. W. Thompson, *Wordsworth's Hawkshead*, ed. Robert Woof (London: Oxford University Press, 1970), 55–56.

8. The lines beginning "There was a boy" appeared in two collections during Wordsworth's lifetime: first in the 1800 edition of the *Lyrical Ballads* and later in the *Poems of 1815*. Wordsworth tells his readers in a note to the latter volume that they were conceived as part of the great "Poem on my own poetical education." They appear in book 5 of *The Prelude* (1805) in slightly altered form and in the 1850 *Prelude*. Wordsworth tweaked several lines of the poem throughout his life but never corrected "has carried." All quotations from the poem in this chapter are taken from the 1800 *Lyrical Ballads* version—the first he published—unless otherwise noted.

9. Wordsworth, "There was a Boy," lines 11–25, in *Lyrical Ballads, and Other Poems, 1797–1800*, ed. James Butler and Karen Green (Ithaca, NY: Cornell University Press, 1992), 140; emphasis added.

10. Ibid., lines 31–32.

11. See Wordsworth, *The Prelude* (1805), 5.408, in *The Thirteen-Book Prelude*, 1:172; and Wordsworth, *The Prelude* (1850), 5.386, in *The Fourteen-Book Prelude*, ed. W.J.B. Owen (Ithaca, NY: Cornell University Press, 1985), 104. The handwritten notebook is held at Dove Cottage (DCMS 16.18).

12. See Pieter Vermeulen, "The Suspension of Reading: Wordsworth's 'Boy of Winander' and Trauma Theory," *Orbis Litterarum* 62, no. 6 (2007): 459–82; and Cathy Caruth, "An Interview with Geoffrey Hartman," in *The Wordsworthian Enlightenment: Romantic Poetry and the Ecology of Reading*, ed. Helen Regueiro Elam and Frances Ferguson (Baltimore: Johns Hopkins University Press, 2005), 296–317.

13. Wordsworth, "There was a Boy," line 28, in *Lyrical Ballads*, 140–41.

14. Geoffrey Hartman, "The Wordsworthian Enlightenment," in *The Wordsworthian Enlightenment*, 33.

15. Ibid.

16. Hartman, *Wordsworth's Poetry: 1787–1814* (New Haven, CT: Yale University Press, 1964), 21.

17. Francis Jeffrey, unsigned review of Crabbe's *Poems* (1807), in *Edinburgh Review*, no. 12 (April 1808): 132–37. Quoted in *Wordsworth: The Critical Heritage*, ed. Robert Woof (London: Routledge, 2001), 227.

18. Susan Wolfson, "Revision as Form: Wordsworth's Drowned Man," in *Formal*

Charges: The Shaping of Poetry in British Romanticism (Stanford, CA: Stanford University Press, 1997), 116.

19. Ibid.

20. Gavin Hopps, "Byron and Grammatical Freedom," in *Liberty and Poetic Licence: New Essays on Byron*, ed. Bernard Beatty, Tony Howe, and Charles E. Robinson (Liverpool: Liverpool University Press, 2008), 173–74.

21. Ibid., 177.

22. Samuel Taylor Coleridge to Robert Southey, Penrith, 14 August 1803, in *The Collected Letters of Samuel Taylor Coleridge: Volume II; 1801–1806*, ed. Earl Leslie Griggs (Oxford: Clarendon Press, 1956), 2:977.

23. William Empson, *Seven Types of Ambiguity*, 2nd ed. (London: Chatto and Windus, 1947), 197.

24. Ibid.

25. Rodney Huddleston, "§ 5.3.2 The experiential perfect," in "The verb," in *The Cambridge Grammar of the English Language*, ed. Rodney Huddleston and Geoffrey K. Pullum et al. (Cambridge: Cambridge University Press, 2002), 143.

26. Ibid., 144.

27. Longman's *A Comprehensive Grammar of the English Language*, ed. Randolph Quirk et al. (New York: Longman, 1985), 188–95, corroborates this definition: "the present perfective indicates that the residence has continued up to the present time (and may even continue into the future)," 190, as does Henry Sweet's late nineteenth-century handbook, *A New English Grammar: Logical and Historical; Part I; Introduction, Phonology, and Accidence* (Oxford: Clarendon Press, 1892), 1:98: "The perfect . . . combines past and present time . . . The perfect . . . expresses an occurrence which began in the past and is connected with the present, either by actual continuance up to the present time . . . or in its results."

28. Transcribed from manuscript "JJ" contained within DCMS 19 (Dove Cottage); my italics.

29. Wordsworth, "Preface to *Lyrical Ballads* (1850)," in *Prose Works*, 1:138.

30. Ibid.

31. Wordsworth, "Essays upon Epitaphs (1)," lines 409–19, in *Prose Works*, 2:59–60.

32. Wordsworth, "Song," lines 1–12, in *Lyrical Ballads*, 163.

33. Wordsworth, "A slumber did my spirit seal," lines 1–7, in *Lyrical Ballads*, 163.

34. Wordsworth, "We Are Seven," lines 13–14, in *Lyrical Ballads*, 74.

35. Ibid., line 15.

36. Ibid., lines 17–24.

37. Ibid., lines 50, 52, 59.

38. Ibid., line 69.

39. William Wordsworth to James Losh, Grasmere, 16 March 1805, in *The Letters of William and Dorothy Wordsworth: The Early Years; 1787–1805*, ed. Ernest de Selincourt, rev. Chester L. Shaver, 2nd ed. (Oxford: Clarendon Press, 1967), 565.

40. Oliver Clarkson, "The Disappointment of Wordsworth's Letters," in *Romanticism and the Letter*, ed. Madeleine Callaghan and Anthony Howe (London: Palgrave, forthcoming in 2020).

41. Ibid.

42. Ibid.

43. For two articles that catalog and describe the poet's use of present-perfect verbs, see John Alexander Alford, "Wordsworth's Use of the Present Perfect," in *Modern Language Quarterly* 33 (1972); and Julian Boyd and Zelda Boyd, "The Perfect of Experience," in *Studies in Romanticism* 16, no. 1 (1977). Neither article mentions his mistake in "There was a boy."

44. Thomas De Quincey, "Lake Reminiscences, [No. II.]—William Wordsworth—*Continued*," in *Works of De Quincey: Volume 11; Articles from "Tait's Magazine" and "Blackwood's Magazine," 1838–41*, ed. Julian North (London: Pickering & Chatto, 2003), 11:74; emphasis added (first published in *Tait's*, o.s. 10, n.s. 6 [February 1839]: 90–103, 94).

45. Ibid., 11:75.

46. See note 9 in this chapter; emphasis added.

47. Frost, "The Most of It," in *Collected Poems, Prose, and Plays*, 307.

48. Wordsworth, "Preface to the Edition of 1815," in *Prose Works*, 3:35.

49. Austin, "A Plea for Excuses," 201; and Eigen, *On Accident*, xxxi.

Chapter 2. Robert Browning's Bad Habit

1. G. K. Chesterton, *English Men of Letters: Robert Browning* (London: Macmillan, 1903), 45.

2. Ibid.

3. Robert Browning, *Pippa Passes*, 4.86–98, in *The Complete Works of Robert Browning*, ed. Morse Peckham, Park Honan, and Warner Barnes (Athens: Ohio University Press, 1971), 3:80–81. All citations of Browning's work come from this edition unless otherwise stated and hereon follow the shortened form: poem/work title, section and line(s), and volume and page(s).

4. "Unsigned Review in *The Athenaeum* (11 December 1841, p. 952)," in *Robert Browning: The Critical Heritage*, ed. Boyd Litzinger and Donald Smalley (London: Routledge & Kegan Paul, 1970), 79.

5. H. F. Chorley, *People's Journal* (18 July 1846, ii. 38–40), in *Critical Heritage*, 128.

6. Thomas Powell, "Robert Browning," in *The Living Authors of England* (New York: D. Appleton, 1849), 83–84.

7. *Pippa Passes*, 4.67–73, 3:81.

8. Quoted in *Pippa Passes*, 4.317n, in *Robert Browning: Selected Poems*, ed. John Woolford, Daniel Karlin, and Joseph Phelan (London: Longman, 2010). Letter from Browning to Furnivall, 20 July 1886, London, in *Browning's Trumpeter: The Correspondence of Robert Browning and Frederick J. Furnivall, 1872–1889*, ed. William S. Peterson (Washington, DC: Decatur House Press, 1979), 135.

9. Donald S. Hair, *Robert Browning's Language* (Toronto: University of Toronto Press, 1999), 9; Chesterton, *Robert Browning*, 2.

10. Quoted in *Pippa Passes*, 4.317n, in *Robert Browning*, ed. Woolford, Karlin, and Phelan.

11. "The influence-relation governs reading as it governs writing, and reading is therefore a miswriting just as writing is a misreading." Harold Bloom, *A Map of Misreading* (Oxford: Oxford University Press, 1975), 2.

12. Ibid., 93.

13. Ibid., 94.

14. Robert Browning to his publisher Edward Moxon, 24 February 1847, Pisa, in *The Brownings' Correspondence: September 1846–December 1847*, ed. Philip Kelley and Scott Lewis (Winfield, KS: Wedgestone, 1998), 14:134.

15. Christopher Ricks, "Literature and the Matter of Fact," 292.

16. "Prince Hohenstiel-Schwangau," 2134n, in *The Poems of Robert Browning: Volume Four, 1862–1871*, ed. John Woolford, Daniel Karlin, and Joseph Phelan (London: Longman, 2014), 568.

17. Ibid.

18. John Fuller, *Who Is Ozymandias? And Other Puzzles in Poetry* (London: Chatto and Windus, 2011), 119–20.

19. H. W. Fay, "A Distressing Blunder," *Academy* 33, no. 841 (16 June 1888): 415.

20. Ibid.

21. John Ruskin to Robert Browning, 2 December 1855, London, in *The Brownings' Correspondence: November 1855–June 1856*, ed. Philip Kelley,

Scott Lewis, Edward Hagan, Joseph Phelan, and Rhian Williams (Winfield, KS: Wedgestone Press, 2015), 22:15.

22. Robert Browning to John Ruskin, 10 December 1855, Paris, in ibid., 22:31.

23. His poem "One Word More" (6:141–50), the closing piece to *Men and Women* (London: Chapman and Hall, 1855), is a notable exception.

24. Browning to Furnivall, 11 October 1881, Venice, in *Browning's Trumpeter*, 34.

25. Browning to William J. Rolfe and Heloise E. Hersey concerning his *Selected Poems*, 10 July 1886, quoted in Philip Drew, *The Poetry of Browning: A Critical Introduction* (London: Methuen, 1970), 13.

26. Browning to Furnivall, 12 February 1888, De Vere Gardens, London, in *Browning's Trumpeter*, 150. The paper was delivered by a scholar named Percy A. Barnett.

27. Yopie Prins, "What Is Historical Poetics?," *Modern Language Quarterly* 77, no. 1 (March 2016): 21.

28. Matthew Campbell, *Rhythm and Will in Victorian Poetry* (Cambridge: Cambridge University Press, 1999), 111.

29. Herbert Tucker, "Dramatic Monologue and the Overhearing of Lyric," in *Lyric Poetry: Beyond New Criticism*, ed. Chaviva Hošek and Patricia A. Parker (Ithaca, NY: Cornell University Press, 1985), 228.

30. Prins, "What Is Historical Poetics?," 17–18.

31. "Essay on Shelley," lines 481–83, 5:148.

32. Prins, "What Is Historical Poetics?," 14.

33. Prins goes on in her essay to explore how this kind of "historical poetics" works in Browning's poem "Pan and Luna," 19–23.

34. See, for example, the introduction ("Beforehand") to Virginia Jackson's *Dickinson's Misery: A Theory of Lyric Reading* (Princeton, NJ: Princeton University Press, 2005), 1–15.

35. Robert Langbaum, *The Poetry of Experience: The Dramatic Monologue in Modern Literary Tradition* (London: Chatto and Windus, 1957), 97–98.

36. Isobel Armstrong, *Victorian Poetry: Poetry, Poetics and Politics* (London: Routledge, 2002), 138.

37. Browning himself certainly believed in a poet's license to draw a world in poetry that does not exactly correspond to the world outside of it. In a footnote to his essay on Shelley, he mentions a moment of "fancifully characterising" in "Julian and Maddalo"; Browning explains the madhouse in San Servolo: "far from being 'windowless,' [it] is as full of windows as a barrack." "Essay on Shelley," 5.149n.

38. Langbaum, *Poetry of Experience*, 107–8.

39. Tucker, "Dramatic Monologue," 228.

40. Ibid.

41. Ibid., 231.

42. Ibid., 243.

43. "One Word More," lines 1–4, 6:141.

44. Hair, *Robert Browning's Language*, 12.

45. Ruskin to Browning, 2 December 1855, London, in *The Brownings' Correspondence: November 1855–June 1856*, 22:14.

46. Fuller, *Ozymandias*, 120.

47. Browning to Ruskin, 10 December 1855, Paris, in *The Brownings' Correspondence: November 1855–June 1856*, 22:29.

48. Hair, *Robert Browning's Language*, 110–11.

49. Wordsworth, *Prose Works*, 1:124.

50. James Murray, quoted in K. M. Elisabeth Murray, *Caught in the Web of Words: James Murray and the "Oxford English Dictionary"* (New Haven, CT: Yale University Press, 1977), 235.

51. Herbert Tucker, *Browning's Beginnings: The Art of Disclosure* (Minneapolis: University of Minnesota Press, 1980), 9.

52. Ibid., 129–30.

53. "Bishop Blougram's Apology," line 996, 5:330.

54. Drew, *The Poetry of Browning*, 262.

55. Chesterton, *Robert Browning*, 1.

56. Browning, *The Ring and the Book*, book 11, lines 635–40, 9:185.

57. Barbara Melchiori, *Browning's Poetry of Reticence* (Edinburgh: Oliver and Boyd, 1968), 14n.

58. John Stuart Mill, "What Is Poetry?" (1833), in *The Collected Works of John Stuart Mill*, ed. John M. Robson (Toronto: University of Toronto Press, 1981), 1:348–49.

59. Francis T. Russell, "His Saving Grace of Pessimism," in *The Browning Critics*, ed. Boyd Litzinger and K. L. Knickerbocker (Lexington: University of Kentucky Press, 1965), 135; Roma A. King Jr., *The Focusing Artifice: The Poetry of Robert Browning* (Athens: Ohio University Press, 1968), 47; and Chesterton, *Robert Browning*, 47.

60. Jacob Korg, "A Reading of *Pippa Passes*," *Victorian Poetry* 6, no. 1 (1968): 7–8.

61. For more on the play's coded language and symbols, see Marvin P. Garrett,

"Language and Design in *Pippa Passes*," *Victorian Poetry* 13, no. 1 (Spring 1975): 47–60.

62. *Pippa Passes*, 1.1–5, 3:13.

63. Ibid., 1.10–12, 3:13.

64. Drew, *Poetry of Browning*, 183.

65. Ibid.

66. *Pippa Passes*, 1.13 and 1.17, 3:13–14.

67. Ibid., 2.308–9, 3:54.

68. Tucker, *Browning's Beginnings*, 126.

69. Ricks, "Literature and the Matter of Fact," 282.

70. "Childe Roland to the Dark Tower Came," lines 202–4, 5:256.

71. See Hair, *Browning's Language*, 109.

72. Harold Bloom, *The Ringers in the Tower: Studies in the Romantic Tradition* (Chicago: University of Chicago Press, 1971), 157–67.

73. Daniel Karlin, *Browning's Hatreds* (Oxford: Clarendon Press, 1993), 253.

74. "Essay on Chatterton," lines 743–44, 3:179.

75. Ibid., lines 744–58, 3:179.

76. See Catherine Maxwell, *The Female Sublime from Milton to Swinburne: Bearing Blindness* (Manchester: Manchester University Press, 2001), 147.

77. Roma King, *The Focusing Artifice*, 92.

78. Seamus Heaney, "Glanmore Sonnets II," line 11, in *Opened Ground* (New York: Farrar, Straus and Giroux, 1998), 157.

79. Thomas Carlyle to Robert Browning, 21 June 1841, in *New Letters of Thomas Carlyle*, ed. Alexander Carlyle (London: Bodley Head, 1904), 234.

80. Tucker, *Browning's Beginnings*, 5.

81. "Essay on Shelley," lines 500–501, 5:149.

Chapter 3. Wondering About John Clare

1. John Clare, "Solitude," line 50, in *The Early Poems of John Clare: 1804–1822*, ed. Eric Robinson and David Powell (Oxford: Clarendon Press, 1989), 2:340; hereafter abbreviated as *EP*. All references to Clare's poetry come from this edition and follow the form poem title, line number(s), abbreviated book title, and volume and page number(s). See "Works Cited" for full details.

2. "The Woodman," line 62, in *EP*, 2:290.

3. John Clare, "The Mores," line 3, in *John Clare: Poems of the Middle Period: 1822–1837*, ed. Eric Robinson, David Powell, and P.M.S. Dawson (Oxford: Clarendon Press, 1996), 2:347; hereafter abbreviated as *MP*.

4. "The cowboy sees the spring & hears the crows," line 13, in *MP*, 5:253.

5. "Rural Morning," line 37, in *EP*, 2:613.

6. "Summer Morning," line 5, in *EP*, 2:381; "Evening," line 2, in *EP*, 2:84.

7. "The Authors Address to His Book," lines 58 and 64, in *EP*, 1:427; "Love Epistles between Richard and Kate," line 72, in *EP*, 1:66.

8. *OED Online*, s.v. "blunder, *v.*," sense 1a, 3a, and 7a (unrevised entry 1989).

9. "AUTOGRAPH: Peterborough MS A61, p. 47," in *MP*, 5:268.

10. Sarah Guyer, *Reading with John Clare: Biopoetics, Sovereignty, Romanticism* (New York: Fordham University Press, 2015), 81.

11. Jonathan Bate, *John Clare: A Biography* (London: Picador, 2003), 405.

12. Ibid.

13. The enclosure acts of the early nineteenth century went into effect in the 1820s, just as Clare was beginning to publish his first poems. Without any land of his own, Clare's relation to and sense of his local landscape was greatly altered by these changes. See, for example, John Barrell's *The Idea of Landscape and the Sense of Place, 1730–1840: An Approach to the Poetry of John Clare* (Cambridge: Cambridge University Press, 1972).

14. Stephanie Kuduk Wiener, *Clare's Lyric: John Clare and Three Modern Poets* (Oxford: Oxford University Press, 2014), 34.

15. Simon Kövesi, "Beyond the Language Wars: Towards a Green Edition of John Clare," *John Clare Society Journal* 26 (July 2007): 72.

16. Wordsworth, "Essay, Supplementary to the Preface," line 452, in *Prose Works*, 3:74.

17. Coleridge, quoted in Peter Swaab, "'Wonder' as a Complex Word," *Romanticism* 18, no. 3 (October 2012): 270.

18. Samuel Taylor Coleridge, Aphorism IX, in *Aids to Reflection*, in *The Collected Works of Samuel Taylor Coleridge*, ed. John Beer (Princeton, NJ: Princeton University Press, 1993), 9:236.

19. Clare, "The Autobiography: 1793–1824," in *The Prose of John Clare*, ed. J. W. and Anne Tibble (London: Routledge & Kegan Paul, 1951), 80.

20. "The passing traveler with wonder sees," lines 1–6, Peterborough MS A61 (p. 106), in *MP*, 5:314; emphasis added.

21. "I know a little nook," lines 23–24, Peterborough MS A61 (pp. 34–35), in *MP*, 5:260; emphasis added.

22. "I found a ball of grass among the hay," lines 1–8, Peterborough MS A61 (p. 6), in *MP*, 5:246; emphasis added.

23. Simon Kövesi, *John Clare: Nature, Criticism, History* (London: Palgrave Macmillan, 2017), 108.

24. Andrew Hodgson, "Form and Feeling in John Clare's Sonnets," *John Clare Society Journal* 31 (2012): 61–62.

25. Clare, "Autobiography," in *Prose*, 13; emphasis added.

26. Guyer, *Reading with John Clare*, 90.

27. Ibid., 86.

28. David Higgins, *Romantic Englishness: Local, National, and Global Selves, 1780–1850* (New York: Palgrave Macmillan, 2014), 90–91.

29. Kövesi, *John Clare*, 108.

30. Erica McAlpine, "Keeping Nature at Bay: John Clare's Poetry of Wonder," *Studies in Romanticism* 50 (Spring 2011): 97.

31. Ibid., 98.

32. Ibid.

33. Plato, *Theaetetus*, in *Plato: Volume II; Theaetetus, Sophist*, trans. H. N. Fowler, Loeb Classical Library (London: William Heinemann, 1921), 55.

34. Aristotle, *Metaphysics: Book I (A)*, 2:983a14, in *The Complete Works of Aristotle*, ed. Jonathan Barnes, Bollingen Series (Princeton, NJ: Princeton University Press, 1984), 6.

35. *OED Online*, s.v. "err, v.," "Etymology: Middle English erre, < French *errer*, Provençal *errar*, Spanish *errar*, Italian *errare*, Latin *errāre* < prehistoric **ersāre*, cognate with Gothic *aírzjan* transitive to lead astray, Old High German *irrôn* transitive and intransitive (German *irren*)" (unrevised entry 1989).

36. "One day when all the woods where bare & blea," Peterborough MS A61 (p. 77), in *MP*, 5:290.

37. Peterborough MS A61 (p. 47), John Clare Manuscripts, Peterborough Museum and Art Gallery.

38. In "The Authors Address to His Book" (*EP*, 1:424–31), "Epistle 1st from Richard" (*EP*, 1:64–66), and "The Quack and the Cobler" (*EP*, 1:164–70), respectively.

39. In "Song" [There's suns in the dew blebs] (*Later Poems*, 2:486), "Song" [Mary charming Mary] (*EP*, 2:51), and "Still Unchangeable" (*MP*, 5:220), respectively.

40. "Sketch Lolham brigs where strangers come & go," Peterborough MS A61 (p. 8), in *MP*, 5:246.

41. Clare, quoted in Barrell, *Idea of Landscape*, 126.

42. John Taylor, "Introduction to *Poems Descriptive of Rural Life and Scenery*," in *John Clare: The Critical Heritage*, ed. Mark Storey (London: Routledge and Kegan Paul, 1973), 47.

43. Barrell, *Idea of Landscape*, 125.

44. Clare, *MP*, 5:xii–xiii.

45. Mina Gorji, *John Clare and the Place of Poetry* (Liverpool: Liverpool University Press, 2008), 18.

46. Ibid., 17.

47. Ibid., 22–23.

48. "The path goes through the farm I often turn," lines 1–2, Peterborough MS A61 (p. 21), *MP*, 5:251.

49. "The cowboy sees the spring & hears the crows," line 13, Peterborough MS A61 (p. 23), *MP*, 5:253.

50. See note 11; emphasis added.

51. John Clare, *By Himself*, ed. Eric Robinson (London: Carcanet, 1998), 101.

52. Alan Vardy, *John Clare: Politics and Poetry* (Basingstoke, UK: Palgrave Macmillan, 2003), 70.

53. Ibid., 66.

54. John Goodridge, *John Clare and Community* (Cambridge: Cambridge University Press, 2013), 12.

55. Andrew Elfenbein, "Romantic Poetry and the Standardization of English," in *Cambridge Companion to British Romantic Poetry*, ed. James Chandler and Maureen McLane (Cambridge: Cambridge University Press, 2008), 94.

56. Kövesi, *John Clare*, 110.

57. Ibid., 109.

58. Ibid., 110.

Chapter 4. Emily Dickinson's Eloquent Lies

1. Emily Dickinson, *The Poems of Emily Dickinson*, ed. R. W. Franklin (Cambridge, MA: Harvard University Press, 1998), F261A, line 7, F124C, line 10. All citations of Dickinson's poetry are from this edition unless otherwise specified. References are to the Franklin number and line(s); where whole poems have been quoted, line numbers are omitted.

2. F1410.

3. Yvor Winters, *In Defense of Reason* (Denver, CO: Alan Swallow, 1937), 283.

4. David Porter, *Dickinson: The Modern Idiom* (Cambridge, MA: Harvard University Press, 1981), 2.

5. Ibid., 6.

6. Sharon Cameron, *Choosing Not Choosing: Dickinson's Fascicles* (Chicago: University of Chicago Press, 1992), 183.

7. Cristanne Miller, *Emily Dickinson: A Poet's Grammar* (Cambridge, MA: Harvard University Press, 1987), 66.

8. Cameron, *Choosing Not Choosing*, 184.

9. Miller, *Emily Dickinson*, 50.

10. Porter, *Dickinson*, 52.

11. Ibid., 66.

12. F45.

13. F545A, line 1.

14. Virginia Jackson, *Dickinson's Misery: A Theory of Lyric Reading* (Princeton, NJ: Princeton University Press, 2005), 17.

15. Miller, *Emily Dickinson*, 67.

16. R. W. Franklin, *The Editing of Emily Dickinson: A Reconsideration* (Madison: University of Wisconsin Press, 1967), 138.

17. F772B.

18. Miller, *Emily Dickinson*, 4.

19. Thomas H. Johnson, *Emily Dickinson: An Interpretive Biography* (Cambridge, MA: Harvard University Press, 1955), 93.

20. David Porter, *The Art of Emily Dickinson's Earlier Poetry* (Cambridge, MA: Harvard University Press, 1966), 139.

21. F328A, lines 9–16.

22. Dickinson, "Of Tribulation—these are They," J325, in *The Poems of Emily Dickinson*, ed. Thomas H. Johnson (Cambridge, MA: Belknap Press of Harvard University Press, 1955), 1:256–57.

23. Emily Dickinson, *The Letters of Emily Dickinson*, ed. Thomas H. Johnson (Cambridge, MA: Harvard University Press, 1958), 2:412. References to Dickinson's letters are hereafter abbreviated to *L* (number in the Johnson edition) and volume and page.

24. In fact, Dickinson spells the word wrong in two other poems as well (F291 and F656).

25. Brita Lindberg Seyersted, *Emily Dickinson's Punctuation* (Oslo: American Institute, 1976), 24.

26. Emily Dickinson to Austin Dickinson, 26 March 1854, *L*159, 1:292.

27. Willis J. Buckingham, "Emily Dickinson's 'Lone Orthography,'" *Papers of the Bibliographical Society of America* 75, no. 4 (1981): 419–35.

28. Emily Dickinson to Austin Dickinson, early June 1854, *L*165, 1:296.

29. Emily Dickinson to Mrs. J. G. Holland, March 1883, *L*806, 3:763.

30. Ibid., *L*820, 3:774.

31. Buckingham, "Emily Dickinson's 'Lone Orthography,'" 419–20.

32. F1380E.

33. Cited in Buckingham, "Emily Dickinson's 'Lone Orthography,'" 425. His

citation comes from the edition of Webster's dictionary that the Dickinson family owned.

34. Ibid., 427.

35. F430B.

36. Buckingham, "Emily Dickinson's 'Lone Orthography,'" 428.

37. F1263, line 1.

38. Emily Dickinson to T. W. Higginson, 2 July 1862, *L*268, 2:412.

39. F1010A.

40. Buckingham, "Emily Dickinson's 'Lone Orthography,'" 430.

41. Emily Dickinson to Susan Gilbert Dickinson, Autumn 1872, *L*378, 2:498. Cf. Franklin's note: "The poem was published in the *Springfield Daily Republican* on 14 February 1866 under the title 'The Snake.' . . . ED wrote [Higginson] a letter, postmarked 17 March, in which she complained of the punctuation between lines 3 and 4 as published 'You may have met him— did you not? / His notice instant is,' and disavowed the publication." Franklin, *The Poems of Emily Dickinson*, 2:951–52.

42. F1096C, lines 1–4.

43. Emily Dickinson to T. W. Higginson, early 1866, *L*316, 2:450.

44. Sharon Cameron, *Lyric Time: Dickinson and the Limits of Genre* (Baltimore, MD: Johns Hopkins University Press, 1979), 16.

45. F1489G.

46. F1489B–G. See poem variants and notes in Franklin, ed., *The Poems of Emily Dickinson*, 3:1305–8.

47. Emily Dickinson, *Emily Dickinson's Poems: As She Preserved Them*, ed. by Cristanne Miller (Cambridge, MA: Belknap Press of Harvard University Press, 2016), 618.

48. Emily Miller Budick explains that in the language of this poem, "there is a hint of frenzy that is intended not simply to replicate the motion of a bird but to warn us that both the bird and the poem are teetering at the edge of confusion and disarray." Emily Miller Budick, *Emily Dickinson and the Life of Language: A Study in Symbolic Poetics* (Baton Rouge: Louisiana State University Press, 1985), 10. See also Roland Hagenbüchle, "Precision and Indeterminacy in the Poetry of Emily Dickinson," *ESQ: A Journal of the American Renaissance* 20, no. 1 (1974): 33–56.

49. Howard explains: "*Cochineal* (5) occurs as the name of a food coloring in cooking recipes of the early nineteenth century, and in the 1870s it was a common enough word to appear in the lines of a somewhat ribald domestic comedy in which one of the characters uses a fictitious board meeting of 'the

Compressed Cochineal Company' as an excuse to his wife for an evening out." William Howard, "Emily Dickinson's Poetic Vocabulary," *PMLA* 72, no. 1 (March 1957): 231.

50. In *The Tempest*, Shakespeare writes of the Queen of Tunis: "She that dwells / Ten leagues beyond man's life; she that from Naples / Can have no note— unless the sun were post" (2.1.241–43).

51. F204B, lines 1–4.

52. F261.

53. F1247, line 4.

54. F570, line 3.

55. Archibald MacLeish, "The Private World: Poems of Emily Dickinson," in *Emily Dickinson: A Collection of Critical Essays*, ed. Richard B. Sewall (Engle- wood Cliffs, NJ: Prentice-Hall, 1963), 152. Paul Muldoon writes a whole essay attending to this phrase ("polar expiation"), revealing its underpinnings in a pun on "polar expedition" and giving an account of Dickinson's particu- lar interest in the expedition of Sir John Franklin, which led to the discovery of the Northwest Passage—a name Dickinson had affectionately given to a particular hallway in her family's homestead. Paul Muldoon, *The End of the Poem* (New York: Farrar, Straus and Giroux, 2006), 116–39.

56. Seyersted, *Emily Dickinson's Punctuation*, 27.

57. See Jack L. Capps, *Emily Dickinson's Reading: 1836–1886* (Cambridge, MA: Harvard University Press, 1966), 103–5.

58. F1161.

59. F1691.

60. Miller, *Emily Dickinson's Poems*, 791.

61. Jack L. Capps, *Emily Dickinson's Reading*, 106.

62. Emily Dickinson to unknown recipient, ca. 1861, *L*233, 2:374.

63. F1410.

64. *OED Online*, s.v. "flake, *n*.", sense 10a: "A small fracture or 'chip,'" and 10b, "One who is 'flaky' or liable to act in an eccentric or crazy manner, a 'screw- ball'; also, a foolish, slow-witted, or unreliable person" (unrevised entry 1989).

65. See, for example, the several versions of F277: "Going to them, happy let- ter!" (F277A), "Going – to – Her! / Happy – Letter! Tell her –" (F277B), and "Going to Him! Happy letter! / Tell him –" (F277C).

66. F1268A.

67. Emily Dickinson to Mrs. J. G. Holland, early March 1866, *L*315, 2:449. Quoted in Porter, *Dickinson*, 56.

68. F122.

69. Cameron, *Lyric Time*, 18.

70. Ibid., 19.

71. F1304B.

CHAPTER 5. HART CRANE'S WRAPTURE

1. Hart Crane to Clarence Arthur Crane, Cleveland, 2 June 1910, in *Complete Poems and Selected Letters*, ed. Langdon Hammer (New York: Library of America, 2006), 181. All citations of Crane's work and correspondence are from this edition, hereafter abbreviated as *CPSL*.

2. Crane to Elizabeth Beldon Hart, 26 January 1916, in *CPSL*, 182.

3. Ibid.

4. Hart Crane to Clarence Arthur Crane, New York, 1 April 1917, in *CPSL*, 186.

5. Ibid., 7 April 1917, in *CPSL*, 187.

6. Allen Tate, "Hart Crane," in *Collected Essays* (Denver, CO: Alan Swallow, 1959), 226. See also Allen Tate, "Introduction to *White Buildings*," in *Hart Crane: A Collection of Critical Essays*, ed. Alan Trachtenberg (Englewood Cliffs, NJ: Prentice-Hall, 1982), 18–22.

7. Yvor Winters, "The Progress of Hart Crane," in *Hart Crane: A Collection of Critical Essays*, ed. Alan Trachtenberg (New Jersey: Prentice-Hall, 1982), 27.

8. Ibid., 31.

9. See William Logan's review of this edition, "Hart Crane's Bridge to Nowhere," *New York Times*, 28 January 2007, Sunday Book Review, https://www.nytimes.com/2007/01/28/books/review/Logan.t.html, as well as his defense of that review in *Poetry Magazine*: William Login, "The Hart Crane Controversy," *Poetry Magazine*, October 2008, https://www.poetryfoundation.org/poetrymagazine/articles/69119/the-hart-crane-controversy.

10. "Voyages II," lines 17–26, in *CPSL*, 25.

11. Crane to Yvor Winters, 27 January 1927, in *CPSL*, 517.

12. A. Alvarez, *The Shaping Spirit: Studies in Modern English and American Poets* (London: Chatto and Windus, 1958), 116–17.

13. Milton, *Comus*, line 546, in *Complete Shorter Poems*, 105; and *Macbeth*, 1.3.145, in *Tragedies*, in *Mr. William Shakespeares Comedies, Histories, & Tragedies: Published According to the True and Originall Copies* (London: Printed by Isaac Iagaard and Edward Blount, 1623), 132.

14. "Atlantis," lines 73–75, in *CPSL*, 74.

15. In addition to Milton and Shakespeare, D. H. Lawrence—of whom Crane was a serious devotee—uses "wrapt" several times in his novels, short stories, and poems. While Lawrence's editors have corrected some of these instances, Crane may well have come across the misspelling in early editions of the work. Examples of "wrapt" can be found in Lawrence's *The White Peacock* (1911), "Daughters of the Vicar" (1914), *Aaron's Rod* (1922), and the poem "Cypresses," written in 1920 and published in *Birds, Beasts, and Flowers* (1923). Crane mentions Lawrence several times in his letters, but no editions of his work remain in what is left of the poet's library. See Kenneth Lohf, "The Library of Hart Crane," in *Proof: Yearbook of American Bibliographical and Textual Studies* 3 (1973): 283–334.

16. Sherman Paul, *Hart's Bridge* (Chicago: University of Illinois Press, 1972), 145.

17. Crane, Draft of "Voyages II" [ca. 1923–24], Brooklyn, Lohf A41, 42681D Bancroft, Hart Crane Papers, Rare Book and Manuscript Library, Columbia University, New York.

18. Herbert Leibowitz, *Hart Crane: An Introduction to the Poetry* (New York: Columbia University Press, 1968), 97.

19. Philip Horton, *Hart Crane: The Life of an American Poet* (New York: Viking Press, 1957), 310.

20. Leibowitz, *Hart Crane*, 101; emphasis added.

21. Ibid., 219; emphasis added.

22. Richard Warrington Baldwin Lewis, *The Poetry of Hart Crane: A Critical Study* (Princeton, NJ: Princeton University Press, 1967), 156.

23. Thomas Yingling, *Hart Crane and the Homosexual Text: New Thresholds, New Anatomies* (Chicago: University of Chicago Press, 1990), 94.

24. Crane to Waldo Frank, New York, 21 April 1924, in *CPSL*, 383.

25. Brian M. Reed, *Hart Crane: After His Lights* (Tuscaloosa: University of Alabama Press, 2006), 112.

26. Marjorie Perloff, *The Poetics of Indeterminacy: Rimbaud to Cage* (Princeton, NJ: Princeton University Press, 1981).

27. Ibid., 4.

28. "General Aims and Theories," in *CPSL*, 163.

29. "To Emily Dickinson," lines 7–8, in *CPSL*, 87.

30. *OED Online*, s.v. "momently, adv." (3rd ed.).

31. Tate, *Collected Essays*, 226.

32. William Logan, "On Reviewing Hart Crane," in *Our Savage Art: Poetry and the Civil Tongue* (New York: Columbia University Press, 2009), 177.

33. See Joseph Warren Beach, "Hart Crane and Moby Dick," *Western Review* 20 (Spring 1956): 183–85.
34. Crane to Sherwood Anderson, Cleveland, 10 January 1922, in *CPSL*, 265.
35. Crane to Harriet Monroe, 1926, in *CPSL*, 165.
36. See "Crane in His Letters," in David Bromwich, *Skeptical Music: Essays on Modern Poetry* (Chicago: University of Chicago Press, 2001), 54. Bromwich notes that Crane's famous letter to Monroe shows "a kind of forthrightness, almost simplicity of heart, on behalf of aesthetic intensity" that can be found in all his letters to friends and poets.
37. Crane to Harriet Monroe, 1926, in *CPSL*, 166.
38. Wallace Stevens, "Thirteen Ways of Looking at a Blackbird," section 5, lines 13–17, *Collected Prose and Poetry*, 75.
39. Crane to Gorham Munson, November 1919, in *CPSL*, 217.
40. Helen Vendler, *On Extended Wings: Wallace Stevens; Longer Poems* (Cambridge, MA: Harvard University Press, 1969), 76.
41. Paul Ramsey, "The Bidding Place: Reflections on Hart Crane," *Parnassus* 5, no. 1 (Fall/Winter 1976): 195.
42. Leibowitz, *Hart Crane*, 81–82.
43. Crane to Jean Toomer, 16 June 1924, in *CPSL*, 390.
44. John T. Irwin, "Naming Names: Hart Crane's 'Logic of Metaphor,'" *Southern Review* 11, no. 2 (April 1975): 286.
45. Crane, "General Aims and Theories," in *CPSL*, 161.
46. Langdon Hammer, *Hart Crane and Allen Tate: Janus-Faced Modernism* (Princeton, NJ: Princeton University Press, 1993), 132.
47. Lewis Carroll, *Through the Looking-Glass*, in *Alice's Adventures in Wonderland and Through the Looking-Glass*, ed. Peter Hunt (Oxford: Oxford University Press, 2009), 136.
48. *Henry IV, Part One*, 5.5.2.
49. Crane, "Voyages III," lines 15–19, in *CSPL*, 26.
50. Hammer, *Crane and Tate*, 166.
51. Paul, *Hart's Bridge*, 151.
52. Leibowitz, *Hart Crane*, 101.
53. Lewis, *The Poetry of Hart Crane*, 168.
54. R. P. Blackmur, *Form and Value in Modern Poetry* (New York: Doubleday Anchor Books, 1957), 277.
55. Leibowitz, *Hart Crane*, 99.
56. Ibid., 101.

57. Ibid.

58. Crane to Monroe, 1926, in *CPSL*, 167–68.

59. Blackmur, *Form and Value*, 273.

60. Reed, *Hart Crane*, 114.

61. For Crane's processes of writing, see Reed, "How to Write a Lyric," in *After His Lights*, 97–125.

62. Crane to Grace Hart Crane, New York, 16 November 1924, in *CPSL*, 401.

CHAPTER 6. FACT-CHECKING ELIZABETH BISHOP

1. Elizabeth Bishop, "The Bight," lines 20–31, in *Poems, Prose and Letters*, ed. Robert Giroux and Lloyd Schwartz (New York: Library of America, 2008), 47. All citations from Bishop's writing are taken from this edition (hereafter abbreviated *PPL*) unless otherwise stated.

2. Ibid.

3. "The Country Mouse," in *PPL*, 426.

4. "In the Waiting Room," in *PPL*, 149–51.

5. David Kalstone, *Becoming a Poet: Elizabeth Bishop with Marianne Moore and Robert Lowell* (Ann Arbor: University of Michigan Press, 2001), 246.

6. Jamie McKendrick, "Bishop's Birds," in *Elizabeth Bishop: Poet of the Periphery*, ed. Linda Anderson and Jo Shapcott (Newcastle: Bloodaxe Books, 2002), 142.

7. Bishop, interview by George Starbuck, "A Conversation with Elizabeth Bishop" (1977), in *Conversations with Elizabeth Bishop*, ed. George Monteiro (Jackson: University Press of Mississippi, 1996), 87.

8. Anne Stevenson, "Chapter One: In the Waiting Room," in *Five Looks at Elizabeth Bishop* (London: Bellew, 1998), 35.

9. Kalstone, *Becoming a Poet*, 245–46.

10. Ibid., 246.

11. Lee Edelman, "The Geography of Gender: Elizabeth Bishop's 'In the Waiting Room,'" *Contemporary Literature* 26, no. 2 (Summer 1985): 180.

12. Ibid., 184.

13. Bishop to Robert Lowell, 19 August 1967, in *Words in Air: The Complete Correspondence between Elizabeth Bishop and Robert Lowell*, ed. Thomas Travisano with Saskia Hamilton (London: Faber and Faber, 2008), 629.

14. Bishop to Lowell, 30 August 1967, in *Words in Air*, 630.

15. Ibid.

16. See Brett C. Millier, *Elizabeth Bishop: Life and the Memory of It* (Berkeley: University of California Press, 1993), 444–45.

17. Elizabeth Bishop to Frank Bidart, 27 July 1971, in *One Art: Letters*, ed. Robert Giroux (New York: Farrar, Straus and Giroux, 1994), 545–46.

18. "In the Waiting Room," lines 80–86, in *PPL*, 150.

19. "The Bight," lines 32–35, in *PPL*, 47.

20. Bishop to Howard Moss, 15 June 1970, in *Elizabeth Bishop and "The New Yorker": The Complete Correspondence*, ed. Joelle Biele (New York: Farrar, Straus and Giroux, 2011), 319; hereafter abbreviated as *EB and TNY*.

21. Ibid., 319.

22. Robert Hemenway to Elizabeth Bishop, 30 June 1970, in *EB and TNY*, 320.

23. Bishop, interview by George Starbuck, "A Conversation with Elizabeth Bishop," in *Conversations*, 87.

24. Bishop, interview by Wesley Wehr, "Elizabeth Bishop: Conversations and Class Notes" (1966), in *Conversations*, 42.

25. Bishop, interview by Elizabeth Spires, "The Art of Poetry, XXVII: Elizabeth Bishop" (1978), in *Conversations*, 117.

26. "The Fish," lines 54, 20, 63–64, in *PPL*, 34.

27. "The Colder the Air," line 1, in *PPL*, 5.

28. "Brazil, January 1, 1502," lines 10–11, in *PPL*, 72.

29. "The Armadillo," lines 9–13, in *PPL*, 83.

30. "Sandpiper," lines 8–9, in *PPL*, 125.

31. "Love Lies Sleeping," lines 57–59, in *PPL*, 14.

32. "The Monument," lines 2–3, in *PPL*, 18.

33. "The Gentleman of Shalott," lines 41–42, in *PPL*, 8.

34. Bishop, interview by David W. McCullough, "David McCullough's Eye on Books" (1977), in *Conversations*, 73.

35. Colm Tóibín, *On Elizabeth Bishop* (Princeton, NJ: Princeton University Press, 2015), 7.

36. "Crusoe in England," lines 10 and 144, in *PPL*, 151, 155.

37. Ibid., lines 96–97, in *PPL*, 154.

38. Ibid., lines 132–33, in *PPL*, 155.

39. Marianne Moore, *The Complete Poems of Marianne Moore* (New York: Macmillan/Viking, 1967), n.p.

40. "The Man-Moth," line 29, in *PPL*, 10–11.

41. "On 'The Man-Moth,'" in *PPL*, 715.

42. Bishop to Lowell, 21 March 1972, in *Words in Air*, 707–8.

43. "At the Fishhouses," lines 78–83, in *PPL*, 52.

44. Bishop, in *Words in Air*, 719.

45. Paul Muldoon, interview with Tracy K. Smith, "*The New Yorker* Poetry Podcast," audio podcast, n.d., http://downloads.newyorker.com/mp3/poetry/140123_poetry_smith.mp3.

46. Ibid.

47. "Writing poetry is an unnatural act . . . ," in *PPL*, 703.

48. Ibid., 706.

CHAPTER 7. MISREMEMBERING SEAMUS HEANEY

1. Seamus Heaney, "Wordsworth's Skates," in *District and Circle* (New York: Farrar, Straus and Giroux, 2006), 24.

2. Neil Corcoran, *The Poetry of Seamus Heaney: A Critical Study* (London: Faber and Faber, 1998), 165.

3. Wordsworth, *The Prelude* (1805), 1.453–91, in *The Thirteen-Book Prelude*, ed. Mark L. Reed (Ithaca, NY: Cornell University Press, 1991), 2:279–81.

4. Ibid., 1.474, 1.461, 2:280.

5. Ibid., 1.566–70, 2:511.

6. For a recent, wide-ranging study of Heaney's regionalism, see Richard Rankine Russell, *Seamus Heaney's Regions* (Notre Dame, IN: University of Notre Dame Press, 2014).

7. Heaney, interview with Dennis O'Driscoll, in *Stepping Stones: Interviews with Seamus Heaney* (London: Faber and Faber, 2008), 162.

8. Heaney, "Glanmore Sonnet 3," *Field Work* (New York: Farrar, Straus and Giroux, 1979), 35.

9. Barbara Hardy, "Allusions, Appropriations, Assimilations," in *Seamus Heaney: Poet, Critic, Translator*, ed. Ashby Bland Crowder and Jason David Hall (London: Palgrave Macmillan, 2007), 193.

10. Seamus Heaney, "The Makings of a Music: Reflections on Wordsworth and Yeats," in *Preoccupations: Selected Prose, 1968–1978* (New York: Farrar, Straus and Giroux, 1980), 67–68.

11. Wordsworth, *The Prelude*, 1.479–80, in *The Thirteen-Book Prelude*, 1:119.

12. Russell notes how "Heaney celebrates the perduring, memory-evoking qualities of the steel in Wordsworth's skates that enabled him to score the surface of frozen Lake Windermere. Such things have a literal cutting edge, implying the continuing importance of words that are sharp, that can slice into a subject and get a grip on it." Richard Rankine Russell, *Seamus Heaney: An Introduction* (Edinburgh: Edinburgh University Press, 2016), 198.

13. See, for example, Heaney's Nobel lecture "Crediting Poetry," in *Opened Ground* (New York: Farrar, Straus and Giroux, 1998), 415–30. Unless

otherwise stated, all citations of Heaney's poetry are from this edition and follow the format Heaney, title, line number(s), *OG*, page number(s).

14. Dorothy Wordsworth to Mary Lamb, 9 January 1830, in *The Letters of William and Dorothy Wordsworth: The Later Years; Part II: 1829–1834*, ed. Alan G. Hill, 2nd ed. (Oxford: Clarendon Press, 1979), 5:191.

15. Wordsworth, *The Prelude*, 3.191, in *The Thirteen-Book Prelude*, 1:140.

16. Heaney, "Feeling into Words," in *Preoccupations*, 54.

17. Heaney, "The Triumph of Spirit," *Guardian*, 11 February 2006, https://www.theguardian.com/books/2006/feb/11/poetry.classics, paragraph 2.

18. David Bromwich, *Disowned by Memory*, 149.

19. Ibid., 149.

20. Ibid., 166.

21. Heaney, "Fosterling," in *OG*, 331.

22. See Heaney, "Place and Displacement: Recent Poetry from Northern Ireland," in *Finders Keepers* (London: Faber and Faber, 2002), 112–33. Heaney draws his argument from *The Prelude*, book 10.

23. Ibid., 118.

24. Elmer Andrews, *The Poetry of Seamus Heaney: All the Realms of Whisper* (London: Macmillan, 1988), 15.

25. Ibid., 202.

26. Andrew Murphy, *Seamus Heaney*, 3rd ed. (Tavistock, UK: Northcote House, 2009), 22.

27. Robert Welch, " 'A rich young man leaving everything he had': Poetic Freedom in Seamus Heaney," in *Seamus Heaney: A Collection of Critical Essays*, ed. Elmer Andrews (London: Macmillan, 1992), 152.

28. Heaney, "The Given Note," lines 13–18, in *OG*, 36.

29. Heaney, "Whitby-sur-Moyola," lines 7–11, in *OG*, 397.

30. Heaney, "The Settle Bed," lines 16–25, in *OG*, 321.

31. Heaney, "Wheels within Wheels," lines 18–19, in *OG*, 329.

32. Eugene O'Brien comments that in *Seeing Things*, "the power of the imagination to alter the 'givens' of reality has become a seminal preoccupation . . . the transformation from the actual to the imagined is repeated in different contexts." *Seamus Heaney: Creating Irelands of the Mind* (Dublin: Liffey Press, 2002), 98. See also Welch, " 'A rich young man leaving everything he had,' " 153.

33. Heaney, "Squarings xlviii," lines 1–4, in *OG*, 366.

34. Corcoran writes, the "punning title raises the possibility of delusion in the

same phrase in which it declares the possibility of revelation." *The Poetry of Seamus Heaney*, 163.

35. Ibid., 165.

36. Catharine Molloy, "Seamus Heaney's *Seeing Things*: 'Retracing the Path Back,'" in *Seamus Heaney: The Shaping Spirit*, ed. Catharine Molloy and Phyllis Carey (London: Associated University Presses, 1996), 158.

37. "[I]n maturity, the myths of the classical world and Dante's *Commedia* (where my Irish Catholic subculture received high cultural ratification) and the myths of other cultures matched and mixed and provided a cosmology that corresponded well enough to the original: you learned that, from the human beginnings, poetic imagination had proffered a world of light and a world of dark, a shadow region—not so much an afterlife as an afterimage of life. Getting older has therefore been a matter of dwelling with and imagining in terms of those archetypical patterns—which is why I called myself 'Jungian.'" Heaney, interview with O'Driscoll, in *Stepping Stones*, 472.

38. Michael Cavanagh, *Professing Poetry: Seamus Heaney's Poetics* (Washington, DC: Catholic University of America Press, 2009), 97.

39. Ibid., 96.

40. Ibid., 167. He is quoting here from Heaney's introduction to *The Essential Wordsworth* (Hopewell, NJ: Ecco, 1988), 3–14.

41. Bromwich, *Disowned by Memory*, 149.

42. Corcoran, *The Poetry of Seamus Heaney*, 193.

43. Douglas Dunn, "Quotidian Miracles: *Seeing Things*," in *The Art of Seamus Heaney*, ed. Tony Curtis (Bridgend, Wales: Seren, 1982), 220.

44. Henry Hart, "What Is Heaney Seeing in *Seeing Things?*," *Colby Quarterly* 30, no. 1 (March 1994): 33.

45. "Whither is fled the visionary gleam? / Where is it now, the glory and the dream?" Wordsworth, "Ode," lines 56–57, in *Poems, in Two Volumes, and Other Poems*, ed. Jared Curtis (Ithaca, NY: Cornell University Press, 1982), 272.

46. Heaney, "Squarings vi," in *OG*, 336.

47. Heaney, "Squarings iii," lines 5–8, in *OG*, 334.

48. Wordsworth, "Expostulation and Reply," line 24, in *Lyrical Ballads* (1798), in *Lyrical Ballads, and Other Poems, 1797–1800*, ed. James Butler and Karen Green (Ithaca, NY: Cornell University Press, 1992), 108.

49. Heaney, "Lightenings vii," lines 1–12, in *OG*, 337.

50. Heaney, "Scrabble," in "Glanmore Revisited," lines 4–5, in *OG*, 322.

51. Heaney, "Place and Displacement," in *Finders Keepers*, 119.

52. Helen Vendler, *Seamus Heaney* (Cambridge, MA: Harvard University Press, 1998), 151–52.

53. Heaney, "Joy or Night: Last Things in the Poetry of W. B. Yeats and Philip Larkin," in *The Redress of Poetry* (London: Faber and Faber, 1995), 152.

54. Heaney, *The Redress of Poetry*, xiii.

55. Florence Emily Hardy, *The Later Years of Thomas Hardy, 1892–1928* (Cambridge: Cambridge University Press, 2011), 263.

56. Bishop to Lowell, 21 March 1972, in *Words in Air*, 707.

57. Barbara Hardy, "Allusions, Appropriations, Assimilations," in *Seamus Heaney: Poet, Critic, Translator*, ed. Ashby Bland Crowder and Jason David Hall (London: Palgrave Macmillan, 2007), 199–200.

58. Ibid., 199.

59. Corcoran, *The Poetry of Seamus Heaney*, 183–84.

60. Heaney, "The Birthplace," lines 36–43, in *OG*, 210.

61. Bernard O'Donoghue, *Seamus Heaney and the Language of Poetry* (Hemel Hempstead, Hertfordshire: Harvester Wheatsheaf, 1994), 97–98.

62. Heaney, "The Loose Box," lines 11–14, in *Electric Light* (New York: Farrar, Straus and Giroux, 2001), 15.

63. Ibid., line 75.

64. Ibid., lines 35–40.

65. Ibid., line 57.

66. Hardy, "Allusions, Appropriations, Assimilations," 197–98.

67. Heaney, "Squarings xlviii," lines 3–4, in *OG*, 366.

68. Heaney, "Squarings xl," line 8, in *OG*, 358.

69. Ibid., lines 1–3, in *OG*, 358.

70. Ibid., lines 10–12, in *OG*, 358.

71. Heaney, "Squarings xli," lines 1–8, in *OG*, 359.

72. Robert Pinsky, "In Praise of Memorizing Poetry—Badly," *Slate*, 1 November 2008, http://www.slate.com/articles/arts/poem/2011/11/william_butler _yeats_on_being_asked_for_a_war_poem_.html.

73. Christopher Ricks, "Walter Pater, Matthew Arnold and Misquotation," in *The Force of Poetry* (Oxford: Clarendon Press, 1984), 392–416.

74. Heaney, interview with Blake Morrison, "Seamus Famous: Time to Be Dazzled," *Independent on Sunday*, 19 May 1991, 26. Quoted in Elmer Andrews, "The Spirit's Protest," in *Seamus Heaney*, 225.

75. Christopher Ricks, "Seamus Heaney: Field Work," in *Reviewery* (London: Penguin, 2002), 297.

76. Heaney, "Feeling into Words," in *Preoccupations*, 52.

77. Heaney, interview with O'Driscoll, in *Stepping Stones*, 321.

78. Heaney, "Frontiers of Writing," in *The Redress of Poetry*, 190.

79. Heaney, interview with O'Driscoll, in *Stepping Stones*, 467.

80. Ricks, "Seamus Heaney: Field Work," 297.

81. Heaney, "Clearances IV," lines 12–14, in *OG*, 286.

82. O'Donoghue, *Seamus Heaney*, 113.

83. Heaney, "Clearances II," lines 4–8, in *OG*, 284.

84. Liam Harte, "Kibird's Classical Canon," *Irish Times*, 2 December 2000. The anecdote, which comes from a keynote address Heaney gave at a conference in Cork, is mentioned both in this article and a subsequent one published a few days later, on 7 December 2000, also in the *Irish Times*.

85. Heaney, "Squarings viii," in *OG*, 338.

86. O'Donoghue, *Seamus Heaney*, 127.

87. Heaney, interview with O'Driscoll, in *Stepping Stones*, 321–22.

88. Seamus Heaney, "Frontiers of Writing," in *The Redress of Poetry*, 203.

89. Heaney, *The Government of the Tongue: Selected Prose, 1978–1987* (New York: Farrar, Straus and Giroux, 1988), 100.

90. Wordsworth, "Preface to *Lyrical Ballads*," in *Lyrical Ballads*, 751.

Conclusion. Mistaking on Purpose

1. David Bromwich, *Skeptical Music: Essays on Modern Poetry*, xiv.

2. Thomas Hardy to an unidentified correspondent, December 1919, in *The Collected Letters of Thomas Hardy*, ed. Richard Little Purdy and Michael Millgate (Oxford: Oxford University Press, 1985), 5:345.

3. W. H. Auden, "Journey to Iceland," lines 1–2, in W. H. Auden and Louis MacNiece, *Letters from Iceland* (London: Faber and Faber, 1937), 25.

4. Ibid., 27.

5. W. H. Auden, "Journey to Iceland," lines 1–2, in *Collected Poems*, ed. Edward Mendelson (London: Faber and Faber, 1991), 149.

6. John Fuller, *Who Is Ozymandias? And Other Puzzles in Poetry* (London: Chatto and Windus, 2011), 126.

7. James Joyce, *A Portrait of the Artist as a Young Man*, ed. Jeri Johnson (Oxford: Oxford University Press, 2001), 196; and Thomas Nashe, *Summer's Last Will and Testament*, line 1590, in *The Works of Thomas Nashe*, ed. Ronald B. McKerrow, rev. F. P. Wilson (Oxford: Blackwell, 1966), 3:283. For a detailed history of the debate over this error, see Andrew Hadfield, "How to Read

Nashe's 'Brightness Falls from the Air,'" *Forum for Modern Language Studies* 51, no. 3 (1 July 2015): 239–47.

8. See Alexander Freer, "Faith in Reading: Revisiting the Midrash–Theory Connection," *Paragraph: A Journal of Modern Critical Theory* 39, no. 3 (November 2016): 335–57; and also Lerer, *Error and the Academic Self,* 11.

9. Frank Kermode, "The Uses of Error," in *The Uses of Error* (Cambridge, MA: Harvard University Press, 1991), 431.

10. Ibid.

11. Ibid.

12. Robert Hass, "Time and Materials," line 34, in *Time and Materials* (New York: Ecco Press, 2007), 25.

13. Dan Chiasson, "Scared by the Smallest Shriek of a Pig, and When Wounded, Always Give Ground," lines 60–64, in *Natural History and Other Poems* (New York: Alfred A. Knopf, 2005), 59.

14. Brunella Antomarini, *Thinking through Error: The Moving Target of Knowledge* (Lanham, MD: Lexington Books, 2012), 8.

15. James Merrill, "164 East 72nd Street," lines 11–13, in *Collected Poems*, ed. J. D. McClatchy and Stephen Yenser (New York: Knopf, 2001), 661.

16. Ibid., lines 48–50, in *Collected Poems*, 662.

17. For more examples of this kind of psychoanalytically inflected wordplay in Merrill, see Erica McAlpine, "James Merrill's Puns," *Essays in Criticism* 68, no. 4 (October 2018): 488–509.

18. Robert Lowell, "Sailing Home from Rapallo," lines 39–40, in *Life Studies* (New York: Farrar, Straus and Cudahy, 1959), 78.

19. Anne Carson, "Essay on What I Think About Most," lines 128–32, in *Men in the Off Hours* (London: Jonathan Cape, 2000), 35.

20. Nerys Williams, *Reading Error: The Lyric and Contemporary Poetry* (Oxford: Peter Lang, 2007), 26.

21. Ibid., 26.

22. Ibid., 35.

23. John Ashbery, "Errors," in *Collected Poems, 1956–1987*, ed. Mark Ford (New York: Library of America, 2008), 23; hereafter abbreviated *CP*.

24. John Ashbery, "Poetical Space," in *John Ashbery: Selected Prose*, ed. Eugene Richie (Manchester: Carcanet, 2004), 214.

25. Dan Chiasson, "American Snipper: New Poems from John Ashbery," *New Yorker*, 15 May 2015, https://www.newyorker.com/magazine/2015/06/01/american-snipper-books-chiasson.

26. Terence Killeen, "John Ashbery: Snatching Joy from the Poetry of Defeat,"

Irish Times, 20 September 2017, https://www.irishtimes.com/culture/books/john-ashbery-snatching-joy-from-the-poetry-of-defeat-1.3226627.

27. John Ashbery, "Preface," in *Other Traditions* (Cambridge, MA: Harvard University Press, 2000), n.p.

28. Ibid., 8; Ashbery, "The Bungalows," in *CP*, 225.

29. Ashbery, "Self-Portrait in a Convex Mirror," lines 1–2, in *CP*, 474.

30. Ibid., lines 16–17, in *CP*, 474.

31. Ibid., lines 190–91, in *CP*, 478.

32. Ibid., lines 198–99, in *CP*, 478.

33. John Ashbery, "Poem," quoted in John Shoptaw, *On the Outside Looking Out: John Ashbery's Poetry* (Cambridge, MA: Harvard University Press, 1994), 178.

34. David Lehman, *The Last Avant-garde: The Making of the New York School of Poets* (New York: Doubleday, 1998), 314.

35. James A. W. Heffernan, *Museum of Words: The Poetics of Ekphrasis from Homer to Ashbery* (Chicago: University of Chicago Press, 1993), 177.

36. Ben Hickman, *John Ashbery and English Poetry* (Edinburgh: Edinburgh University Press, 2012), 43.

37. William Elford Rogers, *Interpreting Interpretation: Textual Hermeneutics as an Ascetic Discipline* (University Park: Pennsylvania State University Press, 1994), 475–76.

38. Shoptaw, *On the Outside Looking Out*, 182.

39. Ibid.

40. Paul Muldoon, "Errata," lines 1–8, in *Poems, 1968–1998* (London: Faber and Faber, 2001), 445.

41. Walker Percy, "Metaphor as Mistake," *Sewanee Review* 66, no. 1 (Winter 1958): 81.

42. Muldoon, "Author's Note," in *Poems*, xv.

43. Percy, "Metaphor as Mistake," 94.

44. Muldoon, "Errata," in *Poems*, 445.

45. Ibid.

46. Paul Muldoon, interview with Patrick McGuinness, in "Speculating: Patrick McGuinness Interviews Paul Muldoon," *Irish Studies Review* 17, no. 1 (12 February 2009): 105

47. Muldoon, "Yarrow," in *Poems*, 347.

48. Ibid., 355.

49. Ibid., 366.

50. Ibid., 387–88.

51. Muldoon quoted by Michael Allen, "Pax Hibernica/Pax America: Rhyme and Reconciliation in Muldoon," in *Paul Muldoon: Critical Essays* (Liverpool: Liverpool University Press, 2004), 64.

52. Muldoon, "Yarrow," in *Poems*, 378.

53. For other purposeful "slips" in this poem and elsewhere in Muldoon's work, see John Kerrigan, "Paul Muldoon's Transits: Muddling Through after *Madoc*," in *Paul Muldoon: Critical Essays*, ed. Tim Kendall and Peter McDonald (Liverpool: Liverpool University Press, 2004).

54. Muldoon, "Yarrow," in *Poems*, 384.

55. Matthew Campbell has written convincingly about Muldoon's hesitance at pinning down the object of loss in his elegies: "it is frequently the case that Muldoon draws the forms of his elegies together. It is as if he contrives to show that there is as little distinction between poems as there is in the feeling of loss for distinct persons." Campbell, "Muldoon's Remains," in *Paul Muldoon: Critical Essays*, ed. Tim Kendall and Peter McDonald (Liverpool: Liverpool University Press, 2004), 179.

56. Muldoon, "Cuthbert and the Otters," lines 59–60, in *One Thousand Things Worth Knowing* (London: Faber and Faber, 2015), 5.

57. Muldoon, "The More a Man Has the More a Man Wants," in *Poems*, 134.

58. Kerrigan, "Paul Muldoon's Transits," 136.

59. *OED Online*, s.v. "reaction formation" in *Compounds* for "reaction, *n*."

60. Geoffrey Hill, "Poetry as 'Menace' and 'Atonement,'" in *Collected Critical Writings*, ed. Kenneth Haynes (Oxford: Oxford University Press, 2008), 15; hereafter abbreviated *CCW*.

61. Geoffrey Hill, "In Memory of Jane Fraser," line 1, in *Broken Hierarchies: Poems, 1952–2012* (Oxford: Oxford University Press, 2013), 9.

62. See Vincent Sherry, *The Uncommon Tongue: The Poetry and Criticism of Geoffrey Hill* (Ann Arbor: University of Michigan Press, 1987), 47.

63. Geoffrey Hill, "In Memory of Jane Fraser," lines 10–16, in *Broken Hierarchies*, 9.

64. Geoffrey Hill, "In Memory of Jane Fraser," lines 15–16, in *For the Unfallen: Poems, 1952–1958* (London: Andre Deutsch, 1959), 23.

65. Geoffrey Hill, *King Log* (London: Andre Deutsch, 1968), 69.

66. Ibid., 70.

67. Hill, "Poetry as 'Menace' and 'Atonement,'" in *CCW*, 19.

68. Ibid., 9.

69. See Gillian White, *Lyric Shame: The "Lyric" Subject of Contemporary American Poetry* (Cambridge, MA: Harvard University Press, 2014).

70. Hill, "Poetry as 'Menace' and 'Atonement,'" in *CCW*, 9 and 19.

71. Ibid., 9.

72. See, for instance, *Errears and Erroriboose: Joyce and Error*, ed. Matthew Creasy (New York: Rodopi, 2011); and Michael Anesko, *Generous Mistakes: Incidents of Error in Henry James* (Oxford: Oxford University Press, 2017).

73. Anesko, *Generous Mistakes*, x.

74. Ibid., 14.

75. Henry James, *The Portrait of a Lady*, ed. Roger Luckhurst (Oxford: Oxford World Classics, 2009), 483.

76. William Empson, *Seven Types of Ambiguity*, 2nd ed. (London: Chatto and Windus, 1947), 244.

Works Cited

Alford, John Alexander. "Wordsworth's Use of the Present Perfect." *Modern Language Quarterly* 33 (1972): 119–29.

Allen, Michael. "Pax Hibernica/Pax America: Rhyme and Reconciliation in Muldoon." In *Paul Muldoon: Critical Essays*, edited by Tim Kendall and Peter McDonald, 62–95. Liverpool: Liverpool University Press, 2004.

Alvarez, A. *The Shaping Spirit: Studies in Modern English and American Poets.* London: Chatto and Windus, 1958.

Ammons, A. R. "The Poem Is a Walk." In *Claims for Poetry*, edited by Donald Hall, 1–8. Ann Arbor: University of Michigan Press, 1982.

Andrews, Elmer. *The Poetry of Seamus Heaney: All the Realms of Whisper.* London: Macmillan, 1988.

Anesko, Michael. *Generous Mistakes: Incidents of Error in Henry James.* Oxford: Oxford University Press, 2017.

Antomarini, Brunella. *Thinking through Error: The Moving Target of Knowledge.* Lanham, MD: Lexington Books, 2012.

Aristotle. *The Complete Works of Aristotle.* Edited by Jonathan Barnes. 2 vols. Bollingen Series. Princeton, NJ: Princeton University Press, 1984.

———. *On the Art of Poetry.* Translated by Ingram Bywater. Oxford: Clarendon Press, 1920.

Armstrong, Isobel. *Victorian Poetry: Poetry, Poetics and Politics.* London: Routledge, 2002.

Arnold, Matthew. *Poetry and Prose.* Edited by John Bryson. London: Rupert Hart-Davis, 1954.

Ashbery, John. *Collected Poems, 1956–1987*. Edited by Mark Ford. New York: Library of America, 2008.

———. *Other Traditions*. Cambridge, MA: Harvard University Press, 2000.

———. *Selected Prose*. Edited by Eugene Richie. Manchester: Carcanet, 2004.

Auden, W. H. *Collected Poems*. Edited by Edward Mendelson. London: Faber and Faber, 1991.

Auden, W. H., and Louis MacNiece. *Letters from Iceland*. London: Faber and Faber, 1937.

Austin, J. L. *Philosophical Papers*. 3rd edition. Oxford: Oxford University Press, 1979.

Barrell, John. *The Idea of Landscape and the Sense of Place, 1730–1840: An Approach to the Poetry of John Clare*. Cambridge: Cambridge University Press, 1972.

Bate, Jonathan. *John Clare: A Biography*. London: Picador, 2003.

———. *Soul of the Age: The Life, Mind and World of William Shakespeare*. London: Penguin, 2008.

Beach, Joseph Warren. "Hart Crane and Moby Dick." *Western Review* 20 (Spring 1956): 183–85.

Bennett, Andrew. *Ignorance: Literature and Agnoiology*. Manchester: Manchester University Press, 2009.

Bishop, Elizabeth. *Conversations with Elizabeth Bishop*. Edited by George Monteiro. Jackson: University Press of Mississippi, 1996.

———. *Elizabeth Bishop and "The New Yorker": The Complete Correspondence*. Edited by Joelle Biele. New York: Farrar, Straus and Giroux, 2011.

———. *One Art: Letters*. Edited by Robert Giroux. New York: Farrar, Straus and Giroux, 1994.

———. *Poems, Prose and Letters*. Edited by Robert Giroux and Lloyd Schwartz. New York: Library of America, 2008.

Bishop, Elizabeth, and Robert Lowell. *Words in Air: The Complete Correspondence between Elizabeth Bishop and Robert Lowell*. Edited by Thomas Travisano with Saskia Hamilton. London: Faber and Faber, 2008.

Blackmur, R. P. *Form and Value in Modern Poetry*. New York: Doubleday Anchor Books, 1957.

Bloom, Harold. *Dramatists and Dramas*. Philadelphia: Chelsea House, 2005.

———. *A Map of Misreading*. Oxford: Oxford University Press, 1975.

———. *The Ringers in the Tower: Studies in the Romantic Tradition*. Chicago: University of Chicago Press, 1971.

Boyd, Julian, and Zelda Boyd. "The Perfect of Experience." *Studies in Romanticism* 16, no. 1 (1977): 3–14.

Bromwich, David. *Disowned by Memory: Wordsworth's Poetry of the 1790s*. Chicago: University of Chicago Press, 1998.

———. *Skeptical Music: Essays on Modern Poetry*. Chicago: University of Chicago Press, 2001.

Browning, Robert. *The Brownings' Correspondence: September 1846–December 1847*. Edited by Philip Kelley and Scott Lewis. Winfield, KS: Wedgestone Press, 1998.

———. *The Brownings' Correspondence: November 1855–June 1856*. Edited by Philip Kelley, Scott Lewis, Edward Hagan, Joseph Phelan, and Rhian Williams. Winfield, KS: Wedgestone Press, 2015.

———. *Browning's Trumpeter: The Correspondence of Robert Browning and Frederick J. Furnivall, 1872–1889*. Edited by William S. Peterson. Washington, DC: Decatur House Press, 1979.

———. *The Complete Works of Robert Browning*. Edited by Morse Peckham, Park Honan, and Warner Barnes. 17 vols. Athens: Ohio University Press, 1969–2011.

———. *The Poems of Robert Browning: Volume Four, 1862–1871*. Edited by John Woolford, Daniel Karlin, and Joseph Phelan. London: Longman, 2014.

———. *Robert Browning: Selected Poems*. Edited by John Woolford, Daniel Karlin, and Joseph Phelan. London: Longman, 2010.

Buckingham, Willis J. "Emily Dickinson's 'Lone Orthography.'" *Papers of the Bibliographical Society of America* 75, no. 4 (1981): 419–35.

Budick, E. Miller. *Emily Dickinson and the Life of Language: A Study in Symbolic Poetics*. Baton Rouge: Louisiana State University Press, 1985.

Burke, Sean. *The Death and Return of the Author: Criticism and Subjectivity in Barthes, Foucault and Derrida*. 3rd edition. Edinburgh: Edinburgh University Press, 1998.

Byron, George Gordon, Lord. *The Complete Poetical Works*. Edited by Jerome J. McGann. 7 vols. Oxford: Clarendon Press, 1980–93.

Cameron, Sharon. *Choosing Not Choosing: Dickinson's Fascicles*. Chicago: University of Chicago Press, 1992.

———. *Lyric Time: Dickinson and the Limits of Genre*. Baltimore, MD: Johns Hopkins University Press, 1979.

Campbell, Matthew. "Muldoon's Remains." In *Paul Muldoon: Critical Essays,* edited by Tim Kendall and Peter McDonald, 170–88. Liverpool: Liverpool University Press, 2004.

Campbell, Matthew. *Rhythm and Will in Victorian Poetry*. Cambridge: Cambridge University Press, 1999.

Capps, Jack L. *Emily Dickinson's Reading: 1836–1886*. Cambridge, MA: Harvard University Press, 1966.

Carlyle, Thomas. *New Letters of Thomas Carlyle*. Edited by Alexander Carlyle. London: Bodley Head, 1904.

Carroll, Lewis. *Through the Looking-Glass*. In *Alice's Adventures in Wonderland and Through the Looking-Glass*, edited by Peter Hunt. Oxford: Oxford University Press, 2009.

Carson, Anne. *Men in the Off Hours*. London: Jonathan Cape, 2000.

Caruth, Cathy. "An Interview with Geoffrey Hartman." In *The Wordsworthian Enlightenment: Romantic Poetry and the Ecology of Reading*, edited by Helen Regueiro Elam and Frances Ferguson, 296–317. Baltimore, MD: Johns Hopkins University Press, 2005.

Cavanagh, Michael. *Professing Poetry: Seamus Heaney's Poetics*. Washington, DC: Catholic University of America Press, 2009.

Chesterton, G. K. *English Men of Letters: Robert Browning*. London: Macmillan, 1903.

Chiasson, Dan. "American Snipper: New Poems from John Ashbery." *New Yorker*, 15 May 2015. https://www.newyorker.com/magazine/2015/06/01/american-snipper-books-chiasson.

———. *Natural History and Other Poems*. New York: Alfred A. Knopf, 2005.

Clare, John. *By Himself*. Edited by Eric Robinson. London: Carcanet, 1998.

———. *The Early Poems of John Clare: 1804–1822*. Edited by Eric Robinson and David Powell. 2 vols. Oxford: Clarendon Press, 1989.

———. *John Clare: Poems of the Middle Period; 1822–1837*. Edited by Eric Robinson, David Powell, and P.M.S. Dawson. 5 vols. Oxford: Clarendon Press, 1996.

———. *The Later Poems of John Clare: 1837–1864*. Edited by Eric Robinson and David Powell. 2 vols. Oxford: Clarendon Press, 1984.

———. *The Prose of John Clare*. Edited by J. W. and Anne Tibble. London: Routledge & Kegan Paul, 1951.

Clarkson, Oliver. *Romanticism and the Letter*. Edited by Madeleine Callaghan and Anthony Howe. London: Palgrave, forthcoming in 2020.

Coleridge, Samuel Taylor. *The Collected Letters of Samuel Taylor Coleridge*. Edited by Earl Leslie Griggs. 3 vols. Oxford: Clarendon Press, 1956.

————. *The Collected Works of Samuel Taylor Coleridge*. Edited by John Beer and Kathleen Coburn. 16 vols. Princeton, NJ: Princeton University Press, 1969–2002.

Corcoran, Neil. *The Poetry of Seamus Heaney: A Critical Study*. London: Faber and Faber, 1998.

Corngold, Stanley. "Error in Paul de Man." *Critical Inquiry* 8, no. 3 (1982): 489–507.

Crane, Hart. *Complete Poems and Selected Letters*. Edited by Langdon Hammer. New York: Library of America, 2006.

————. Draft of "Voyages II" [ca. 1923–24], Brooklyn, Lohf A41, 42681D Bancroft, Hart Crane Papers, Rare Book and Manuscript Library, Columbia University, New York.

Creasy, Matthew, ed. *Errears and Erroriboose: Joyce and Error*. New York: Rodopi, 2011.

De Quincey, Thomas. *The Works of Thomas De Quincey: Volume 11; Articles from "Tait's Magazine" and "Blackwood's Magazine," 1838–41*. Edited by Julian North. 20 vols. London: Pickering & Chatto, 2003.

Dickinson, Emily. *Emily Dickinson's Poems: As She Preserved Them*. Edited by Cristanne Miller. Cambridge, MA: Belknap Press of Harvard University Press, 2016.

————. *The Letters of Emily Dickinson*. Edited by Thomas H. Johnson. 3 vols. Cambridge, MA: Harvard University Press, 1955.

————. *The Poems of Emily Dickinson*. Edited by R. W. Franklin. 3 vols. Cambridge, MA: Harvard University Press, 1998.

————. *The Poems of Emily Dickinson*. Edited by Thomas H. Johnson. 3 vols. Cambridge, MA: Belknap Press of Harvard University Press, 1955.

Dodsley, Robert, ed. *A Collection of Poems*. 4 vols. London: Printed by J. Hughs, 1755.

Drew, Philip. *The Poetry of Browning: A Critical Introduction*. London: Methuen, 1970.

Dunn, Douglas. "Quotidian Miracles: *Seeing Things*." In *The Art of Seamus Heaney*, edited by Tony Curtis, 205–26. Bridgend, Wales: Seren, 1982.

Edelman, Lee. "The Geography of Gender: Elizabeth Bishop's 'In the Waiting Room.'" *Contemporary Literature* 26, no. 2 (Summer 1985): 179–96.

Eigen, Edward. *On Accident: Episodes in Architecture and Landscape*. Cambridge, MA: MIT Press, 2018.

Elfenbein, Andrew. "Romantic Poetry and the Standardization of English." In *Cambridge Companion to British Romantic Poetry*, edited by James Chandler and Maureen McLane, 76–97. Cambridge: Cambridge University Press, 2008.

Eliot, T. S. *The Sacred Wood: Essays on Poetry and Criticism.* London: Faber and Faber, 1997.

Empson, William. *Seven Types of Ambiguity.* 2nd edition. London: Chatto and Windus, 1947.

Fay, H. W. "A Distressing Blunder." *Academy* 33, no. 841 (16 June 1888): 415.

Ferry, Anne. *By Design: Intention in Poetry.* Stanford, CA: Stanford University Press, 2008.

Finney, Claude. *The Evolution of Keats's Poetry.* 2 vols. Cambridge, MA: Harvard University Press, 1936.

Franklin, R. W. *The Editing of Emily Dickinson: A Reconsideration.* Madison: University of Wisconsin Press, 1967.

Freer, Alexander. "Faith in Reading: Revisiting the Midrash–Theory Connection." *Paragraph: A Journal of Modern Critical Theory* 39, no. 3 (November 2016): 335–57.

Freud, Sigmund. *The Psychopathology of Everyday Life.* Translated by Anthea Bell. London: Penguin, 2002.

Frost, Robert. *Collected Poems, Prose, and Plays.* Edited by Richard Poirier and Mark Richardson. New York: Library of America, 1995.

Fuller, John. *Who Is Ozymandias? And Other Puzzles in Poetry.* London: Chatto and Windus, 2011.

Garrett, Marvin P. "Language and Design in *Pippa Passes.*" *Victorian Poetry* 13, no. 1 (Spring 1975): 47–60.

Goodridge, John. *John Clare and Community.* Cambridge: Cambridge University Press, 2013.

Gorji, Mina. *John Clare and the Place of Poetry.* Liverpool: Liverpool University Press, 2008.

Guyer, Sarah. *Reading with John Clare: Biopoetics, Sovereignty, Romanticism.* New York: Fordham University Press, 2015.

Hadfield, Andrew. "How to Read Nashe's 'Brightness Falls from the Air.'" *Forum for Modern Language Studies* 51, no. 3 (1 July 2015): 239–47.

Hagenbüchle, Roland. "Precision and Indeterminacy in the Poetry of Emily Dickinson." *ESQ: A Journal of the American Renaissance* 20, no. 1 (1974): 33–56.

Hair, Donald. *Robert Browning's Language.* Toronto: University of Toronto Press, 1999.

Hammer, Langdon. *Hart Crane and Allen Tate: Janus-Faced Modernism.* Princeton, NJ: Princeton University Press, 1993.

Hardy, Barbara. "Literary Allusions, Appropriations and Assimilations." In *Seamus Heaney: Poet, Critic, Translator,* edited by Ashby Bland Crowder and Jason David Hall, 189–209. London: Palgrave Macmillan, 2007.

Hardy, Florence Emily. *The Later Years of Thomas Hardy, 1892–1928.* Cambridge: Cambridge University Press, 2011.

Hardy, Thomas. *The Collected Letters of Thomas Hardy.* Edited by Richard Little Purdy and Michael Millgate. 8 vols. Oxford: Oxford University Press, 1985.

Hart, Henry. "What Is Heaney Seeing in *Seeing Things?*" *Colby Quarterly* 30, no. 1 (March 1994): 33–42.

Harte, Liam. "Kibird's Classical Canon." *Irish Times,* 2 December 2000.

Hartman, Geoffrey. "The Wordsworthian Enlightenment." In *The Wordsworthian Enlightenment: Romantic Poetry and the Ecology of Reading,* edited by Helen Regueiro Elam and Frances Ferguson, 29–44. Baltimore, MD: Johns Hopkins University Press, 2005.

———. *Wordsworth's Poetry: 1787–1814.* New Haven, CT: Yale University Press, 1964.

Hass, Robert. *Time and Materials.* New York: Ecco Press, 2007.

Heaney, Seamus. *District and Circle.* New York: Farrar, Straus and Giroux, 2006.

———. *Electric Light.* New York: Farrar, Straus and Giroux, 2001.

———. *Field Work.* New York: Farrar, Straus and Giroux, 1979.

———. *Finders Keepers: Selected Prose, 1971–2001.* London: Faber and Faber, 2002.

———. *The Government of the Tongue: Selected Prose, 1978–1987.* New York: Farrar, Straus and Giroux, 1988.

———. Interview with Blake Morrison. "Seamus Famous: Time to Be Dazzled." *Independent on Sunday,* 19 May 1991, 26.

———. Interviews with Dennis O'Driscoll. In *Stepping Stones: Interviews with Seamus Heaney.* London: Faber and Faber, 2008.

———. "Introduction." In *The Essential Wordsworth,* edited by Seamus Heaney, 3–14. Hopewell, NJ: Ecco, 1988.

———. *Opened Ground: Selected Poems, 1966–1996.* New York: Farrar, Straus and Giroux, 1998.

———. *Preoccupations: Selected Prose, 1968–1978.* New York: Farrar, Straus and Giroux, 1980.

———. *The Redress of Poetry.* London: Faber and Faber, 1995.

Heaney, Seamus. "The Triumph of Spirit." *Guardian*, 11 February 2006. https://www.theguardian.com/books/2006/feb/11/poetry.classics.

Heffernan, James A. W. *Museum of Words: The Poetics of Ekphrasis from Homer to Ashbery*. Chicago: University of Chicago Press, 1993.

Hickman, Ben. *John Ashbery and English Poetry*. Edinburgh: Edinburgh University Press, 2012.

Higgins, David. *Romantic Englishness: Local, National, and Global Selves, 1780–1850*. New York: Palgrave Macmillan, 2014.

Hill, Geoffrey. *Broken Hierarchies: Poems, 1952–2012*. Oxford: Oxford University Press, 2013.

———. *Collected Critical Writings*. Edited by Kenneth Haynes. Oxford: Oxford University Press, 2008.

———. *For the Unfallen: Poems, 1952–1958*. London: Andre Deutsch, 1959.

———. *King Log*. London: Andre Deutsch, 1968.

Hirsch, E. D. *Validity in Interpretation*. New Haven, CT: Yale University Press, 1967.

Hodgson, Andrew. "Form and Feeling in John Clare's Sonnets." *John Clare Society Journal* 31 (2012): 111–22.

Hopps, Gavin. "Byron and Grammatical Freedom." In *Liberty and Poetic Licence: New Essays on Byron*, edited by Bernard Beatty, Tony Howe, and Charles E. Robinson, 165–80. Liverpool: Liverpool University Press, 2008.

Howard, William. "Emily Dickinson's Poetic Vocabulary." *PMLA* 72, no. 1 (March 1957): 225–48.

Huddleston, Rodney, and Geoffrey K. Pullum et al., eds. *The Cambridge Grammar of the English Language*. Cambridge: Cambridge University Press, 2002.

Irwin, John T. "Naming Names: Hart Crane's 'Logic of Metaphor.'" *Southern Review* 11, no. 2 (April 1975): 284–99.

Jackson, Virginia. *Dickinson's Misery: A Theory of Lyric Reading*. Princeton, NJ: Princeton University Press, 2005.

James, Henry. *The Portrait of a Lady*. Edited by Roger Luckhurst. Oxford: Oxford World Classics, 2009.

Johnson, Thomas H. *Emily Dickinson: An Interpretive Biography*. Cambridge, MA: Harvard University Press, 1955.

Joyce, James. *A Portrait of the Artist as a Young Man*. Edited by Jeri Johnson. Oxford: Oxford University Press, 2001.

Kalstone, David. *Becoming a Poet: Elizabeth Bishop with Marianne Moore and Robert Lowell*. Ann Arbor: University of Michigan Press, 2001.

Kandl, John. "The Politics of Keats's Early Poetry." In *The Cambridge Companion to Keats*, edited by Susan Wolfson, 1–20. Cambridge: Cambridge University Press, 2001.

Karlin, Daniel. *Browning's Hatreds*. Oxford: Clarendon Press, 1993.

Keats, John. *John Keats: Selected Letters*. Edited by Robert Gittings. Oxford: Oxford University Press, 2002.

———. *The Major Works*. Edited by Elizabeth Cook. Oxford: Oxford University Press, 2001.

Kermode, Frank. *The Uses of Error*. Cambridge, MA: Harvard University Press, 1991.

Kerrigan, John. "Paul Muldoon's Transits: Muddling Through after *Madoc*." In *Paul Muldoon: Critical Essays*, edited by Tim Kendall and Peter McDonald, 125–49. Liverpool: Liverpool University Press, 2004.

Killeen, Terence. "John Ashbery: Snatching Joy from the Poetry of Defeat." *Irish Times*, 20 September 2017. https://www.irishtimes.com/culture/books/john-ashbery-snatching-joy-from-the-poetry-of-defeat-1.3226627.

King, Roma A., Jr. *The Focusing Artifice: The Poetry of Robert Browning*. Athens: Ohio University Press, 1968.

Knapp, Steven, and Walter Benn Michaels. "Against Theory." *Critical Inquiry* 8, no. 4 (Summer 1982): 723–42.

Korg, Jacob. "A Reading of *Pippa Passes*." *Victorian Poetry* 6, no. 1 (1968): 5–19.

Kövesi, Simon. "Beyond the Language Wars: Towards a Green Edition of John Clare." *John Clare Society Journal* 26 (July 2007): 61–75.

———. *John Clare: Nature, Criticism, History*. London: Palgrave Macmillan, 2017.

Langbaum, Robert. *The Poetry of Experience: The Dramatic Monologue in Modern Literary Tradition*. London: Chatto and Windus, 1957.

Lehman, David. *The Last Avant-garde: The Making of the New York School of Poets*. New York: Doubleday, 1998.

Leibowitz, Herbert. *Hart Crane: An Introduction to the Poetry*. New York: Columbia University Press, 1968.

Lerer, Seth. *Error and the Academic Self: The Scholarly Imagination, Medieval to Modern*. New York: Columbia University Press, 2002.

Levinson, Marjorie. *Keats's Life of Allegory: The Origins of a Style*. Oxford: Basil Blackwell, 1988.

Litzinger, Boyd, and Donald Smalley, eds. *Robert Browning: The Critical Heritage*. London: Routledge & Kegan Paul, 1970.

Logan, William. "The Hart Crane Controversy." *Poetry Magazine*, October

2008. https://www.poetryfoundation.org/poetrymagazine/articles/69119/the
-hart-crane-controversy.

Logan, William. "Hart Crane's Bridge to Nowhere." *New York Times*, Sunday
Book Review, 28 January 2007. https://www.nytimes.com/2007/01/28
/books/review/Logan.t.html.

———. *Our Savage Art: Poetry and the Civil Tongue.* New York: Columbia University Press, 2009.

Lohf, Kenneth. "The Library of Hart Crane." *Proof: Yearbook of American Bibliographical and Textual Studies* 3 (1973): 283–334.

Lowell, Robert. *Collected Poems.* Edited by Frank Bidart. New York: Farrar,
Straus and Giroux, 2003.

———. *Life Studies.* New York: Farrar, Straus and Cudahy, 1959.

MacLeish, Archibald. "The Private World: Poems of Emily Dickinson." In *Emily
Dickinson: A Collection of Critical Essays*, edited by Richard B. Sewall, 150–
61. Englewood Cliffs, NJ: Prentice-Hall, 1963.

Matthews, G. M., ed. *Keats: The Critical Heritage.* London: Routledge and
Kegan Paul Books, 1971.

Maxwell, Catherine. *The Female Sublime from Milton to Swinburne: Bearing
Blindness.* Manchester: Manchester University Press, 2001.

McAlpine, Erica. "James Merrill's Puns." *Essays in Criticism* 68, no. 4 (October
2018): 488–509.

———. "Keeping Nature at Bay: John Clare's Poetry of Wonder." *Studies in Romanticism* 50 (Spring 2011): 79–104.

McGann, Jerome. *The Poetics of Sensibility: A Revolution in Literary Style.* Oxford:
Clarendon Press, 1996.

McGuinness, Patrick. "Speculating: Patrick McGuinness Interviews Paul Muldoon." *Irish Studies Review* 17, no. 1 (12 February 2009): 103–10.

McKendrick, Jamie. "Bishop's Birds." In *Elizabeth Bishop: Poet on the Periphery*,
edited by Linda Anderson and Jo Shapcott, 123–42. Newcastle, UK:
Bloodaxe Books, 2002.

Melchiori, Barbara. *Browning's Poetry of Reticence.* Edinburgh: Oliver and Boyd,
1968.

Merrill, James. *Collected Poems.* Edited by J. D. McClatchy and Stephen Yenser.
New York: Knopf, 2001.

Mill, John Stuart. *The Collected Works of John Stuart Mill: Volume I; Autobiography and Literary Essays.* Edited by John M. Robson. 33 vols. Toronto: University of Toronto Press, 1981.

Miller, Cristanne. *Emily Dickinson: A Poet's Grammar*. Cambridge, MA: Harvard University Press, 1987.

Miller, Tracy. "What Remains: Matthew Arnold's Poetics of Place and the Victorian Elegy." *Victorian Poetry* 50, no. 2 (Summer 2012): 147–65.

Millier, Brett C. *Elizabeth Bishop: Life and the Memory of It*. Berkeley: University of California Press, 1993.

Milton, John. *Complete Shorter Poems*. Edited by Stella P. Revard. Oxford: Wiley Blackwell, 2009.

Molloy, Catharine. "Seamus Heaney's *Seeing Things*: 'Retracing the Path Back.'" In *Seamus Heaney: The Shaping Spirit*, edited by Catharine Molloy and Phyllis Carey, 157–73. London: Associated University Presses, 1996.

Moore, Marianne. *The Complete Poems of Marianne Moore*. New York: Macmillan/Viking Press, 1967.

Muldoon, Paul. *The End of the Poem*. New York: Farrar, Straus and Giroux, 2006.

———. Interview with Patrick McGuinness. "Speculating: Patrick McGuinness Interviews Paul Muldoon," *Irish Studies Review* 17, no. 1 (12 February 2009): 105.

———. Interview with Tracy K. Smith. "*The New Yorker* Poetry Podcast," audio podcast, n.d. http://downloads.newyorker.com/mp3/poetry/140123_poetry _smith.mp3.

———. *One Thousand Things Worth Knowing*. London: Faber and Faber, 2015.

———. *Poems, 1968–1998*. London: Faber and Faber, 2001.

Murphy, Andrew. *Seamus Heaney*. 3rd edition. Tavistock, UK: Northcote House, 2009.

Murray, K. M. Elisabeth. *Caught in the Web of Words: James Murray and the "Oxford English Dictionary."* New Haven, CT: Yale University Press, 1977.

Nashe, Thomas. *The Works of Thomas Nashe*. Edited by Ronald B. McKerrow. Revised by F. P. Wilson. 5 vols. Oxford: Blackwell, 1966.

O'Brien, Eugene. *Seamus Heaney: Creating Irelands of the Mind*. Dublin: Liffey Press, 2002.

O'Donoghue, Bernard. *Seamus Heaney and the Language of Poetry*. Hemel Hempstead, Hertfordshire: Harvester Wheatsheaf, 1994.

O'Driscoll, Dennis. *Stepping Stones: Interviews with Seamus Heaney*. London: Faber and Faber, 2008.

O'Neill, Michael. *Romanticism and the Self-Conscious Poem*. Oxford: Clarendon Press, 1997.

Palgrave, Francis. *The Golden Treasury*. Revised and enlarged edition. London: Macmillan, 1902.

Paul, Sherman. *Hart's Bridge*. Chicago: University of Illinois Press, 1972.

Percy, Walker. "Metaphor as Mistake." *Sewanee Review* 66, no. 1 (Winter 1958): 79–99.

Perloff, Marjorie. *The Poetics of Indeterminacy: Rimbaud to Cage*. Princeton, NJ: Princeton University Press, 1981.

Perry, Seamus. "What the Poem 'Knows.'" *Times Literary Supplement*, no. 4962 (22 May 1998): 32.

Pessoa, Fernando. *The Book of Disquiet*. Translated by Richard Zenith. London: Penguin Classics, 2002.

Phillips, Adam. *One Way and Another: New and Selected Essays*. London: Penguin, 2013.

———. *Promises, Promises: Essays on Literature and Psychoanalysis*. London: Faber and Faber, 2000.

Pinsky, Robert. "In Praise of Memorizing Poetry—Badly." *Slate*, 1 November 2008. http://www.slate.com/articles/arts/poem/2011/11/william_butler _yeats_on_being_asked_for_a_war_poem_.html.

Plato. *Plato: Volume II; Theaetetus, Sophist*. Translated by H. N. Fowler. Loeb Classical Library. London: William Heinemann, 1921.

Porter, David. *Dickinson: The Modern Idiom*. Cambridge, MA: Harvard University Press, 1981.

Powell, Thomas. *The Art of Emily Dickinson's Earlier Poetry*. Cambridge, MA: Harvard University Press, 1966.

———. *The Living Authors of England*. New York: D. Appleton, 1849.

Prins, Yopie. "What Is Historical Poetics?" *Modern Language Quarterly* 77, no. 1 (March 2016): 13–40.

Quint, David. *Inside "Paradise Lost": Reading the Designs of Milton's Epic*. Princeton, NJ: Princeton University Press, 2014.

Quirk, Randolph, et al., eds. *A Comprehensive Grammar of the English Language*. London: Longman, 1985.

Ramsey, Paul. "The Biding Place: Reflections on Hart Crane." *Parnassus* 5, no. 1 (Fall/Winter 1976): 187–99.

Reed, Brian M. *Hart Crane: After His Lights*. Tuscaloosa: University of Alabama Press, 2006.

Ricks, Christopher. *Essays in Appreciation*. Oxford: Oxford University Press, 1998.

————. *The Force of Poetry*. Oxford: Clarendon Press, 1984.

————. *Reviewery*. London: Penguin, 2002.

Rogers, William Elford. *Interpreting Interpretation: Textual Hermeneutics as an Ascetic Discipline*. University Park: Pennsylvania State University Press, 1994.

Russell, Francis T. "His Saving Grace of Pessimism." In *The Browning Critics*, edited by Boyd Litzinger and K. L. Knickerbocker, 131–41. Lexington: University of Kentucky Press, 1965.

Russell, Richard Rankine. *Seamus Heaney's Regions*. Notre Dame, IN: University of Notre Dame Press, 2014.

————. *Seamus Heaney: An Introduction*. Edinburgh: Edinburgh University Press, 2016.

Rzepka, Charles. " 'Cortez: Or Balboa, or Somebody like That': Form, Fact, and Forgetting in Keats's 'Chapman's Homer' Sonnet." *Keats-Shelley Journal* 51 (2002): 35–75.

Scarry, Elaine. *On Beauty and Being Just*. Princeton, NJ: Princeton University Press, 2001.

Seyersted, Brita Lindberg. *Emily Dickinson's Punctuation*. Oslo: American Institute, 1976.

Shakespeare, William. *The Norton Shakespeare*. Edited by Stephen Greenblatt. New York: W. W. Norton, 1997.

————. *The Works of Shakespear*. Edited by Sir Thomas Hanmer. 6 vols. London: Printed for J. and P. Knapton, 1745.

————. *Mr. William Shakespeares Comedies, Histories, & Tragedies: Published According to the True and Originall Copies*. London: Printed by Isaac Iagaard and Edward Blount, 1623.

Sherry, Vincent. *The Uncommon Tongue: The Poetry and Criticism of Geoffrey Hill*. Ann Arbor: University of Michigan Press, 1987.

Shoptaw, John. *On the Outside Looking Out: John Ashbery's Poetry*. Cambridge, MA: Harvard University Press, 1994.

Spenser, Edmund. *The Faerie Queene*. Edited by A. C. Hamilton. 2nd edition. London: Routledge, 2013.

Spiegelman, Willard. *Majestic Indolence: English Romantic Poetry and the Work of Art*. Oxford: Oxford University Press, 1995.

Stevens, Wallace. *Wallace Stevens: Collected Poetry and Prose*. Edited by Frank Kermode and Joan Richardson. New York: Library of America, 1997.

Stevenson, Anne. *Five Looks at Elizabeth Bishop*. London: Bellew, 1998.

Stillinger, Jack. *Romantic Complexity: Keats, Coleridge, and Wordsworth*. Chicago: University of Illinois Press, 2006.

Sutherland, John. *Is Heathcliff a Murderer? Great Puzzles in Nineteenth-Century Fiction*. Oxford: Oxford University Press, 2002.

Sutherland, Keston. "Wrong Poetry." *Textual Practice* 24, no. 4 (2010): 765–82.

Swaab, Peter. " 'Wonder' as a Complex Word." *Romanticism* 18, no. 3 (October 2012): 270–80.

Sweet, Henry. *A New English Grammar: Logical and Historical*. 2 vols. Oxford: Clarendon Press, 1892.

Tate, Allen. *Collected Essays*. Denver, CO: Alan Swallow, 1959.

Taylor, John. "Introduction to *Poems Descriptive of Rural Life and Scenery*." In *John Clare: The Critical Heritage*, edited by Mark Storey, 43–54. London: Routledge and Kegan Paul, 1973.

Tennyson, Alfred, Lord. *Tennyson: A Selected Edition*. Edited by Christopher Ricks. Berkeley: University of California Press, 1989.

Thompson, T. W. *Wordsworth's Hawkshead*. Edited by Robert Woof. Oxford: Oxford University Press, 1970.

Tóibín, Colm. *On Elizabeth Bishop*. Princeton, NJ: Princeton University Press, 2015.

Tucker, Herbert. *Browning's Beginnings: The Art of Disclosure*. Minneapolis: University of Minnesota Press, 1980.

———. "Dramatic Monologue and the Overhearing of Lyric." In *Lyric Poetry: Beyond New Criticism*, edited by Chaviva Hošek and Patricia A. Parker, 226–43. Ithaca, NY: Cornell University Press, 1985.

Vardy, Alan. *John Clare: Politics and Poetry*. Basingstoke, UK: Palgrave Macmillan, 2003.

Vendler, Helen. *On Extended Wings: Wallace Stevens' Longer Poems*. Cambridge, MA: Harvard University Press, 1969.

———. *Seamus Heaney*. Cambridge, MA: Harvard University Press, 1998.

Vermeulen, Pieter. "The Suspension of Reading: Wordsworth's 'Boy of Winander' and Trauma Theory." *Orbis Litterarum* 62, no. 6 (2007): 459–82.

Von Lippmann, Edmund O. "Shakespeare's Ignorance?" *New Review* 4 (1891): 250–54.

Watkins, Daniel. *Keats's Poetry and the Politics of the Imagination*. London: Associated University Presses, 1989.

Welch, Robert. " 'A rich young man leaving everything he had': Poetic Freedom in Seamus Heaney." In *Seamus Heaney: A Collection of Critical Essays*, edited by Elmer Andrews, 150–81. New York: St. Martin's Press, 1992.

White, Gillian. *Lyric Shame: The "Lyric" Subject of Contemporary American Poetry.* Cambridge, MA: Harvard University Press, 2014.

Wiener, Stephanie Kuduk. *Clare's Lyric: John Clare and Three Modern Poets.* Oxford: Oxford University Press, 2014.

Williams, Nerys. *Reading Error: The Lyric and Contemporary Poetry.* Oxford: Peter Lang, 2007.

Wimsatt, W. K. *The Verbal Icon.* New York: Noonday Press, 1954.

Winters, Yvor. *In Defense of Reason.* Denver, CO: Alan Swallow, 1937.

———. "The Progress of Hart Crane." In *Hart Crane: A Collection of Critical Essays,* edited by Alan Trachtenberg, 23–31. New Jersey: Prentice-Hall, 1982.

Wittgenstein, Ludwig. *Philosophical Investigations.* New York: Macmillan, 1958.

Wolfson, Susan J. *Formal Charges: The Shaping of Poetry in British Romanticism.* Stanford, CA: Stanford University Press, 1997.

———. *The Questioning Presence: Wordsworth, Keats and the Interrogative Mode in Romantic Poetry.* Ithaca, NY: Cornell University Press, 1986.

Woodhouse, Richard. *The Keats Circle, Letters and Papers, 1816–1878.* Edited by Hyder Edward Rollins. 2 vols. Cambridge, MA: Harvard University Press, 1948.

Woof, Robert, ed. *Wordsworth: The Critical Heritage.* London: Routledge, 2001.

Wordsworth, William. *The Fenwick Notes of William Wordsworth.* Edited by Jared Curtis. London: Bristol Classical Press, 1993.

———. *The Fourteen-Book "Prelude."* Edited by W.J.B. Owen. Ithaca, NY: Cornell University Press, 1985.

———. *Lyrical Ballads, and Other Poems, 1797–1800.* Edited by James Butler and Karen Green. Ithaca, NY: Cornell University Press, 1992.

———. Manuscript "JJ." DCMS 19. Dove Cottage. Grasmere.

———. *Poems, in Two Volumes, and Other Poems.* Edited by Jared Curtis. Ithaca, NY: Cornell University Press, 1982.

———. *The Prose Works of William Wordsworth.* Edited by W.J.B. Owen and Jane Worthington Smyser. 3 vols. Oxford: Clarendon Press, 1974.

———. *The Thirteen-Book Prelude.* Edited by Mark L. Reed. 2 vols. Ithaca, NY: Cornell University Press, 1991.

Wordsworth, William, and Dorothy Wordsworth. *The Letters of William and Dorothy Wordsworth: The Early Years; 1787–1805.* Edited by Ernest de Selincourt. Revised by Chester L. Shaver. 2nd edition. Oxford: Clarendon Press, 1967.

Wordsworth, William, and Dorothy Wordsworth. *The Letters of William and Dorothy Wordsworth: The Later Years; Part II: 1829–1834*. Edited by Alan G. Hill. 2nd edition. Oxford: Clarendon Press, 1979.

Yingling, Thomas. *Hart Crane and the Homosexual Text: New Thresholds, New Anatomies*. Chicago: University of Chicago Press, 1990.

Index

accidents: during compositional process, 2, 82, 175, 182; "external accidents" and unintended creativity, 45–46; Heaney on role of accident in poetry, 181–83; identifying, 85–86, 135–36; as involuntary, 22, 45–46, 68–69, 150; vs. mistakes, x, 17–18, 22, 45–46, 85–86, 118, 150, 193–94; transformed into "accuracy," 175, 181–82; as valuable to poets, 2, 45–46, 79, 150, 175, 181, 182–83, 193–94; and will, 150. *See also* chance

accuracy: accidents transformed into, 175, 181–82; "accurate" mistakes, 155; Bishop and importance of, 25, 137–38, 142–44, 148–50, 153–55, 194; Browning and, 52–53; descriptive accuracy of errors, 107–9, 122–23, 124, 192–93; errors and interpretive possibility, 107–9; errors as "impressionistically correct," 33; imagination as counter to reality, 182–83; individual parameters for truth and, 153, 167, 194; as less important than art, 3, 68, 190, 211; poems as accurate representations, 194–95; subjectivity and, 137–38, 143–44, 183–86; Tennyson and 38, 143–44, 183–86; Tennyson and

focus on, 12; thematic *vs.* literal, 145. *See also* factual errors

acknowledgment of errors: and atonement, 207–10; Bishop and, 145–50; and confessional poems, 192; and correction during revision, 10, 52–54, 98–99, 117, 133; by critics, 11; Dickinson and, 24, 97–100, 116–17; in errata, 5–7, 201–2; as evidence of diligence, 150; Heaney and, 167, 170–72, 178, 180, 183, 186–87; justification and, 41; and preservation or resistance to correction, 50–51, 113–16, 145–47, 150, 190, 204; as resolution, 116–17; and respect for poet's craft and intention, 27, 69, 73, 82–83, 86, 89, 106, 126, 131–36, 153–54, 187–90, 194, 200–201; and self-corrections within poems, 87, 149, 170–71, 206–7; Spenser and, 5; subjectivity and, 5–6; Tennyson and, 12; and value of mistakes, 25–26, 34, 46, 69, 72, 116–17, 168–69, 190–91, 193; and willingness to use errors productively, 192

"Against Theory" (Knapp and Michaels), 17